Between Threats and War

Between Threats and War

U.S. DISCRETE MILITARY OPERATIONS
IN THE POST–COLD WAR WORLD

Micah Zenko

STANFORD SECURITY SERIES
An Imprint of Stanford University Press
Stanford, California
A Council on Foreign Relations Book

Stanford University Press
Stanford, California

Special discounts for bulk quantities of Stanford Security Studies are available to
corporations, professional associations, and other organizations. For details and discount
information, contact the special sales department of Stanford University Press.
Tel: (650) 736-1782, Fax: (650) 736-1784

Printed in the United States of America on acid-free, archival-quality paper

Library of Congress Cataloging-in-Publication Data

Zenko, Micah.
Between threats and war : U.S. discrete military operations in the post-Cold War world /
Micah Zenko.
p. cm.
"A Council on Foreign Relations book."
Includes bibliographical references and index.
ISBN 978-0-8047-7190-0 (cloth : alk. paper)—ISBN 978-0-8047-7191-7 (pbk.)
1. United States—Military policy. 2. Limited war. 3. United States—Foreign relations—1989-
I. Title.
UA23.Z446 2010
355.4'77309049—dc22
2010011549

Typeset by Bruce Lundquist in 10/14 Minion

The Council on Foreign Relations (CFR) is an independent, nonpartisan membership
organization, think tank, and publisher dedicated to being a resource for its members,
government officials, business executives, journalists, educators and students, civic and
religious leaders, and other interested citizens in order to help them better understand the
world and the foreign policy choices facing the United States and other countries. Founded
in 1921, CFR carries out its mission by maintaining a diverse membership, with special
programs to promote interest and develop expertise in the next generation of foreign policy
leaders; convening meetings at its headquarters in New York and in Washington, D.C.,
and other cities where senior government officials, members of Congress, global leaders,
and prominent thinkers come together with CFR members to discuss and debate major
international issues; supporting a Studies Program that fosters independent research,
enabling CFR scholars to produce articles, reports, and books and hold roundtables that
analyze foreign policy issues and make concrete policy recommendations; publishing *Foreign
Affairs*, the preeminent journal on international affairs and U.S. foreign policy; sponsoring
Independent Task Forces that produce reports with both findings and policy prescriptions on
the most important foreign policy topics; and providing up-to-date information and analysis
about world events and American foreign policy on its website, www.cfr.org.

The Council on Foreign Relations takes no institutional position on policy issues and has
no affiliation with the U.S. government. All statements of fact and expressions of opinion
contained in its publications are the sole responsibility of the author or authors.

CONTENTS

ACKNOWLEDGMENTS

This book began out of a dissertation with committee members Robert Art, Shai Feldman, and Steve Miller, as well as Seyom Brown, who provided early, detailed comments. An extra debt of gratitude goes to Bob, who helped make it better at every stage, and Steve, who turned a conversation into a topic and an acronym. The Department of Politics at Brandeis University; Belfer Center for Science and International Affairs and Carr Center for Human Rights Policy at Harvard University; and the Center for Preventive Action (CPA) and International Institutions and Global Governance (IIGG) program at the Council on Foreign Relations (CFR) provided institutional support and employment. I am grateful for the assistance and encouragement from the leaders of these esteemed institutions, including Steve Berg, Jytte Klausen, and Daniel Kryder at Brandeis; Graham Allison at the Belfer Center; and Sarah Sewall at the Carr Center. At CFR, Richard N. Haass and James M. Lindsay, the president and director of studies, respectively, as well as Paul Stares within CPA and Stewart Patrick within IIGG, provided essential guidance and support. I would also like to thank the Carnegie Corporation of New York and the Robina Foundation for providing financial support via generous grants to the Council on Foreign Relations. Numerous friends and colleagues also offered suggestions, comments, or collaborative support, including Max Abrahms, Kevin Benson, Steve Biddle, Arnold Bogis, Matt Bunn, Matan Chorev, Angelina Clarke, Amy Cunningham, David Dagan, Patricia Lee Dorff, Ehud Eiran, Jason Forrester, Rebecca R. Friedman, Dana Stern Gibber, Kelly Greenhill, Rebecca Johnson, Alexander Noyes, Abby O'Brient, Mike Pryce, Kevin Ryan, Julian Schofield, Todd Sechser, Amanda Swanson, and Lawrence Woocher. Finally, an enormous thanks goes to Adam Zenko for making this possible. In addition, the thirty-one civilian and military officials and experts gracious enough to be interviewed about proposed or actual military operations—some of which remain classified—must be mentioned:

Amb. Richard Armitage, Assistant Secretary of Defense for International Security Policy (1983–1989), Deputy Secretary of State (2001–2005)

Dr. Robert Baumann, U.S. Army Command and General Staff College

Col. Kevin Benson, U.S. Army planner, and Director, School of Advanced Military Studies (2003–2007)

Amb. Barbara Bodine, Ambassador to the Republic of Yemen (1997–2001)

Col. Dallas Brown, Director, Joint Interagency Coordination Group, U.S. Central Command (2005–2007); Director for Global Issues and Multilateral Affairs on the NSC (1994–1997)

Xenia Dormandy, Director for South Asia on the NSC (2004–2005)

Douglas Feith, Undersecretary of Defense for Policy (2001–2005)

Vice Adm. Scott Fry, Deputy Director for Strategy and Policy, J-5 (1995–1997), Director of Operations, J-3 (1998–2001)

Sen. Bob Graham, senator from Florida (1987–2005), Chairman of Senate Select Committee on Intelligence (2001–2005)

Maj. Gen. Jonathan "Scott" Gration, Commander of the Northern No-Fly Zone (1996–1998), Director of Plans and Policy Directorate, Headquarters, U.S. European Command (2004–2006)

Amb. Marc Grossman, Ambassador to Turkey (1994–1997), Assistant Secretary of State for European Affairs (1997–2000), Undersecretary of State for Political Affairs (2001–2005)

Brig. Gen. Michael Jones, Deputy Director for Politico-Military Affairs (Middle East), J-5 (2005–2007)

Gen. John "Jack" Keane, Army Vice Chief of Staff (1999–2003)

Gen. Paul Kern, Senior Military Assistant to Secretary of Defense William Perry (1995–1997), Commanding General, Army Materiel Command (2001–2004)

Lt. Gen. Donald Kerrick, Deputy Assistant to the President for National Security Affairs (1997–1999), Deputy National Security Advisor (2000–2001)

Dr. Michael Knights, writer and Middle East expert

Lt. Gen. Barry McCaffrey, Principal Staff Assistant to the Chairman of the Joint Chiefs of Staff and later Director of Strategic Planning, J-5 (1992–1994), Commander of U.S. Southern Command (1994–1996)

Franklin Miller, Special Assistant to President George W. Bush and Senior Director for Defense Policy and Arms Control on the NSC (2001–2005)

Gen. Richard Myers, Vice Chairman of the Joint Chiefs of Staff (2000–2001), Chairman of the Joint Chiefs of Staff (2001–2005)

Maj. Gen. Larry New, Director of Operations and Plans, Joint Task Force Southwest Asia (Southern No-Fly Zone) (1996–1997)

Lt. Gen. Gregory Newbold, Director of Operations, J-3 (2000–2002)

Gen. David Petraeus, Executive Assistant to the Director of the Joint Staff and later to the Chairman of the Joint Chiefs of Staff (1997–1999), Commander of U.S. Central Command (2008–present)

Paul Pillar, Deputy Chief of the Counterterrorist Center at the CIA (1997–1999), National Intelligence Officer for the Near East and South Asia (2000-2005)

Gen. Joseph Ralston, Vice Chairman of the Joint Chiefs of Staff (1996–2000), Commander of the U.S. European Command (2000–2003)

Bruce Riedel, Senior Director for Near East Affairs on the NSC, Deputy Assistant Secretary of Defense for Near East and South Asian Affairs (1995–1997), Special Assistant to the President and Senior Director for Near East Affairs on the NSC (1997–2002)

Brig. Gen. Kevin Ryan, Deputy Director for Strategy, Plans and Policy, Office of the Deputy Chief of Staff, U.S. Army (2003–2005)

Kori Schake, Director of Defense Strategy and Requirements on the NSC (2002–2005)

James Steinberg, Deputy National Security Advisor (1996–2000)

Gen. Anthony Zinni, Commander of U.S. Central Command (1997–2000)

Former George W. Bush administration official, intelligence operations

Former Clinton administration official, Middle East policy

Former Clinton administration Pentagon official

U.S. Air Force colonel, Special Operations Forces

ACRONYMS USED IN THIS BOOK

AAA	anti-aircraft artillery
AMRAAM	Advanced Medium-Range Air-to-Air Missile
AQI	Al Qaeda in Iraq
AWACS	Airborne Warning and Control System
CALCM	Conventional Air-Launched Cruise Missile
CENTCOM	U.S. Central Command
CIC	Council of Islamic Courts
CSG	Counterterrorism Security Group
DC	Deputies Committee (NSC)
DMO	Discrete Military Operation
EUCOM	U.S. European Command
FATA	Federally Administered Tribal Areas (Pakistan)
FFZ	free-fly zone
GWOT	Global War on Terrorism
HIMARS	High Mobility Artillery Rockets
IADS	Iraqi Air Defense System
IAEA	International Atomic Energy Agency
IMK	Islamic Movement of Iraqi Kurdistan
IrAF	Iraqi Air Force
ISI	Inter-Services Intelligence directorate (Pakistan)
JSOC	Joint Special Operations Command
JSOW	Joint Stand-Off Weapon
KDP	Kurdish Democratic Party
NATO	North Atlantic Treaty Organization
NFZ	no-fly zone

NIF   National Islamic Front

NSA   National Security Agency

NSC   National Security Council

OBL   Osama Bin Laden (Unit)

ONW   Operation Northern Watch (Iraq)

OPLAN 1003   Operation Plan 1003

OSW   Operation Southern Watch (Iraq)

PKK   Kurdish Workers Party

PUK   Patriotic Union of Kurdistan

ROE   rules of engagement

SAM   surface-to-air missile

SOCOM   Special Operations Command

SOF   Special Operation Forces

TLAM   Tomahawk Land Attack Missile

UNPROFOR   UN Protection Force

UNSCOM   UN Special Commission

WMD   weapons of mass destruction

1 INTRODUCTION

"The thesis, then, must be repeated: war is an act of force, and there is no logical limit to the application of that force."[1]

Major General Carl von Clausewitz, Prussian Army

"[The use of force] doesn't have to be all or nothing. We should be able to use limited force in limited areas."[2]

Madeline Albright, U.S. Secretary of State

"As soon as they tell me it is limited, it means they do not care whether you achieve a result or not. As soon as they me tell me 'surgical,' I head for the bunker."[3]

General Colin Powell, Chairman of the Joint Chiefs of Staff

WHEN CONFRONTED with a persistent foreign policy problem that threatens U.S. interests, one that cannot be adequately addressed through economic or political pressure, American policymakers routinely resort to using limited military force. Current and former government officials, foreign policy analysts, and citizens call for the limited use of force with the belief that it potentially can resolve the problem expediently and without resulting in unwanted U.S. military or local civilian casualties. Proponents of such operations are found across the entire political spectrum, and their proposals range from the practical to the satirical: from centrist former senior Pentagon and State Department officials proposing to bomb North Korean ballistic missiles poised to launch; to a liberal *Washington Post* columnist calling for a Predator missile strike to kill Zimbabwean president Robert Mugabe—a scheme that was one-upped by a former diplomat and human rights advocate who suggested a "messy in the short run" invasion to oust Mugabe; to a White House spokesperson advocating the assassination of Iraqi president Saddam Hussein because "the cost of one bullet . . . is substantially less" than the cost of war—a scheme echoed by a conservative pastor who himself encouraged the assassination of Venezuelan president Hugo Chavez because "it's a whole lot cheaper than starting a war."[4] Out of anger, empathy, or impatience with an ongoing foreign policy dilemma, advocates in and out of the U.S. government continually propose the subject of this book—Discrete Military Operations (DMOs).

America's use of limited military force and DMOs since the end of the Cold War is important because the United States continues to be the dominant international actor and because U.S. decisionmakers have increasingly turned to the use of limited force against other states or non-state actors to achieve their policy goals. In addition, rapid technological advances in the U.S. military's capacity to conduct precise strikes from a safe distance, and an international setting in which the United States faces a potentially open-ended threat from non-state terrorist networks, make it likely that the reliance on limited force will remain a persistent feature of U.S. foreign policy. Despite the rising significance of DMOs, however, it is unclear and understudied whether limited uses of force have succeeded at achieving their intended military and political objectives.

To clarify and illuminate recent U.S. limited uses of force, this book presents a new concept: "Discrete Military Operations." Here, DMOs are defined as a single or serial physical use of kinetic military force to achieve a defined military and political goal by inflicting casualties or causing destruction, without seeking to conquer an opposing army or to capture or control territory. DMOs usually consist of a single attack or series of sortie strikes, lasting just minutes, hours, or a few days. DMOs usually involve only one combat arm and one mode of attack directed against an adversary's military capabilities or infrastructure, regime or organizational assets, or key leadership. DMOs are also proscribed by strict rules of engagement to ensure that the intensity and scope of the strike does not exceed levels necessary to attempt to achieve the political objectives.[5]

In investigating U.S. DMOs from 1991 through June 1, 2009, thirty-six in all,[6] this book answers three basic questions: "Why were they used?" "Did they achieve their intended military and political objectives?" and "What variables determined their success or failure?" By broadly addressing these questions, the book evaluates the policy choices of U.S. officials over the past two decades and offers recommendations for how limited military force can be better used in the future. In addition, because U.S. uses of DMOs have now been a reality for four successive administrations, the insights and recommendations from this book are increasingly relevant to making predictions about the development of American grand strategy and military policy.[7]

The available evidence demonstrates that U.S. DMOs achieved all of their military objectives just over half of the time, and all political objectives less than 6 percent of the time. However, this large gap between political goals and military outcomes is predictable: identifying and destroying a target is a far easier task than affecting the behavior of an adversary, or potential future adversaries, through the use of force. The primary political objectives can be summarized as any one, or a combination, of the following goals: *punishment*, or revenge, for an adversary's past behavior with no intention of altering future behavior; *deterrence*, to attempt to maintain the status quo by discouraging an adversary from initiating a specific action; and *coercion*, to attempt to compel a change in an adversary's future behavior. For punishment to succeed, the military objective of a DMO must be met: if you miss the target, your adversary experiences little or no cost and may even be emboldened. For deterrence or coercion to succeed, the adversary must either maintain the status quo or change its own desired course of action because it was targeted by a limited strike. Determining whether political objectives have been met as a consequence of a DMO is a difficult analytical undertaking, but possible after careful reconstruction of the intended and actual outcomes of each case.

If DMOs have been so unsuccessful at achieving their political objectives, why do they continue to be so enthusiastically proposed and utilized by U.S. decisionmakers? The key explanation lies in divergent opinions between senior civilian and military officials over the utility of limited force. In the United States, the military is responsible for planning and executing DMOs, but only at the explicit authorization of the president of the United States and the secretary of defense (collectively, formally known as the National Command Authority). As a general proposition—supported by recent history and interviews with dozens of national security officials—senior civilian officials support the use of DMOs, while senior military officials do not. An explanation for this split, detailed in Chapter 2, is that those authorizing the use of DMOs believe that they will achieve some set of primary political objectives. In practice, however, they overwhelmingly do not.

In addition, policymakers and the general public, conditioned by round-the-clock television news coverage repeatedly showing video clips of America's armed forces surgically destroying cross-haired targets from afar, would be surprised to discover that only five in ten DMOs achieve all of their military objectives. Despite military and intelligence budgets of over $700 billion and unparalleled air, sea, and space capabilities, human error, weapon malfunctions, and poor intelligence hamper DMOs just like they do many other U.S. military operations.[8] Even DMOs that attempt to destroy an easily observable, fixed target can encounter a range of problems: planes carrying out the operation can be damaged or shot down before they release their ordnance; guidance data can be incorrectly programmed; unsuitable weapons systems can be selected; precision-guided munitions can veer off course, or be pushed by high winds; and cloud cover, smog, or dust storms can obscure targets that require visual acquisition at the last minute. Attempting to successfully destroy a mobile target—especially an individual—is even more difficult. The primary reason is that despite all of the intelligence collection assets utilized by the United States and its allies, human beings who believe they are targeted are adaptive, resilient, and hard to kill from a distance. Throughout the years, efforts to eliminate from afar such adversaries of the United States as Muammar Qadhafi, Slobodan Milosevic, Saddam Hussein, and Osama Bin Laden have generally failed. For these reasons, as well as countless other problems that arise in the fog of limited operations, U.S. DMOs fail to achieve their military objective as often as they succeed.

UNDERSTANDING DISCRETE MILITARY OPERATIONS

The ultimate tool of diplomacy, force is utilized with varying degrees of destructiveness, duration, and effectiveness according to the objective and military capabilities available.

The U.S. military conceives of conflict occurring along a spectrum of five general operational themes, of which the middle three could include DMOs: peacetime military engagement, limited intervention, peace operations, irregular warfare, and major combat operations.[9] Another way to consider DMOs is along a use-of-force continuum as described by the following list—with peace at one end and total war at the other. DMOs exist in an as yet poorly defined zone between threat of force and limited war.

Discrete Military Operations Typology of Force:

Peace with potential adversaries

Show of force to influence an adversary with no certain intent of war

Threat of force to achieve a change in an adversary's behavior

Demonstrative force to achieve a change in an adversary's behavior

Limited force to punish an adversary or achieve a change in behavior

Limited war with no certain intent of escalation

Total war of unrestrained use of capabilities to eliminate an adversary

As an illustrative metaphor for understanding international uses of force, consider an assailant pointing a gun at a person's head. If the aggressor pulls the trigger and kills the target without making a political demand, this action would be an act of punishment, or brute force. If the aggressor threatens to pull the trigger but does not, and affects some change of behavior in the target as a result of the threat, it is a *threat of force*. If the aggressor makes a specific demand of a change in behavior, seeks to maintain the status quo, or simply seeks to punish the target, and puts a bullet into the target's foot, those are all the equivalents of a *discrete military operation*. The foot-shot type of DMO may be undertaken for one or several primary or secondary reasons: to achieve a tactical military objective, to punish, to deter, to coerce, or to demonstrate resolve to a domestic or international audience.[10]

From a strategic perspective, what ultimately distinguishes a DMO from more ambitious and destructive uses of force is that it is usually undertaken without a theory of victory—a hypothetical narrative detailing how the ensuing conflict could be permanently resolved on favorable terms.[11] Although DMOs rarely have a theory of victory, they can be evaluated as being successful on the basis of the intended political and military objectives. DMOs can also be the iterative application of limited force against an adversary during an ongoing hostile relationship. After the DMO is completed, there is no clear military or political resolution between the two adversaries. For example, President George H.W. Bush in 1989 declared his "war" on drugs, which he claimed that "together we will win."[12] In 1993, U.S. Special Forces either assisted in, or were directly responsible for, the death of Colombian drug lord Pablo Escobar. While Escobar's death might have momentarily slowed the supply of cocaine from Columbia, and even deterred other drug lords, it hardly resulted in a U.S. victory in the war on drugs. Similarly, while three presidents used DMOs between 1993 and 2003 against Iraq, none were "fight and win" operations undertaken with the clear intent of resolving the state of hostilities with Saddam Hussein's regime. By contrast, the 2003 invasion and occupation of Iraq—Operation Iraqi Freedom—intended to depose the ruling regime and install a new political authority into power, thereby resolving America's long-standing contentious relationship with Hussein.

There are two terms used by political scientists and military historians that should not be confused with DMOs. The first is the historical *limited war* concept ascribed to North Atlantic Treaty Organization powers during the Cold War, which attempted to find a use for conventional tank-based armies without risking the escalation of a strategic nuclear exchange with the Soviet Union.[13] As defined by Robert Osgood, "limited war is one in which the belligerents restrict the purposes for which they fight to concrete, well-defined objectives that do not demand the utmost military effort of which the belligerents are capable. . . . It demands of the belligerents only a fractional commitment of their human and physical resources."[14] Second, DMOs should not be considered alongside the *small wars* of the late nineteenth and early twentieth centuries, conducted by imperial powers to politically and militarily control overseas territories, extract natural resources, or brutally eliminate colonial resistance movements.[15] These wars were rarely small in their intensity or intent, but are defined as such by the size of the adversarial target—that is, any state that is not also a great or middle power.

DMOs also do not include humanitarian or refugee relief operations, in which the military essentially provides protection or basic provisions for displaced persons;[16] peacekeeping, counterinsurgency, or stability operations, in which the military attempts to shape or control the operational environment of a defined territory through shows of force, direct actions, or policing;[17] or noncombatant evacuation operations in non-hostile environments, such as those the U.S. Marines have undertaken in Liberia (October 1992 and April 1996), Yemen (May 1994), and the Central African Republic (May 1996).[18] Although force may have been used to protect U.S. troops or citizens during these operations, none of them were undertaken with the intent to create casualties or damage.

There are yet two more types of military operations that are not counted as DMOs. First, DMOs in support of civilian authorities that occurred within the United States are not assessed, such as the April 19, 1993, armored invasion of the Branch Davidian complex in Waco, Texas, which resulted in seventy-five deaths.[19] This omission is because the scope of this book only considers limited military force as a tool of U.S. foreign policy. Second, DMOs that received covert or overt intelligence or logistical support from U.S. military or intelligence agencies, but that are conducted by other countries, are also excluded. Recent examples include Turkey's 2007 and 2008 limited air and ground campaign against suspected members of the Kurdish Workers Party (PKK) in Northern Iraq, which received real-time intelligence and overhead imagery from U.S. aircraft and unmanned drones;[20] the intelligence and logistics assistance given by the George W. Bush administration to the Ugandan government in its efforts to kill Joseph Kony, the leader of the Lord's Resistance Army;[21] and the Obama administration's provision of planning support, firepower, and intelligence for more than two dozen ground raids and airstrikes in Yemen in late 2009 and early 2010.[22] While such operations benefited from direct U.S. assistance, they ultimately were both authorized and conducted by foreign military or intelligence agencies.

U.S. DISCRETE MILITARY OPERATIONS USE AND ISSUES

Since the collapse of the Soviet Union, American foreign policy decision-makers have faced a radically changed international landscape. First, the United States is a unipolar power in the international system, so far lacking a competing superpower to substantially constrain its actions.[23] Second, many new threats have arisen, including rogue states that are harder to deter than was the Soviet Union; the spread of weapons of mass destruction to such states; and transnational terror networks lacking an identifiable military force and operating from stateless zones, where the government does not or cannot maintain oversight or political control. Despite the widely held belief among academics and policymakers that "everything changed after 9/11," a close reading of the U.S. national security strategy documents published in the past decade demonstrates that there has been little variation in America's declared national interests and security threats.[24] These threats are much less clearly identifiable and smaller in scope than was the Soviet threat, and far less state-centric. To counter these current and other foreseeable security threats, a troubling dilemma emerges when leaders shape America's policy responses: while each threat clearly contains the potential to endanger vital or secondary U.S. interests such that they necessitate the use of military force, they usually fail to justify the costs of a conventional war. Consequently, American political leaders keep returning to the use of DMOs.

As a unipolar power, America also remains the military hegemon in the post–Cold War world. No other state maintains a comparable cumulative military capability to project force against an adversary anywhere in the world. No other government has committed the sustained resources needed to research and develop more advanced capabilities to rapidly project offensive military power—be it through ground forces or missiles.[25] In addition, only the United States has the range of international interests that could compel intervention anywhere, as well as forty-eight reported off-the-shelf warplans that contemplate attacking other countries through, among other military options, prompt global strikes.[26]

Despite being a growth industry over the past two decades, limited force as a tool of statecraft remains undefined, and largely unexamined in an analytical manner. Simply put, scholars and military historians of the United States have shown a substantial bias toward studying major incidents rather than smaller ones.[27] In fact, the most-utilized dataset for security studies scholars of warfare—the Correlates of War Inter-State War Dataset—does not include any use of force that resulted in fewer than 1,000 battle-related deaths. An advantage to studying DMOs over conventional wars is that limited applications of force are increasingly perceived by both civilians and the armed forces as a more "usable" and internationally palatable military option.[28] One reason for this, according to a survey of all public opinion polls on the U.S. uses of force abroad between 1981 and 2005, is that Americans show higher levels of support for airstrikes than for the deployment of U.S. ground troops.[29] A second reason is that military planners—often employing worst-case planning assumptions—offer civilian decisionmakers ground combat options that include a larger number of troops to deploy overseas than civilians find politically acceptable.[30] Thus, although the United States occasionally used DMOs prior to the Cold War's end, a review of the political-military debates over using force in Bosnia, Kosovo, Afghanistan, Pakistan, Somalia, and elsewhere demonstrates that they have been much more regularly "on the table" since 1991.

The lack of scholarly attention to DMOs is troubling because such limited attacks have become the norm among American uses of military force since the First Gulf War. The United States has used direct military force against another country at least forty-one times during the time period covered in this book. Of these, five are not DMOs, as they had the intended goal of controlling, or altering the control of, the territory of another sovereign state or overthrowing a governing regime: Haiti, Somalia, Kosovo, Afghanistan since 1991, and the Iraq war that started in 2003. As listed in the appendix, thirty-six of the U.S. post–Cold War direct uses of force were Discrete Military Operations—88 percent of all uses of force.

Even as the employment of DMOs has increased, their use has been questioned and even ridiculed at times by political and military leaders as being ineffective. For example, George W. Bush, while campaigning for the presi-

dency in 2000, derided the use of "pinprick strikes" in retaliation for suspected Al Qaeda terror attacks. President Bush later spelled out his low regard
for DMOs: "When I take action," he said, "I'm not going to fire a $2 million
missile at a $10 empty tent and hit a camel in the butt. It's going to be deci-
sive."[31] Yet President Bush found DMOs to be an attractive option when he approved a Predator attack against suspected terrorists in Yemen in November
2002, in addition to dozens of other instances in Pakistan, Somalia, and Syria.
But later, as detailed in Chapter 6, Bush did not, prior to March 2003, authorize a DMO against a terrorist training camp in Northern Iraq that might
have eliminated terrorist operative Abu Musab Al Zarqawi, his followers, and
a potential WMD production facility. The Clinton administration used limited force on multiple occasions, and President Clinton himself had an affinity
for creative DMOs, once telling Chairman of the Joint Chiefs of Staff General
Hugh Shelton, "You know, it would scare the shit out of al-Qaeda if suddenly
a bunch of black ninjas rappelled out of helicopters in the middle of their
camp. It would get us enormous deterrence and show those guys we're not
afraid."[32] Yet throughout 1998–1999, when there were reportedly at least ten
opportunities to capture or kill Osama Bin Laden, the Clinton administration
repeatedly decided not to act.[33]

The American military, meanwhile, has generally held a strong institutional opposition to DMOs. Despite the battlefield necessity since 2006 to
adapt and integrate counterinsurgency principles into the Army and Marine
Corps, since World War II, the U.S. military has preferred large-scale conventional wars of annihilation to smaller-in-scope, low-intensity operations.[34]
Historically, America's military doctrine, force structure, global military
posture, education and training, and career promotional incentives have all
overwhelmingly supported a preference for big wars.[35] Military officials perceive that civilians prefer DMOs because they are an immediately responsive
tool of statecraft that will result in fewer U.S. and target-state casualties, have
fewer domestic political costs, and quickly demonstrate America's resolve and
willingness to use force. Many generals and admirals disagree with the latter point, and furthermore argue that DMOs have little long-term impact on
changing an adversary's behavior, but have the inherently dangerous potential
to uncontrollably escalate into a larger unwanted war. Military officials ideally
prefer some version of the Powell Doctrine, in which force is used in an overwhelming manner, with clearly defined political goals, the sustained support
of the American public, and an achievable exit strategy.[36] As a consequence of

that mind-set, senior military leaders have decried DMOs as "tank plinking," "salami-tactics," "a wrist-slap plan," "token retaliation," "pissing in the wind," "pure fantasy," "cowboy Hollywood stuff," "quasi military," "a waste of good ordnance," or simply "political."[37]

In his excellent study of the military's influence on decisionmaking for U.S. uses of force during the Cold War, Richard Betts provided an institutional logic behind the civilian-military split highly relevant to intra-administration debates over DMOs. Betts's rationale is worth quoting at length:

> The military's natural professional impulse is toward worst-case contingency planning for any conceivable disaster. The standard rationale is that enemy intentions cannot usually be perceived with certainty, and even if they are, they can change abruptly (such as in a cabinet or presidium shuffle), while lead-time requirements mean that enemy capabilities cannot be matched in a comparably short time. Political leaders, on the other hand, have to be more sensitive to competing nonmilitary needs. Their natural tendency is to "satisfice" rather than optimize, to shave as much as possible from the military estimates of their requirements. Because scarcity prevents providing resources for all hypothetical contingencies but because paralysis of policy is also undesirable, political authorities may sometimes be more prone to take risks by selecting options that have only a probability of success rather than a guarantee.[38]

Contrary to the opinion of some civilian and almost all military leaders, DMOs have several clear advantages over both conventional warfare or choosing not to use force at all. First, DMOs can support a wide range of military objectives, including destroying suspected WMD production facilities, damaging anti-aircraft systems, demolishing an adversary's runways or aircraft, killing political leaders or terrorist suspects, and rescuing hostages. Second, DMOs can achieve any combination of primary political goals against an adversary such as deterrence, compellence, or punishment, and secondary goals before a wider audience, such as signaling resolve, alliance-management, or domestic political gain. Third, because DMOs pursue more limited political objectives than full-scale warfare, presidents are rarely penalized for those that are a mixed success, or even an outright failure. Success in a conventional war is easier to measure with yes-no questions: adversary's military defeated?; regime changed?; territory conquered and controlled?; adversary's behavior changed?; political leaders killed or captured? Presidents have authorized several DMOs that failed, or were at best mixed successes, in the past thirty-five years. For example: Ford—the May 15, 1975, bungled assault and bombing raids against Koh Tang, Cambodia, over the *Mayaguez* incident;[39] Carter—*Desert One*, the April 24–25, 1980, unsuccessful hostage rescue operation in Iran;[40] Reagan—the December 4, 1983, raid on Syrian anti-aircraft sites in Lebanon that resulted in two downed planes, one killed U.S. pilot, and another taken hostage;[41] and George W. Bush—the February 16, 2001, airstrikes against five Iraqi command and control sites in which all but two of the twenty-eight Joint Stand-Off Weapons used missed their targets.[42] In each instance, even though the key military and political objectives of the DMO went unfulfilled, the president did not suffer a noticeable decline in public support and did not encounter persistent criticism among elite observers for the decision. Furthermore, American DMOs are conducted without a formal presidential declaration of war, and sometimes covertly, allowing the Executive Branch a relatively free hand, basically unchecked by congressional, media, or public oversight.[43] Fourth, since most DMOs are conducted with stand-off precision strike weapons, they greatly reduce the risk of casualties to soldiers, sailors, airmen, or Marines. Finally, DMOs generally do not require extensive logistical support in the form of basing or staging rights from other countries. Because they lack the same heavy footprint as larger uses of force, DMOs do not have many of the political-military cooperation problems associated with full-scale warfare.

RESEARCH FINDINGS

Senior civilian officials are more likely to support the use of DMOs than are the uniformed military. Recent research, as reinforced by first-person interviews, shows that top-level civilian decisionmakers tend to have more interventionist foreign policy agendas, are more willing to use the military to achieve those foreign policy goals, and are more willing to place constraints on the manner in which force will be used.[44] As mentioned earlier, senior military officials, in contrast, prefer overwhelming and decisive force in support of clear political objectives. Measuring the validity of this proposition throughout the case studies in this book requires determining to what extent there was a split between the most influential military and civilian decisionmakers.

Senior civilian officials favor the use of DMOs more than do the uniformed military for four reasons. First, civilians believe that DMOs are effective in achieving their limited military or political objectives, whereas, as noted earlier, military officials generally find DMOs ineffective. Second, civilians believe that DMOs are controllable uses of force that will not escalate to a wider conflict between the attacking state and the target. In contrast, military leaders believe that it is difficult, if not impossible, to manage "firebreaks" between different intensities of force, and that even small uses of force can trigger an incremental chain of events that can unleash a full-scale war.[45] Third, senior civilian leaders believe that the domestic political costs of a failed DMO will be low. Senior military officials, on the other hand, believe that unsuccessful DMOs have deleterious domestic political effects, because they can potentially harm the American public's perception of the military. Fourth, civilians believe that the use of some DMOs demonstrates resolve both to targeted adversaries and to a wider international audience.[46] In contrast, many military leaders believe that DMOs are actually a sign of weakness to the world regarding America's willingness to use overwhelming military force. This "all or nothing" school of thought,[47] best articulated by General Colin Powell, finds DMOs to be nothing more than "gratification without commitment."[48]

In general, U.S. use of DMOs since 1991 has been tactically successful at meeting most military objectives, but strategically ineffective in achieving specific political goals. Appendix I codes the level of success in meeting the stated military and political objectives of thirty-six instances of U.S. use of DMOs. It also contains a short description of each instance, aside from the four studied in depth in the case studies in this book. These assessments admittedly are subjective, though it is more straightforward to determine the objective military success of a DMO than the political success.

The findings are not promising for DMOs as a political solution. A detailed analysis of the evidence shows that five of the thirty-six cases had an undetermined military outcome. Of the remaining thirty-one, sixteen (52 percent) met all of the intended military objectives, while only two (6 percent) met all of the intended political objectives. When success and mixed success are combined, the results even out: twenty-two cases met roughly one-half of the intended military objectives (71 percent), twenty-seven cases met at least one-half of the intended political objectives (75 percent). Nine cases totally failed to meet their intended military goals—all of which were assassination attempts (Osama Bin Laden, Saddam Hussein, Abu Hamza Rabia, an as-yet unidentified Al Qaeda member, Ayman Al-Zawahiri, and four attempts on Al Qaeda officials in Somalia)—while nine completely failed to meet the intended political goal. Thus the data demonstrate that DMOs are a useful tool for destroying a target but that the attacks are generally unsuccessful in punishing, deterring, or compelling an adversary.

CASE STUDIES TELL THE STORY

Collecting and analyzing data is a dry and insufficient means of evaluating complex decisionmaking processes, such as whether or not to attack another country or sub-state actor. Examination of case studies allows for a broader geostrategic, psychological, and historical understanding of the adversary against whom U.S. officials considered using limited military force. The four cases that are studied in-depth to better understand DMOs are as follows.

Iraqi No-Fly Zones (NFZ) (July 1991–April 2003). The no-fly zones operated under three names: Provide Comfort II, which included tens of thousands of sorties (July 24, 1991–December 31, 1996); Northern Watch, which included around 16,000 sorties (January 1, 1997–April 30, 2003); and Southern Watch, which included over 200,000 sorties (August 26, 1992–April 30, 2003).[49] The no-fly zones were intended to deny Iraq the ability to fly fixed-wing flights against the perceived internal political enemies of Saddam Hussein's regime. The typical enforcement flight included a package of four to five aircraft flying inside the zones for thirty minutes to two hours, under strict rules of engagement created in collaboration with the host country from which the planes originated. Although British and French planes participated, only U.S. planes attacked Iraqi anti-aircraft and radar sites, and only after the planes were threatened.[50]

Operation Infinite Reach (August 20, 1998). In retaliation for bombings against U.S. embassies in Kenya and Tanzania, the United States simultaneously launched thirteen Tomahawk cruise missiles against a pharmaceutical plant in Khartoum, Sudan, suspected of producing nerve gas and sixty-six Tomahawks against six sites within an Al Qaeda training complex in southern Afghanistan with the intention of killing Osama Bin Laden and other terrorist leaders. Between twenty and sixty people in the camps were killed and several dozen others injured—many of whom were reportedly Pakistani militants training for operations in Kashmir. Neither Bin Laden nor his chief lieutenants were killed.[51]

Yemeni Assassination (November 3, 2002). A Central Intelligence Agency–operated Predator drone originating and controlled from Djibouti launched a Hellfire missile at a car carrying six suspected Al Qaeda members one hundred miles east of the capital, Sana'a. All six were killed, including Abu Ali al-Harithi, suspected mastermind of the *U.S.S. Cole* attack, and Ahmed Hijazi, a naturalized U.S. citizen and alleged ringleader of a purported terrorist sleeper cell in Lackawanna, New York.[52]

Khurmal, Iraq (Summer 2002). In early 2002, U.S. intelligence got word that in Iraqi Kurdistan, near the city of Khurmal, a Kurdish terrorist organization—Ansar al-Islam—was running a training camp and reportedly producing cyanide gas, toxic poisons, and ricin for terrorist attacks by its affiliated cells in Western Europe. The U.S. military developed a combined air-ground operation option that anticipated striking the camp on July 4, 2002. That option was unanimously supported by the Joint Chiefs of Staff and proposed to the White House. President Bush ultimately opted not to strike the camp because the DMO potentially could have derailed the goal of removing Saddam Hussein from power.[53]

These cases were selected for five reasons. First, they involve all of the services of the U.S. military and CIA, thus negating any single-service bias in the sample. In addition, some of the DMOs are multi-service. Second—with the exception of the still-covert Yemen targeted killing—the cases have produced a wealth of available data that include participants who were willing to discuss them on the record, thus providing a deeper understanding of each case. Third, they differ in terms of length of duration, intensity of operations, and type of operation. Fourth, there are enough variations across the cases with regard to political and military intent—such as revenge, punishment, deterrence, national morale, and so on—that any initial findings developed in this book will be applicable to other countries that employ DMOs.[54] Finally, the decisionmaking processes behind the three actual—and one proposed—DMOs reviewed have not been presented or analyzed in detail elsewhere. For scholars and historians, the careful presentation of the facts supported by first-person interviews reveals new details about each event. For the lay reader, the strategic setting and decision-making processes of the cases are meant to illustrate how intra-administration debates are occurring today over whether to strike Al Qaeda operatives in Pakistan, attack pirate infrastructure onshore in East Africa, or bomb suspected Iranian nuclear facilities.

The Khurmal case is an example of the dog that did not bark. Social scientists refer to such non-events as *negative cases*, in which an expected and relevant outcome of interest did not occur, even though it was a strong possibility.[55] The case was included because, for the purposes of studying and evaluating U.S. limited uses of military force, it is important to understand the causes and conditions of negative cases, when limited force is proposed and debated among senior officials but never implemented. To be sufficiently comprehensive, one cannot only look at DMOs that were executed.

Recent examples of negative cases run the gamut from the oversized extreme with indeterminate political objectives to a very limited plan with well-defined political goals to initially limited operations that expanded beyond what was politically acceptable when logistics and support elements were included. An example of the first would be the decision by the NSC in June 1996 not to execute the "Eisenhower option," a ground invasion in retaliation for the June 25, 1996, bombing of the Khobar Towers that ranged to as many as 500,000 troops, cruise missile strikes against strategic assets on Iran's coast and WMD sites, and strikes against Iranian-sponsored terror camps in Lebanon.[56] An example of the second would be President George H.W. Bush's decision in August 1990 to not attack an Iraqi oil tanker to disable it and prevent it from traveling to South Yemen, an operation initially planned to coerce Saddam Hussein to withdraw his forces from Kuwait.[57] And an example of the third would be the refusal, moments before it began, of Secretary of Defense Donald Rumsfeld to authorize in late 2005 a complex U.S. Navy Seal operation to attempt to capture Ayman al-Zawahiri in northern Pakistan.[58] Within this spectrum, between these extremes, lies a wide range of limited military operations—such as the potential Khurmal operation—that were developed, proposed, and debated, but ultimately rejected by senior officials as inappropriate instruments of national power to tackle a specific foreign policy dilemma.

CONCLUSION

Even in a globalized era characterized by increased trade and transactions, freely flowing capital, relatively open borders, and unprecedented interconnectedness, the world remains stubbornly anarchic, and military force continues to be a fungible tool for achieving foreign policy goals. Whether it is the September 2007 Israeli airstrike on a suspected nuclear facility in Syria, Colombia's March 2008 small-scale raid against suspected Revolutionary Armed Forces of Colombia (FARC) officials located just inside Ecuador, or Israel's attack against a suspected Hezbollah weapons convoy in northern Sudan in January 2009, limited military operations against other countries are an important instrument of international statecraft. Such operations are conducted with political and military objectives that foreign decisionmakers believe cannot be met—in the timeframe required—through available non-kinetic solutions. The United States has both the widest and the deepest range of global interests, and the most available military capabilities to use limited force in support of those interests. It is no surprise, therefore, that the United States both considers at the most senior levels and conducts vastly more DMOs than any other country in the world. The goal of this book is to determine if those DMOs have been the correct course of action for the United States since 1991, and to prescribe the causes and conditions for their potential success in the future.

2 POLITICAL USES OF FORCE AND THE CIVILIAN-MILITARY SPLIT

"In politics force is said to be the ultima ratio. In international politics force serves, not only as the ultima ratio, but indeed as the first and constant one."[1]

Kenneth Waltz, political scientist

"And perhaps when they see that our actual strength is keeping pace with the language that we use, they will be more inclined to give way, since their land will still be untouched and, in making up their minds, they will be thinking of advantages which they still possess and which have not yet been destroyed."[2]

Archidamus II, King of Sparta

"It was my experience over the years that one of the biggest misimpressions held by the public has been that our military is always straining at the leash, wanting to use force in any situation. The reality is just the opposite. In more than twenty years of attending meetings in the Situation Room, my experience was that the biggest doves in Washington wear uniforms."[3]

Robert Gates, Director of Central Intelligence

BEFORE EXAMINING THE FOUR CASE STUDIES, it is useful to provide a brief sketch of the foundations of the three main political uses of force—compellence, deterrence, and punishment—and to outline the enduring differences between senior civilian and military officials over the use of Discrete Military Operations.

POLITICAL USES OF FORCE

In a note revising his manuscript *On War*, the Prussian general and strategist Carl von Clausewitz put forth his oft-quoted dictum that "war is nothing but the continuation of policy with other means."[4] This proposition captures the notion that inter-state war in general does not arise from minor disagreements or primal hatred between adversarial states. Nor is war a self-generated phenomenon isolated from a state's larger strategic goals. The British general Rupert Smith underscored this notion as recently as 2007, noting, "Armies enter combat not merely because two or more of them happen to be hanging around an empty battlefield and decide to fill in some time but because an issue between two or more political entities cannot be settled in other ways and then military means are resorted to."[5] What generals such as Clausewitz and Smith have encouraged politicians and military commanders to recognize is that there is a political purpose to every aspect of military force, regardless of its operational objectives, intensity, or duration. Even if a soldier acting without political intent or orders from a superior launches a tank round across a border and into an adversary's territory, there undoubtedly will be political consequences. To increase the likelihood of success for the strategic use of military force, a state's leadership should clearly define its intended political objectives before deploying forces in an effort to achieve them.

In the 1950s and 1960s, the economist Thomas Schelling utilized a game theoretical approach to help develop and popularize the archetypal labels that are still relevant for the political goals behind military power. Schelling envisioned the threat or use of force to be but one component of an ongoing bargaining relationship between two adversarial states "in which communication is incomplete, or impossible."[6] He found that, in seeking to avoid war, but to influence the behavior of an adversary, "violence is most purposive and most successful when it is threatened and not used."[7] The use of brute force, or "pure hurting" as Schelling termed it, was a distinct alternative to the bargaining process, not a component of it. In addition, committing to the use of overwhelming military power against an adversary has a terminal effect—it saves nothing in reserve, is more costly and risky, increases an enemy's resolve, and makes a negotiated solution less likely.[8] As a consequence, Schilling contended, the threat or use of limited military power is a more adaptive and fungible tool and has a more enduring utility in the bargaining process between two adversaries.

The three primary political purposes of force developed by Schelling and others are compellence, deterrence, and punishment.[9] (*Compellence* in its latter-day guise of coercive diplomacy is discussed further on.) *Deterrence* refers to the strategy of persuading a state to refrain from taking a certain action by threatening something it values. Successfully employed, deterrence persuades another state that the costs of challenging the status quo outweigh the costs of enduring it.[10] Deterrence strategies can be either specific (or immediate), where a targeted adversary is warned against undertaking a specific behavior, or general, where a standing but unspecified threat is broadcast to actual or potential adversaries to convince them not to undertake a certain behavior or range of behaviors. One successful example of specific deterrence (to date) occurred in October 2006, when, after North Korea conducted its first explosive nuclear test, President George W. Bush warned, "The transfer of nuclear weapons or material by North Korea to states or non-state entities would be considered a grave threat to the United States, and we would hold North Korea fully accountable of the consequences of such action."[11] A failed specific deterrent demand was one issued by Bush's father—and reconfirmed by the Clinton administration—in the "Christmas Warning" of 1992, which warned Serbian president Slobodan Milosevic, "In the event of conflict in Kosovo caused by Serbian action, the United States will be prepared to employ military force against the Serbians in Kosovo and in Serbia proper."[12] When Serbia initiated a brutal counterinsurgency campaign in Kosovo in March 1998, however, the Clinton administration refused to back up the ultimatum, and deflected questions about whether it remained in effect.[13]

Deterrence can be either general or specific in nature. Since general deterrence is less clearly articulated than its specific version, and is a component of the normal day-to-day relationships between states, it is much more difficult to quantify and assess.[14] For example, nine days after September 11, 2001, President Bush announced, "From this day forward, any nation that continues to harbor or support terrorism will be regarded by the United States as a hostile regime."[15] Note that Bush's threat extended equally to all 190 other states, over an undefined time period, with unclear consequences. Eight years after Bush made his declaration, terrorists continue to operate from the territory of some states, enjoying varying degrees of direct support; other states, however, have expelled terrorists from their sovereign territory, or ended assistance to them, possibly out of fear of U.S. military, economic, or diplomatic pressure. Thus it is difficult to quantify the extent to which general deterrence has worked. For both specific or general deterrence, however, once either the targeted adversary has undertaken the proscribed behavior or the threat of force has actually been carried out, the strategy has failed.

Punishment is a strategy that has the primary goal of achieving the physical destruction of a target through the direct and kinetic application of force. Punishment strategies usually are attempted in conjunction with secondary objectives, such as deterring or compelling the future actions of both a targeted adversary and similar existing or future ones. The primary goal of the attacks, however, is either to eliminate a target altogether, such as a regime's assets or military capabilities, or to kill an adversary. Among all political uses of military force, punishment is generally the least political, meaning that it is often disconnected from the bargaining process between two adversaries. Each U.S. DMO conducted since 1991 in which punishment was the primary objective sought to extract some degree of revenge for an earlier action by the targeted adversary or its affiliates. In none of the cases was limited force used after making a deterrent or compellent demand. They were, in essence, "bolt from the blue" military strikes. Not surprisingly, punishment uses of force are the easiest to evaluate for success or failure: the intended target is always either almost fully destroyed or killed, or it remains intact or alive. For example, in January 2007, a U.S. Air Force Special Operations AC-130 fired on a convoy of escaping Islamic militants near the village of Ras Kamboni in southern Somalia near Kenya. Its primary target was Aden Hashi Ayro, a militant leader and senior operative in Al Qaeda's East Africa network. Ayro survived, making it a failed punishment operation. But sixteen months later, the U.S. Navy fired four or five Tomahawk cruise missiles into a small compound in the city of Dusa Marreb in central Somalia, killing Ayro and a dozen civilians. In that instance, the punishment component of the operation succeeded, but the secondary objective of deterring Al Qaeda from using Somalia to plan and stage operations did not.[16]

Compellence, as a subset of coercive diplomacy, is worth examining in greater detail to better understand DMOs because it is a strategy that considers either the threat of force or the actual use of kinetic force in a limited manner.[17] In addition, policy and academic debates about the efficacy of coercive diplomacy occurred regularly during the era studied in this book, as reflected in the George H.W. Bush and Clinton administrations' discussions about whether to use force in Iraq, Bosnia, Haiti, Kosovo, and North Korea.[18] The phrase has great political value for U.S. civilian policymakers seeking to be perceived as tough enough to threaten or use military power but also sufficiently open-minded to negotiate with adversaries. While running for president in 2007 and 2008, Senator Hillary Clinton repeatedly attempted to justify her vote in 2002 authorizing the use of force to threaten the removal of Saddam Hussein from power in Iraq as simply a vote for compellence, proclaiming, "I believe in coercive diplomacy," in a February 2008 presidential debate.[19] Though the George W. Bush administration did not attempt coercive diplomacy as often as its immediate predecessor—since the adversary that most threatened U.S. national interests was an inherently harder to compel non-state terrorist organization—it retained its use and language.[20] Initial months of the Barack Obama presidency have seen a restatement of immediate deterrent threats to North Korea, but not any specific coercive diplomatic threats against adversaries of the United States.

The theory of coercive diplomacy, as initially developed by Alexander George, includes three core ingredients.[21] First, a specific demand is placed upon a target. Second, a specific deadline or a sense of urgency to comply is communicated to the target. Third, a credible threat of military punishment is made that is great enough to make the target choose compliance over resistance. Several variants of coercive diplomacy—for example, "try and see," or "turning the screw"—can be attempted with differing applications of the three ingredients depending on the specific situation and the adversary's values. In addition, positive inducements can be offered to the target in conjunction with the declaration of the threat in an effort to increase the likelihood of compliance—such as offering a "carrot" while wielding a "stick." Regardless of which variant is used, coercive diplomacy succeeds in only one way, when the target complies with the demand on the required timeline because of the threat or use of limited force, but it can fail in one of two ways: when the target refuses to comply, or when a greater-than-threatened use of force is used to achieve the desired political objectives. As Robert Art notes, "Wherever one draws the line between limited and full-scale use, if the coercer has to cross that line to achieve its objectives, then, by definition, coercive diplomacy has failed."[22]

Along with actually using limited force, compellence can also be attempted by merely threatening to use force. Investigating foreign policy strategies of threatening force—or even repositioning troops or combat material—to achieve a political effect against a target state is most closely associated with Barry Blechman and Stephen Kaplan's landmark 1977 study, *Force Without War: U.S. Armed Forces as a Political Instrument.* Blechman and Kaplan examined in-depth the efficacy of thirty-three cases—from a universe of 215 total incidents—between 1946 and 1975 in which U.S. armed forces attempted to influence another country's behavior. They found that over a short term (six months), U.S. operational objectives were achieved 75 percent of the time, but that over a longer term (three years), the success rate dropped to 39 percent. Among the types of political objectives, Blechman and Kaplan found that, over the long term, the peaceful use of armed forces was over three times more likely to succeed at deterring a targeted state (64 percent), than at compelling one (19 percent).[23] Philip Zelikow correlated these findings with an updated dataset that included seventy-one incidents of peaceful uses of force between 1975 and 1984.[24]

As an overall strategy of U.S. foreign policy, however, coercive diplomacy generally has failed more often than it has succeeded. Two major studies of U.S. coercive diplomacy efforts have shown that they were clear successes at most 30 percent of the time.[25] A key reason for this is that in an international arena necessarily characterized by incomplete information and uncertainty, states are naturally careful to weigh potential costs and benefits before committing to a course of action. Compellence attempts to stop or alter a purposeful and ongoing state behavior. Deterrence, on the other hand, attempts to persuade a state from beginning a new course of action before it has committed its resources and credibility. Being compelled by the United States to alter one's status-quo behavior could have severe negative consequences to one's reputation and perceived authority, while standing up to the United States could bolster one's credibility and respect domestically, regionally, and even globally. States therefore have consistently—and successfully—resisted America's compellent demands.

DMOs can be included as a subset of coercive diplomacy, but only when actual force is used against an adversary in support of a compellent political objective. The fundamental difference between DMOs and coercive diplomacy is the unit of analysis. Studies of coercive diplomacy consider a unit of analysis to be an interaction between two states in which one issues a demand on a target state that is backed up by the threat of military force. This will always be a subjective measurement, since a targeted state can make demands on the issuing state and back them up with counter-coercive threats, thus making it difficult to determine who is compelling whom.[26] But for DMOs, the unit of analysis consists of an empirically observable military action by one state against another for any number of the primary political goals: compellence, deterrence, or punishment.

CIVILIAN-MILITARY SPLIT IN USING FORCE

A key issue of civil-military relations in democratic societies is the mechanisms used by elected civilian officials to oversee and control the uniformed armed forces.[27] For such relations in the United States, tensions regarding the employment of force in a limited manner are the pertinent component for this book. Despite the common and sometimes popular depiction of military officials dragging reluctant civilian policymakers to war, during the Cold War, the reverse was true for the United States. As Richard Betts found in his careful study of military and civilian influence on decisions to use force during the Cold War, "The stereotype of a belligerent chorus of generals and admirals intimidating a pacific civilian establishment is not supported by the evidence."[28] Since the end of the Vietnam War the evidence supporting the divergence between senior American military and civilian officials has been further developed and refined.[29] At the highest levels there is a significant split in the United States between the uniformed military and their civilian overseers about the use of limited force. This schism is in part a consequence of persistent, differing interpretations over how the policy choices of successive U.S. administrations failed to prevent the fall of South Vietnam to Communism.[30] At the heart of those policy choices is the belief among many generals and admirals who served in Vietnam that the U.S. military "had won all of the battles but had lost the war" in large part because of the "Fight-Talk, Fight-Talk" strategy employed by civilians in Washington, D.C.[31]

The deeper, structural reason for the split, however, is found in the distinct and relatively uniform environment under which military officials are educated, trained, and employed, in contrast with their civilian policymaker counterparts. As Peter Feaver notes, "Military communities have strong identities that mark them as 'different' from those of civilians, and this is deliberately cultivated and signified. . . . there is, in other words, some irreducible difference between military and civilian, and this will naturally extend to different perspectives."[32] Senior officers are educated at the war colleges and command schools that provide similar warnings about the downsides of limited uses of force—as captured in the "Powell Doctrine"—through lectures, group discussions, and student research papers. They have mandatory reading lists—from the War Colleges, Chiefs of Staff, and officer training schools—which provide shared reference points and historical analogies that help shape preferences.[33] Senior officers are also trained within their field to support a common doctrine: those "fundamental principles by which the military forces or elements thereof guide their actions in support of national objectives."[34] Most important, senior military officers serve for at least twenty years before they are promoted to the senior ranks of brigadier general for the Army, Air Force, or Marines, and rear admiral for the Navy. On the other hand, the average length of service for a senior civilian political appointee in the Department of Defense is only two years.[35] Throughout their relatively lengthy tenures of service, such senior military officers are exposed to a set of received beliefs reinforced through institutional pressures regarding the conditions under which force should be used. Yet civilian policymakers—especially political appointees who hold the most influential decisionmaking positions—have no uniform exposure to policy issues, and little institutional loyalty to a position they will leave in a relatively short period of time.

The dissimilar conditions under which civilian and military officials rise through their respective ranks, and the asymmetry in practical knowledge about how military operations are planned and conducted, result in a "reciprocal ignorance" between the two groups about each other's perspectives.[36] As a consequence of this difference, there are two general schools of thought characterizing their corresponding beliefs in using limited force.[37] Senior civilian officials are broadly represented as belonging to the *Surgical Strike School.* When civilian officials perceive a foreign policy dilemma that does not threaten vital U.S. interests but requires a quick response, they often find that limited military force is the most responsive tool available. In addition, limited force has low political costs if it fails, and less risk both to U.S. soldiers conducting the mission and civilians living in the targeted state. Furthermore, the Surgical Strike School assumes a high degree of precision in the application of force. Finally, such officials generally believe that limited force can achieve limited political objectives, and will not necessarily result in escalating uses of force.

Senior military officials, on the other hand, are predominantly characterized by the *Functional Force School. Webster's* defines function as "The action for which a person or thing is specially fitted, used, or responsible or for which a thing exists: the activity appropriate to the nature or position of a person or thing."[38] In confronting a foreign policy dilemma, military officials seek clear guidance from civilian officials about what exactly are the desired political objectives and end state. As former Army Vice Chief of Staff General Jack Keane noted, military officials believe that it is their obligation to force civilians to consider, "What are the objectives, how clear are they, and what is the strategy to achieve them?"[39] Among the available instruments of national power, the Functional Force School perceives military force to be the bluntest, and an often inadequate means to resolving the root problems that it attempts to deal with. If force is to be used at all, it should be overwhelming and attempted as a last resort in the bargaining process with an adversary. In addition, on the basis of technical expertise and historical experience, they know limited force is rarely applied in a precise and low-cost manner. Finally, these military officials envision that small military operations, whether they succeed or fail, can result in a slippery slope down which more lethal military power is employed incrementally either out of revenge for earlier defeats or setbacks, to capitalize on gains already made, or to chase an increasingly elusive victory.

Of course, debates between senior civilian and military officials are highly context dependent, and some participants belong to neither of the two schools.[40] Sometimes, civilian policymakers oppose limited strikes, while military officials will advise that they can be designed and executed to achieve their political objectives. In addition, neither the broad spectrum of civilian national security policymakers nor military officials from each service speaks with a single, coherent voice in administration debates. For example, the Army has consistently been more cautious about using limited force than other U.S. services.[41] Long-serving Pentagon civilian officials are generally more sympathetic to senior military official's positions on DMO-type missions than are politically appointed civilians serving within a specific administration. In addition, civilian officials from State Department regional bureaus are understandably less supportive of small-scale strikes against countries within their portfolio.[42] Nevertheless, civil-military relations scholars have found, as strongly confirmed in interviews conducted for this work, that U.S. civilian decisionmakers are more willing both to rely on military force to achieve their foreign policy goals and to place constraints on the manner in which force is used than are their military counterparts.[43]

These conflicting schools are problematic for the successful employment of DMOs, since, although civilians formally authorize using force, civilians and military officials normally arrive at a joint decision through an iterative bargaining process.[44] This back-and-forth process between senior civilian and military officials occurs within two different arenas. The first arena consists of the formal and informal discussions that take place behind closed doors, over secure phone lines, and via encrypted e-mail, throughout the military planning process. Here, planning staffs at the Combatant Command level develop a range of military options, which are then vetted within the Joint Staff, and the Office of the Secretary of Defense. The vice chairman of the Joint Chiefs, or Director of Operations (J-3), receives further feedback from interagency steering groups, or the Deputies Committee of the National Security Council (NSC). Finally, the chairman of the Joint Chiefs presents several military options to the Principals Committee of the NSC, where the president makes the final decision, in consultation with civilian and military aides. The second arena within which debates over using force occur is the public realm, with opinions disseminated through speeches, congressional testimonies, news stories, real-time leaks to retired officials and media, and op-eds. At each step of the process, within the private and public arena, the demands of civilians and the professional advice of military officers interact to shape, refine, and finalize military operations as politics allow and the conditions on the ground dictate.

A particularly illustrative—and overlooked—real-life example of how the civil-military debate over using force occurs is worth examining. During the summer of 1992, concerned about the deteriorating situation in the former Yugoslavia—represented by photographs of emaciated Bosnian Muslim men in concentration camps—and prodded by statements supporting the use of military power in the Balkans by presidential candidate and then-Governor Bill Clinton, George H.W. Bush administration civilian officials strongly considered using military power, including ground troops, to ensure the delivery of humanitarian aid and deter Serbian aggression.[45] In August, the Senate Armed Services Committee requested that a senior official from the Joint Chiefs of Staff testify at a hearing on U.S. policy toward Bosnia. General Colin Powell, Chairman of the Joint Chiefs, directed Lieutenant General Barry McCaffrey—principal military assistant to the chairman—to testify.[46] In preparing for his Senate appearance, McCaffrey created his own presentation and slides, without having them approved by the Joint Chiefs, the Office of the Secretary of Defense, or the White House. When asked the force level required to end the violence throughout Bosnia-Herzegovina, McCaffrey replied, "It would be around 400,000 troops." For securing the supply of humanitarian aid to Sarajevo he offered "a seat-of-the-pants answer, consisting of 60,000 to 120,000 troops to provide absolute security." To emphasize the difficulty of possible military operations in Bosnia-Herzegovina, McCaffrey also repeatedly highlighted that in four years of fighting in Yugoslavia during World War II, over a million people lost their lives—a testament to the Yugoslavs' perceived innate aggression and intense hatred of foreign occupiers.[47]

Lieutenant General McCaffrey's personal estimates of the forces needed and potentially poor outcomes were shared by many senior military officials, including General Powell. According to David Halberstam, through the remainder of the George H.W. Bush administration, and during the first year of the Clinton administration, "Powell would show his lack of enthusiasm by giving [senior civilians] a high estimate, and they would quickly back off. The figure never went under two hundred thousand troops."[48] As a consequence of the massive ground presence required by Powell, such possible military operations were never seriously considered by civilian officials. The presentation of military options perceived by civilians as being intentionally oversized— to prevent them from ever being executed—was a constant issue that faced the George H.W. Bush, Clinton, and to a lesser extent, George W. Bush and Barack Obama administrations.[49] As Brent Scowcroft recalled about the Bush administration debates over using force to expel the Iraqi Army from Kuwait, "The initial plan for retaking Kuwait . . . had not seemed designed by anyone eager to undertake the task. Similarly, the force requirements for a successful offense given to [Bush] . . . were so large that one could speculate they were set forth by a command hoping their size would change his mind about pursuing a military option."[50] Military planners providing inflated estimates of the forces required to achieve an objective is a clear example of what Feaver refers to as "shirking"—when a military agent does something that undermines the ability of civilians to make future decisions.[51]

U.S. civilian officials also consistently solicit specific military solutions to foreign policy problems that are far from what military officials believe to be reasonable, or logistically achievable.[52] Civilians can underestimate the full range of capabilities required to conduct DMOs, and overlook the likely second- and third-order effects of an operation. To cite a few infamous examples: in 1961, advisor Dean Acheson advocated that President Kennedy send an Army battalion up the Autobahn to West Berlin to probe Soviet reactions;[53] in the summer of 1985, senior NSC civilians envisioned removing Libyan leader Muammar Qadhafi from power by a joint U.S.-Egyptian land-air campaign, which the Joint Chiefs considered "ludicrous;"[54] and late in his administration, President Clinton believed the United States could "scare the shit out of al-Qaeda if suddenly a bunch of black ninjas rappelled out of helicopters in the middle of their camp."[55] Clinton's proposal was one of numerous "silly" options for killing Osama Bin Laden proposed by civilians who "had seen too many movies," according to a knowledgeable Pentagon official.[56] Many such "awfully crazy schemes," as Robert Gates—himself a former Air Force intelligence officer—recalled observing civilians propose during his experiences in five administrations, are squashed at the lower levels of the inter-agency planning process, and never formally presented to the president.[57] They have the effect, however, of convincing military officers that civilian officials have dangerous and unrealistic expectations of what military power can achieve, and are not serious about countering structural issues that created the foreign policy problem in the first place. Former Chairman of the Joint Chiefs of Staff General Richard Myers aptly summarized this tension between military and civilian officials: "A lot of people not wearing military uniforms don't really understand what it takes to conduct military operations."[58]

3 IRAQI NO-FLY ZONES: 1991–2003

BETWEEN JULY 1991 AND MARCH 2003, American pilots patrolled northern and southern Iraq with the principal military mission of preventing the Iraqi Air Force (IrAF) from flying fixed-wing aircraft over these regions. To this end, the Iraqi no-fly zones (NFZs) were a resounding military success: with the exception of a few brief incursions into the zones by the IrAF, Saddam Hussein's airpower was wholly confined to the middle of his country. The NFZs, however, also had two principal political missions. First was protecting the Kurds in northern Iraq and the Shias in the south from attacks by Hussein's security forces. The NFZs were a mixed success in achieving this objective: while Hussein's Baathist Party regime did not threaten Kurdish or Shia populations from the air, Iraqi government troops continued to terrorize them with ground forces. The United States refused to intervene militarily to prevent these ground attacks against Hussein's political enemies. However, the second political mission was to contain Hussein from invading Kuwait and Saudi Arabia, or launching ballistic missiles against his neighbors. The NFZs fully succeeded in this objective: Iraq had the means, motive, and opportunity to break out of the American-led containment regime, but was deterred from doing so. In short, the Iraqi NFZs were a Discrete Military Operation (DMO) that achieved its military goal but had mixed success in achieving its political goals.[1]

This chapter contains six sections. First, it presents the strategic setting in which the northern NFZ was created in the aftermath of Operation Desert Storm. Second, it describes the situation that led to the adoption of a southern NFZ to match the year-old no-fly zone in the north. Third, it details the political environment in which the NFZs were transformed from humanitarian protection to military containment in the first Clinton administration. Fourth, it describes the operation of the NFZs in the second Clinton term, when U.S. policy toward Iraq included the aspiration of regime change. Fifth, it reveals how the NFZs were utilized by the George W. Bush administration to prepare the battlefield before the start of Operation Iraqi Freedom in 2003. Finally, the chapter evaluates the success or failure of the military and political objectives of the NFZs.

THE ACCIDENTAL BIRTH AND EARLY HISTORY OF THE NFZS

On January 17, 1991, a UN coalition led by 500,000 U.S. troops commenced Operation Desert Storm to expel the Iraqi military from Kuwait. Four weeks into the bombing campaign, on February 15, President George H.W. Bush, using identical language, twice—at the White House and later at a Raytheon defense plant in Massachusetts—encouraged "the Iraqi military and the Iraqi people to take matters into their own hands and force Saddam Hussein, the dictator, to step aside."[2] President Bush's message was beamed into Iraq via every international television and radio channel.[3] Leaflets were dropped by coalition aircraft that called on Iraqi soldiers and civilians to "fill the streets and alleys and bring down Saddam Hussein and his aides."[4] Kurdish rebels in the north and the Shias in the south began building upon years of clandestine planning to topple Hussein.[5] On February 28, President Bush declared a cease-fire merely a hundred hours after the ground war component of Desert Storm began, and the following day Iraq exploded in rebellion. Beginning in Basra and spreading throughout the cities of Najaf, Karbala, and Nasiriyya, Shia rebels and Iraqi Army sympathizers attacked government security agents and regime targets.[6] On March 5, Kurdish rebels revolted against Iraqi Army divisions and Baath Party officials, detaining whom they could and massacring resisters.[7] One month after Bush's call to the Iraqi people to rise up, incredibly, fourteen of Iraq's eighteen provinces were no longer under the control of the central government.[8]

On March 3, 1991, the American commander of UN coalition forces, General Norman Schwarzkopf, met with Hussein's generals at the Safwan Airfield in Iraq to discuss the military terms of the cease-fire between Iraq and the international coalition. The Safwan Accords focused on the lines of demarcation between opposing ground forces, the mechanisms for coordinating the exchange of prisoners of war, and an order by Schwarzkopf that Iraq not fly fixed-wing aircraft. Included in the discussion between Schwarzkopf and the Iraqis at Safwan was a request by an Iraqi general for permission to fly helicopters, including armed gunships, to transport government officials above the country's many destroyed roads and bridges. Believing it a legitimate request from a defeated commander, and acting without instructions from the Pentagon or the White House, Schwarzkopf replied, "I will instruct the Air Force not to shoot at any helicopters flying over the territory of Iraq where our troops are not located."[9] President Bush and National Security Advisor Brent Scowcroft's foreign policy memoir succinctly summarized the effect of Schwarzkopf's decision: "Saddam almost immediately began using the helicopters as gunships to put down the uprisings."[10]

The Iraq Air Force's fixed-wing aircraft, however, were never employed to defeat the Kurd or Shia uprisings. Despite formal requests from the Iraqi Revolutionary Command Council, American military officials refused to allow IrAF planes to be "repositioned" within the country because they might attack coalition forces while in transit.[11] On one of the few occasions that an Iraqi combat aircraft violated Schwarzkopf's edict—an SU-22 Fitter flying out of Kirkuk to *avoid* the Kurds, not to attack them—it was shot down by an American F-15C.[12] The U.S. military's demonstrated readiness to shoot down violators of this as-yet-undefined "no-fly zone," and the general unwillingness of the Iraqis to test the American order, strongly suggest that a similar pronouncement would have certainly deterred Iraq from utilizing helicopters as a counterinsurgency tool.[13] While patrolling southern Iraq, U.S. F-15s watched Iraqi helicopters attack Shias; using the fighter aircraft to down the helicopters would have been a simple and straightforward mission.[14] In the end, the IrAF planes were an unnecessary tool for the regime in Baghdad. Using only helicopters, long-range artillery, and armored ground forces, Hussein's Republican Guard divisions brutally counterattacked the uprising, killing between 30,000 and 60,000 Shias in the south, and some 20,000 Kurds in the north.[15] Though the United States had enormous military capabilities in the Persian Gulf, the Bush administration provided no assistance to the uprisings because it feared that Iraq would fragment, Iranian-backed Shias would assume power in Baghdad, and more GIs would be killed in "another Vietnam."[16] By early April 1991, Saddam Hussein's regime had completely crushed both Shia and Kurdish resistances.

As a deliberate tactic of his counteroffensive against the Kurds, Hussein sought to depopulate northern Iraq by panicking its residents into fleeing from their homes.[17] In 1987 and 1988, during a military campaign against Kurdish militias suspected of cooperating with Tehran during the Iran-Iraq War, Iraqi planes and helicopters had dropped mustard and nerve gas on civilians in at least sixty villages.[18] To mimic their earlier WMD attacks, in

April 1991, Republican Guard divisions dumped flour—resembling powdered chemical agents—from helicopters onto displaced Kurds in a successful effort to induce widespread terror.[19] On April 5, the UN Security Council passed Resolution 688, which demanded that the Iraqi regime "immediately end this repression" against the civilian population.[20] This diplomatic initiative, however, was irrelevant to the facts on the ground, as two million Kurds had already been newly displaced and scattered throughout northern Iraq, Iran, and Turkey, facing the possibility of starvation and disease in an inhospitable region with freezing temperatures.

As daily death rates reached 1,000 Kurdish refugees along the Turkish frontier, American and European officials developed a humanitarian assistance plan.[21] The American contribution included an April 6, 1991, demarche to Iraqi diplomats in Washington, D.C., and the April 5 UN resolution warning Iraq against attacking displaced Kurds. According to the *New York Times*, the demarche "included an explicit injunction against the use of helicopters and fixed-wing aircraft in the northernmost corner of Iraq."[22] Believing that Iraq would comply, on April 7, U.S. C-130 cargo planes began airdropping relief packages on the twelve largest Kurdish refugee camps along the Iraq-Turkey border.[23] This limited and uncoordinated effort—dismissed as "dropping popcorns on pigeons" by American military officials—was deemed insufficient by Secretary of State James Baker who, upon surveying the humanitarian catastrophe, vowed to mobilize the world.[24] The combined efforts of Baker and U.S. Ambassador to Turkey Morton Abramowitz resulted in the second component of the U.S. humanitarian assistance plan: Operation Provide Comfort, the largest military relief effort since the Berlin Airlift. This operation deployed U.S. and coalition troops to Iraq to organize, secure, and supply the refugee camps. Beginning on April 15, American soldiers, including the 10th Special Forces Group and 24th Marine Expeditionary Unit, alongside British and French forces, entered northern Iraq to organize and secure the Kurdish refugee camps with humanitarian assistance.[25] To enforce the April 6 demarche and protect the coalition troops operating on the ground, a combined U.S., British, and French air wing—operating out of the Incirlik Air Base in southern Turkey—began flying combat air patrols above the 36th parallel in northern Iraq. Initial NFZ patrols conducted by F-16s and A-10 ground-support aircraft flying at altitudes as low as five hundred feet succeeded in deterring Iraqi ground forces from either attacking coalition forces or disrupting the relief efforts.[26]

In mid-July 1991, as the humanitarian assistance effort wound down, the last coalition forces were withdrawn from northern Iraq. To ensure "that [Saddam] understands that we're deadly serious about . . . protecting the Kurds," in the words of a Pentagon official, American, British, and French officials formed a rapid-reaction force of 2,600 soldiers in southeastern Turkey and continued air patrol flights above the 36th parallel in northern Iraq.[27] On July 24, the mission was renamed Operation Provide Comfort II.[28] It was within the context of first providing support for humanitarian assistance to desperate Kurdish refugees, and preventing Saddam Hussein's airpower from threatening them in northern Iraq, that the open-ended policy of the NFZs emerged.

OPERATION SOUTHERN WATCH

By summer 1992, the cease-fire terms between Iraq and the American-led coalition had begun to unravel over disagreements about the enforcement of two key UN Security Council Resolutions. The first, Resolution 687, detailed specific requirements with which Iraq had to comply to have the economic sanctions lifted: renouncing all claims to Kuwait, accepting the country's international debt, financing the reconstruction of Kuwaiti territory destroyed in the occupation, and repatriating all third-country nationals kidnapped before or during the war. The key final requirement of Resolution 687 demanded that Iraq "accept the destruction, removal, or rendering harmless" of all WMD stockpiles and research, as well as any ballistic missiles with a range of more than ninety miles.[29] Iraq immediately hid components of its WMD-related systems, lied about its earlier weapons and missile developments, and obstructed the UN Special Commission (UNSCOM) and International Atomic Energy Agency (IAEA) inspectors tasked with enforcing Resolution 687. In August and October 1991, the Security Council passed more resolutions calling on Iraq to comply with "the ongoing monitoring and verification" process.[30] International diplomatic pressure, combined with President Bush's threats to use force if Iraq continued its obstructions, compelled Hussein to cooperate through the year's end.[31] By early 1992, however, Iraq had reverted to a pattern of disruptive behavior against the weapons inspectors widely portrayed as "cheat and retreat."[32]

The second relevant Security Council Resolution, 688, which demanded that Hussein refrain from attacking his citizens, was tested once again, this time over Iraq's repression of the Shia. Although the 1991 Shia uprising that exploded in the wake of Desert Storm was defeated, in April 1992, "the Iraqi military began an intensive series of military operations aimed at breaking the back of residual Shiite resistance groups in the south."[33] This counterinsurgency campaign, conducted by elements of ten Iraqi army divisions, included building roadways into the marshlands to bring artillery within range of Shia insurgents, implementing cordon operations against suspected rebel areas, and draining the marshes to eliminate hiding places from the Iraqi troops.[34] In April 1992, Iranian jets penetrated Iraqi airspace to bomb a camp of the Mujahedin-e Khalq, a Shia anti-Tehran armed opposition group.[35] The Iraqi government used the Iranian raids as an excuse to unilaterally terminate its Safwan Accords obligations by restarting aircraft flight over southern Iraq. The United States responded by cataloguing and condemning the IrAF sorties, but made no effort to ground the planes. In May and July, Iraqi Su-25 and PC-7 ground-attack aircraft were used against Shia insurgents, bombing and strafing villages, and dropping napalm and white phosphorous on suspected rebel camps.[36]

The combined effect of Hussein's refusal to comply with Resolution 687—by obstructing the weapons inspections—and Resolution 688—by attacking the Shias in the southern marshlands—persuaded the American-led coalition to take action to compel a change in Iraqi behavior. Coercive strikes against a list of regime targets approved by President Bush were considered but ultimately rejected because Iraq's neighbors disapproved, most strongly Turkey, which refused to allow the coalition aircraft use of Incirlik in offensive attacks.[37] In lieu of military strikes, and acting on intelligence reports that Iraq was planning an even larger military campaign against the Shia, coalition officials imposed a second NFZ—dubbed Operation Southern Watch (OSW)—over southern Iraq.[38] To avoid using solely carrier-based aircraft to enforce OSW, Secretary Baker secured Saudi Arabia's permission to use the Dhahran Air Base, located less than two hundred miles from the Iraqi border.[39] On August 26, President Bush officially announced that on the following day the United States and its coalition partners—the United Kingdom and France—would "begin flying surveillance missions in southern Iraq, south of the 32 degrees north latitude, to monitor the situation there," and that "[the coalition] is establishing a no-fly zone for all Iraqi fixed- and rotary-wing aircraft . . . over this same area."[40] In response, the Iraqi Air Force moved all of its aircraft located within OSW to the free-fly zone (FFZ): the portion of central Iraq located between the northern and southern NFZs.[41]

Anonymous Bush administration officials, policy analysts, and editorial boards collectively wondered what purpose was served in denying Iraq the use of airpower against the Shia when Iraq's punitive and reliable ground forces remained available.[42] Furthermore, it was unclear how enforcing the NFZs would compel Saddam Hussein to reveal the intentions and capabilities of his proscribed WMD and ballistic missile programs. A senior Bush administration official partially addressed these concerns by highlighting a side benefit of having enemy aircraft loitering above Iraqi territory: "One of the effects of this is to deny him the attribute of sovereignty. If that sends the signal that as long as Saddam is in charge, Iraq's sovereignty is eroding, so be it."[43] Though regime change was not yet Washington's declared policy, it would have been welcomed, as Baghdad faced harsh economic sanctions, an embargo on unfettered oil sales, costly reparation payments, and stringent demands to account for its WMD and missile programs. Furthermore, the NFZs provided the United States the unique ability to monitor Iraqi troop movements, collect technical intelligence, and threaten regime assets with airstrikes. With both NFZs operating by 1992, one American official mused hopefully, "How long do you think [Hussein] could last within just four parallels?"[44]

THE NFZS FROM JANUARY 1993 AND SEPTEMBER 1996

From Humanitarianism to Containment

The enforcement of the Iraqi NFZs throughout the first term of the Clinton administration must be considered in light of the Clinton Doctrine. First articulated in September 1993 by National Security Advisor Anthony Lake, the Doctrine sought a "world of multiplying democracies, expanding markets and accelerating commerce." Iraq was identified as an opponent of this vision—a "backlash state." According to Lake, American policy toward such states, "so long as they act as they do, must seek to isolate them diplomatically, militarily, economically, and technologically."[45] While this vision represented a transition from the Bush administration's realist foreign policy characterized by a desire for international stability to one of democratic idealism with respect to Iraq, the early Clinton administration maintained the same key features of its predecessor: economic sanctions and diplomatic isolation to compel the implementation of UN Security Council resolutions, and enforcement of the NFZs to deter potential aggression by Saddam Hussein. As such, the principal political mission of the NFZs shifted somewhat from protecting the Kurds and the Shia to preventing Iraq from threatening its neighbors with its ground forces.

This policy of containing Iraq faced its strongest test in October 1994, when Hussein deployed 70,000 troops, including two Republican Guard divisions, and 1,000 tanks to the Kuwaiti border in an attempt to compel the UN Security Council to lift its economic sanctions on Iraq. Concerned that Iraq would invade Kuwait and push on to the Saudi oil fields, the Clinton administration implemented Operation Vigilant Warrior, which included deploying 36,000 troops to the Persian Gulf and placing another 155,000 on alert.[46] Simultaneously, American pilots simulated bombing runs on Iraqi air-defense command centers and surface-to-air missile (SAM) sites in the southern NFZ.[47] Deterred by this swift U.S. response, the Iraqi dictator quickly redeployed his Republican Guard divisions and heavy equipment back to central Iraq, where they stayed.[48] In this instance, containment, supported in no small part by the coalition planes enforcing Operation Southern Watch, succeeded.

Prior to Hussein's feint of attacking Kuwait, the Security Council had been considering easing the sanctions against Iraq. A UN representative at the time, however, offered a prescient observation that would come to apply throughout the 1990s: "Every time lifting the sanctions comes up, the Iraqis do something to ensure that the sanctions will not be lifted."[49] In addition to maintaining the sanctions regime on Baghdad, the Security Council passed Resolution 949, which demanded that "all military units recently deployed to southern Iraq . . . not redeploy to the south."[50] Washington and London used Resolution 949 as justification for diplomatic notes that were submitted to Iraq on October 20 that declared a "no-drive zone"—or, alternatively, a "no-augmentation zone"—for Iraqi ground forces beneath the 32nd parallel. The objective of this policy was to safeguard Kuwaiti and Saudi oil while avoiding a southern version of an autonomous Kurdistan region that would be dominated by Iranian-backed Shias. As an administration official noted, "We want to avoid the situation that we have in the north where there is essentially a separate protectorate."[51] Meanwhile, the Kurds—for the time being—flourished under the protection of the northern NFZs, establishing a court system, arming their own internal security force, building schools and clinics, and installing an elected parliament in the provincial capital of Irbil.[52]

"Groundhog Day"

By the mid-1990s, day-in and day-out enforcement of the NFZs had become a routinized mission, with standard operating procedures and clear rules of engagement (ROE). Typical of American airmen's need for a challenge, most pilots found enforcing the NFZs tedious and boring. In the words of Major General Scott Gration—who held command positions in both NFZs and flew 274 combat missions over Iraq—patrolling the zones was "boredom interspersed with something interesting, then boredom."[53] To many, the phrase "Groundhog Day" applied, a reference to the 1993 movie in which a weatherman finds himself reliving the same uneventful day over and over again.[54] A typical flight into Iraqi airspace, or "the box" as pilots called it, consisted of a package of F-15 fighter escorts, F-16 suppression of enemy air defense planes, and EF-111 electronic jammers, plus E-3 AWACS radar surveillance planes and KC-135 refueling tankers providing logistical support while loitering just outside the Iraqi border. On special missions American pilots flew U-2 surveillance planes to provide data to UNSCOM weapons inspectors. The more standard NFZ flight, however, was a simple and well-scripted four- to six-hour show-of-force patrol—a muscular reminder to Baghdad that it did not control nearly two-thirds of its airspace. To maintain the element of surprise against the Iraqi Air Defense System (IADS), however, NFZ missions also included training flights, simulated ground attacks, night-time operations, flying with radio silence, collecting signals and technical intelligence, and even provoking air-defense firing by dropping flares over critical targets or swooping low in a threatening manner.[55] In 2003, the remarkable success of airpower at rapidly destroying military and regime targets was a direct reflection of U.S. pilots' repeated prior exposure to Iraq's conditions. As Vice Admiral Scott Fry, the Joint Staff's director of operations from 1998 to 2000, recalled, "We had this wonderful bombing range for years and years in Iraq."[56]

The response options of pilots tracked or fired upon by the IADS were determined by the standing rules of engagement. According to the Pentagon, ROE are "[d]irectives issued by competent military authority that delineate the circumstances and limitations under which United States forces will initiate and/or continue combat engagement with other forces encountered."[57] These directives provide guidance to commanders in answering four questions about using military force: when, where, against whom, and how.[58] In the case of the NFZs, each answer was influenced by conditions imposed by the host nation from where the flights originated. As a rule, Saudi Arabia allowed more flexible and lethal ROE, as well as near-daily missions, while Turkey placed much tighter restrictions on pilots' responses to being threatened, and permitted fewer patrols per week.[59] According to Marc Grossman, U.S. ambassador to Turkey in the mid-1990s, these restrictions "were all designed to remind us that we should not allow an independent Kurdish state in Northern Iraq."[60]

Furthermore, Ankara could order planes out of the northern NFZ whenever Turkish Air Force F-16s entered Iraqi airspace to bomb villages suspected of harboring PKK terrorists or to protest unrelated actions of the United States, such as refusing to sell Turkey cluster bombs.[61] While British and French planes provided support for the flights, only American ROE allowed its pilots to respond to direct threats by bombing Iraq. On average, the American component of enforcing the NFZs required a combined effort of 34,000 sorties a year, at a total annual cost of $1 billion.[62]

The September 1996 Challenge

In the summer of 1996, a cease-fire brokered by the State Department between the two main Kurdish political parties—the Kurdish Democratic Party (KDP) and the Patriotic Union of Kurdistan (PUK)—unraveled over disagreements about their division of oil-smuggling revenues.[63] When the United States refused to decisively mediate this latest of many disputes, the two parties sought assistance from external powers: the PUK turned to Iran for weapons, logistics, and military advisors, while the KDP appealed directly to Saddam Hussein for Iraqi troops to intervene on their behalf.[64] Since the exposure of a CIA-sponsored coup attempt originating in northern Iraq months earlier, Hussein had been eager to use force to reassert his control over the Kurds and score a victory for the Republican Guards.[65] Hussein marshaled two Republican Guard divisions and three regular army divisions, for a battle group of 40,000 troops, 300 tanks, and 300 artillery pieces.[66] Starting as early as August 20, American intelligence from human and technical sources monitored Iraqi forces as they swept over the 36th parallel into Kurdish Iraq.[67] On both August 28 and 30, the United States warned Hussein—through Iraq's UN Mission—not to intervene on the ground in northern Iraq, or else "it would be a serious mistake."[68]

Before dawn on August 31, 1996, Iraqi armored divisions advanced on the Kurdish capital of Irbil. To the cheers of PUK militiamen defending the city from the Republican Guards, American aircraft circled overhead between 10:40 and 11:00 A.M.[69] With American planes enforcing the northern NFZ, and Hussein openly violating Security Council Resolution 688 by using armed force against his citizens, how would the Clinton administration respond? Ultimately, it decided not to intervene and protect the Kurds for four reasons. First, with the presidential election three months away, the White House sought to avoid a foreign policy disaster that could derail a probable second term. Second, the U.S. airwing based at Incirlik enforcing the northern NFZ consisted of only four dozen planes, which were not properly configured to identify and strike mobile Iraqi ground forces.[70] Third, neither Ankara nor Riyadh would have allowed its sovereign territory, nor its airspace, to be used for offensive strike missions against Iraq.[71] Finally, senior civilian and military officials had no appetite for intervening in a Kurdish civil war, especially one in which Baghdad and Tehran were actively involved. In the words of Assistant Secretary of Defense for Near East and South Asian Affairs Bruce Reidel: "Overall, the administration was positively disgusted with the Kurds."[72]

Instead of bombing the Republican Guard and regular army divisions responsible for attacking the Kurds, the Clinton administration paradoxically took two actions to further constrain Hussein in southern Iraq. The first was Operation Desert Strike, a U.S.-only Tomahawk cruise missile strike against fifteen Iraqi air-defense sites, primarily those located between Iraq's 32nd and 33rd parallels that had fired on pilots patrolling OSW.[73] Desert Strike succeeded somewhat in suppressing the Iraqi IADS threat, but it could have achieved more of its objectives if it had included ground-attack aircraft more suitable for destroying air-defense systems. Jordan and Saudi Arabia, however, refused to provide host nation support for such planes, despite a personal appeal from Secretary of Defense William Perry—one official heavily involved in Iraq policy recalled, "We were shocked they said no."[74]

Second, the Clinton administration expanded the area over which the Iraqi Air Force would be forbidden to fly. A range of possibilities were initially considered, including declaring a country-wide no-fly zone; expanding the northern NFZ southward to the 34th parallel (covering all of Kurdistan); including the portion of Iraq west of the 41st or 42nd latitude; or enlarging OSW to the 34th parallel, which would encompass Baghdad. Eventually, the Clinton administration decided on a modified version of the latter option— expanding the northern edge of OSW sixty-nine miles from the 32nd to the 33rd parallel (see Map 1). This option was initially developed during a weekend meeting of senior Pentagon officials at CENTCOM Headquarters in response to the October 1994 Iraqi armor and troop movements toward the Kuwaiti border.[75] According to Air Force and Navy officials, the 34th parallel was not chosen because it would have first required a three-week suppression campaign against the dense air defenses around Baghdad and would have necessitated aerial refueling within Iraq, which would have placed an enormous strain on scarce refueling tankers and combat search-and-rescue assets.[76] The practical impact of this NFZ extension on Hussein's regime was the loss of

Map 1. Iraqi no-fly zones
SOURCE: U.S. Air Force

three airbases and a joint operations training center that were located within this newly expanded NFZ.[77]

While the White House tried to put a brave face on its response to Hussein's aggression against the Kurds, U.S. actions were widely perceived as weak and ineffectual.[78] Even within the Clinton administration, the Tomahawk retaliation was derided, with one State Department official lamenting, "We've not demonstrated a lot of courage. Our actions have not left the region any more secure: Saddam has gotten away with it."[79] Reflecting the global diplomatic consensus regarding the actions of Baghdad and Washington, the Security Council refused to pass a resolution condemning Hussein's attack on the Kurds, while the Saudi-led Gulf Cooperation Council even condemned the U.S. cruise missile strikes.[80] In the end, only Britain, Germany, Japan, Canada, Israel, and Kuwait publicly supported Operation Desert Strike.[81] In his debut testimony before the Senate Select Committee on Intelligence, Director of Central Intelligence John Deutch bluntly summarized the opinion of many analysts in and out of government: "I believe that Saddam Hussein's position has been strengthened in the region recently" and "there is also perception of weakened determination of the coalition to meet Iraqi aggression."[82] For the first time, there was little regional support for U.S. military action in the face of clear Iraqi aggression.

THE NFZS FROM OCTOBER 1996 AND JANUARY 2001

From Containment to Regime Change

After two failed CIA-backed coup attempts, and the relatively weak response to Hussein's attack on the Kurds, the Clinton administration began its second term suffering from Iraq fatigue. Though ready to meet efforts by Iraq to break out of its containment regime with a proportional military response, the Clinton administration was focused on domestic issues and had other more pressing foreign policy priorities—primarily crafting a Middle East peace process and engaging China—and sought to avoid any international crises.[83] As a consequence of this non-confrontational containment of Iraq, Americans and their political leaders largely forgot about the NFZs. General Anthony Zinni, who helped establish the Kurdish safe haven in 1991 and later became the commander in chief of U.S. Central Command (CENTCOM), recalled that in regard to the NFZs, the United States was "piecemealing things without the coherence of a strategy."[84] As one revealing example of this ad-hoc approach, for the first six years, the two NFZs operated independently of each other, in large part because the northern no-fly zone fell under U.S. European Command (EUCOM), while the southern one fell under CENTCOM. In practice, this meant that each NFZ commander was unaware if the other would fly that day, what planes would be included in the package, what mission was planned, and what tactics each routinely faced from the IADS.[85] What should have been a coordinated use of limited force against a common adversary was actually two distinct operations. As Major General Gration, commander of the northern NFZ between 1996 and 1998, recalled, "We were always asking ourselves 'What are we really doing here?'"[86]

By late summer 1997, Saddam Hussein, recognizing that the sanctions regime would persist as long as he remained in power, escalated Iraq's disruptive behavior toward UN weapons inspectors. Baghdad repeatedly obstructed UNSCOM by harassing inspectors, withholding information, hiding sensitive equipment, calling for the expulsion of Americans, and declaring Hussein's palaces off-limits. The one UNSCOM instrument that Iraq was forced to accept, however, were the American U-2 reconnaissance planes, which beamed real-time imagery to a UN ground station.[87] As UNSCOM chairman Rolf Ekeus recalled, "The U-2 is the workhorse. The data it provides is fundamental to UNSCOM planning."[88] This slow-flying plane, which flew unescorted and possessed limited maneuverability, was vulnerable to being shot down by Iraqi fighters or a SAM.[89] To protect the U-2 flights, which were flown by American pilots, the Clinton administration developed more aggressive response options—operational plans Desert Thunder I through V—in case Iraq attempted to intercept a U-2.[90] By November, the serial crises between Iraq and the weapons inspectors, the overt threats to the U-2, and several provocative IrAF sorties into the southern NFZ had galvanized the Clinton administration to refocus on containing Hussein and to get "really serious about military options," according to Deputy National Security Advisor James Steinberg.[91] While the mind-set of the Clinton principals was shifting, senior administration officials still cautioned that "our strategy is containment, not overthrow."[92]

In the summer of 1998, the Clinton administration's review of Iraq concluded that there was no situation in which Saddam Hussein would accept unfettered UNSCOM inspections. If military force was used, it would not be intended to coerce Hussein into allowing the inspectors more freedom of movement, but rather to degrade and damage Iraq's suspected WMD and missile capabilities. As NSC Iraq analyst Kenneth Pollock recalled, "We were looking for a way to end 'cheat and retreat' with a bang. From now on, we were going to rely on means other than inspections to roll back Iraq's WMD."[93] After Iraq failed to meet its commitments to UNSCOM one final time, the weapons inspectors left the country on the afternoon of December 16. Later that evening, the United States and Great Britain commenced Operation Desert Fox. Over the course of this four-day bombing campaign, the two allies launched 415 cruise missiles and dropped over 600 bombs against ninety-seven targets—roughly one-third were dual-use facilities potentially related to WMD production and storage, one-third to the IADS, and the remaining third to the regime's command and control and security forces.[94] Operation Desert Fox achieved its limited military goals: degrading Iraq's WMD efforts and setting back its ballistic missile programs one to two years, and killing or wounding 1,400 of Hussein's elite military and security forces, all while causing few civilian casualties and no U.S. combat deaths.[95] According to a Pentagon official closely involved in Iraq policy, the administration always assumed that Iraq's WMD and ballistic missile sites would be bombed again if they were rebuilt: but, of course, they never were.[96] By the end of 1998, the Clinton administration's Iraq strategy had switched from one of active containment to active containment with the stated aspiration—but without actual plans or concerted efforts—to topple Saddam Hussein.[97]

The aftermath of Operation Desert Fox ushered in a period of intense and sustained confrontations within the NFZs. Hussein declared the NFZs to be a violation of Iraqi sovereignty, and offered a $14,000 bounty to anyone who shot down a coalition plane, with a $2,800 bonus if the pilot were captured alive.[98] Acting on Hussein's initiatives, and for the first time in three years, Iraqi air-defense operators began firing clusters of SAMs at coalition planes. While the SAMs all missed, because they were made without the assistance of tracking radars to avoid counter-strikes, they nevertheless posed a heightened risk to NFZ pilots.[99] Iraq even used its crippled IrAF fighter aircraft to penetrate NFZs on average of twice daily in late 1998 and early 1999, resulting in the first air-to-air engagements between U.S. and Iraqi pilots since 1993.[100]

In January 1999, due to these hostilities, the White House permitted OSW and Operation Northern Watch (ONW, the successor to Operation Provide Comfort II begun on January 1, 1997) commanders to tremendously broaden their response options. In his history of America's military engagement with Iraq throughout the 1990s, Michael Knights described the change in the ROE for American pilots:

> Since the no-fly zones began, ROE trips had been strictly limited to enemy firing of AAA guns, illumination of an aircraft with acquisition or tracking radar, or the launching of SAMs. Now, if desired, the military could launch air strikes to respond to aerial incursions, the deployment of radars and SAMs, the use of general-surveillance radar, or the augmentation of military forces in the south. Furthermore, when it responded, it could strike back indirectly at almost any element of the air-defense system (and even naval systems) within the no-fly zones. . . . The national command authorities had written a blank check.[101]

In OSW, General Zinni's CENTCOM staff applied this newfound freedom with caution. Henceforth, if OSW pilots were threatened, that threat would be "banked" and re-examined that evening to determine if a retaliatory strike was necessary and what target to hit—including command and control centers that were not connected to the IADS. This system of next-day targeting allowed Zinni to dictate the nature and operational tempo of the southern NFZ.[102] In ONW, the White House's blank check was tempered by the constant and intrusive oversight of Turkey. Though Ankara disallowed delayed responses, they permitted threatened pilots to respond within minutes to any element of the IADS but only if it appeared on a preapproved target list.[103]

These revised ROE—in practice far more permissive in the south than in the north—characterized the enforcement of the NFZs over the Clinton administration's last two years. For the United States, the NFZs had become a tool of containment maintained through attrition, since the Iraqis had not covertly procured, indigenously developed, or systematically repaired its IADS faster than air patrols destroyed it. For the Iraqis, their token resistance to the NFZs was a sort of lethal lottery: air-defense operators fired blindly with the hope that a "golden BB" would take down an American plane. The lame-duck White House had no interest or intention of escalating NFZ operations to the point that they would threaten Saddam Hussein, while the Iraqi dictator possessed just enough conventional military—and possibly WMD—capabilities to inhibit a march on Baghdad.

THE NFZS BETWEEN JANUARY 2001 AND MARCH 2003

An Overdue Policy Review

Ten days after assuming office, President George W. Bush convened his first meeting of the Principals Committee of the NSC to discuss "Mideast Policy." The consensus of the senior officials was that Saddam Hussein's regime was destabilizing the region and most likely developing proscribed WMD and ballistic missiles. President Bush tasked the heads of the State Department, the Pentagon, and the CIA to review America's diplomatic and military approach toward Iraq, including the enforcement of the NFZs.[104]

From the start of the military component of the review, three aspects of the no-fly zones troubled the Bush administration. First, military and intelligence officials believed that the Iraqi air-defense threat to the pilots in the NFZs was increasing. In the day-to-day battle of tactics and counter-tactics with American and British pilots, Iraq air-defense operators had learned how to exploit the coalition's ROE in choosing where to place their systems, how to target the aircraft, and when to shoot. The IrAF had developed a tactic whereby its planes nosed into the NFZs and then back into the free-fly zones to draw U.S. planes into "Sambushes"—where an array of surface-to-air missiles faced the NFZ, ready to fire. To support this enterprise, Iraq had tripled its arsenal of mobile SA-6s—from less than ten to three dozen—via purchases from Serbia and Ukraine.[105] More troubling, Iraq had enhanced its ability to track and target aircraft through a system of radars networked by secure fiber-optic cables. Previously, Iraqi air-defense command and control centers had communicated via radio transmissions, which are susceptible to interception, jamming, or spoofing. The fiber-optic data links, supplied and installed by China, allowed the IADS to communicate in real time without outside interference. To degrade this threat, Air Force planners at CENTCOM developed a plan—Response Option 4—to attack Iraqi surveillance radars and fiber-optic nodes dispersed throughout the FFZ. On February 14, Chairman of the Joint Chiefs of Staff General Hugh Shelton presented Response Option 4 to the NSC; the following day Bush approved it.[106] On February 16, U.S. Air Force and Navy planes bombed twenty-five targets at five separate Iraqi IADS sites. The raid was a mixed success: while most air-dropped bombs and cruise missiles struck their targets, all but two of twenty-eight AGM-154A Joint Stand-Off Weapons (JSOW)—cluster bombs containing 145 anti-personnel bomblets—launched by the Navy missed their aim-points by an average of one hundred yards.[107] While reviewing the bomb damage assessments with General Shelton, Vice Admiral Scott Fry, Joint Staff Director of Operations, recalled that "you could see that all of the [JSOW] targets were missed by the exact same small margin."[108]

Second, the Bush administration revamped U.S. contingency plans in case an American pilot was shot down and captured. President Bush specifically tasked Defense Secretary Donald Rumsfeld to develop more robust options "in case we really needed to put some serious weapons on Iraq in order to free a pilot."[109] The Clinton administration response to this distinct possibility was an operational plan—code-named Desert Badger—that could be implemented within four hours. The Clinton plan would have consisted of strikes from U.S. aircraft or cruise missiles launched from ships in the Persian Gulf directly onto the Hussein regime's command and control centers in Baghdad to purportedly disrupt the ability of Iraq to capture the pilot, as well as escalating attacks if the pilot were seized.[110] In 2001, CENTCOM planners expanded Desert Badger into three escalating response options: Red plan (seven days of strikes), White plan (an additional eleven days of strikes), and Blue plan (twenty more days).[111] In the dreaded event that a U.S. plane was brought down or crashed, Rumsfeld would recommend one of the three options, and then President Bush would select America's retaliation.[112]

Finally, the Bush administration questioned the overall efficacy of the NFZs, and considered whether it was worthwhile to continue patrolling them. As a frustrated administration official noted, "Now we have tit for tat. They shoot at one plane, we shoot back. They move a SAM, we take it out.

The question is, what are we doing here? What is our objective? What are we doing to achieve it?"[113] Regardless, the high operational tempo required to police them was placing strains on U.S. Air Force and Navy aircraft and pilots.[114] Furthermore, high-demand intelligence assets used in the NFZs—specifically aerial reconnaissance planes and high-imagery satellites—reduced the ability of the United States to spy on other states of concern, such as Iran and India.[115]

As part of the Pentagon's Iraq review, in late March, General Tommy Franks, Commander in Chief of CENTCOM, presented Rumsfeld with four new NFZ enforcement options: leaving them unchanged; increasing the number of airstrikes; reducing combat patrols in favor of more aerial reconnaissance; and eliminating them altogether, but leaving U.S. and British airpower "over the horizon" elsewhere in the Persian Gulf.[116] Reportedly, Franks and the U.S. Air Force's top commander in Europe, General Joseph Ralston, fought within the administration to sharply reduce the scale of OSW and ONW operations. Franks recommended reducing OSW patrols but maintaining limited overflights to conduct aerial reconnaissance of Iraqi troop movements. Ralston, on the other hand, was exasperated by the limits placed on NFZ patrols by the Saudis and the Turks and was concerned about the continued exposure of U.S. pilots to being shot down.[117] The Air Force commander supported terminating ONW, while preserving a contingent of warplanes at Incirlik to deter Iraqi attacks on the Kurds.[118] According to Undersecretary of Defense for Policy Douglas Feith, in the debate over the NFZs "nobody argued for the status quo."[119]

By the summer of 2001, Baghdad had rebuilt much of the fiber-optic network that was degraded in the February strike; as Secretary Rumsfeld noted in August, "Iraq has been successful in quantitatively and qualitatively improving their air defense."[120] In turn, Iraqi air defense operators became more effective and aggressive in targeting U.S. and British pilots, including a near downing of a U-2 spy plane with an unguided SAM.[121] By September 11, the Bush administration's Iraq review, though overdue, remained unfinished. Soon afterward, Washington's attention became consumed with devising and implementing Operation Enduring Freedom in Afghanistan. According to Lieutenant General Gregory Newbold, after 9/11 the NFZs "went completely cold" with the IADS "not threatening American pilots," as Hussein was uncertain whether he would be next on the White House's hit list.[122] As a consequence of focusing on removing the Taliban from power in Afghanistan, the tempo of operations in the Iraqi NFZs remained static.[123]

Preparing the Battlefield

On November 21, 2001, President Bush asked about the status of America's existing war plans against Iraq.[124] On December 28, General Franks briefed what he termed "Desert Storm II"—actually called Operations Plan 1003 (OPLAN 1003)—to the president and senior administration officials in four phases. As a component of Phase II, "Shaping the Battlespace," Franks proposed degrading Saddam Hussein's air defenses by responding "vigorously" to "Iraqi violations of the no-fly zones."[125] While CENTCOM updated OPLAN 1003, by as early as February 2002, President Bush had begun to signal to key administration officials—with his public pronouncements and in internal debates—that he strongly favored removing Saddam Hussein from power.[126] In fact, on February 16, 2002, Bush signed a top secret intelligence order that directed the CIA to support the U.S. military in conducting regime change in Iraq.[127] As a senior administration official warned at that time, "This is not an argument about whether to get rid of Saddam Hussein. That debate is over. This is . . . how you do it."[128]

As major ground combat operations in Afghanistan ended, in March 2002, CENTCOM planners began developing new options for using the NFZs for "the aerial preparation of the battlefield for a full-scale invasion of Iraq."[129] Since Turkey would not allow ONW to be utilized for this mission, these options applied only to OSW. In keeping with Secretary Rumsfeld's demand to reduce the time between A-Day (start of the bombing campaign) and G-Day (start of the ground war), General Franks's staff compiled a roster of preapproved response options for OSW planes if Iraqi air-defense operators demonstrated aggressive intent by tracking or shooting at them.[130] The White House was briefed in detail about the more expansive CENTCOM plan, and strongly endorsed it with no questions asked.[131] In June, the secret campaign—Operation Southern Focus—began with strikes against air-defense radars, SAMs, the rebuilt IADS fiberoptic network, and command and control centers. OSW pilots also engaged in a massive, though ineffective, propaganda campaign by dropping over four million leaflets that warned air-defense operators that firing on U.S. aircraft would make widows of their wives.[132] In the month before Operation Iraqi Freedom, Southern Focus was further expanded to include "spikes" of 1,000 sorties a day to confuse Iraq about when war would start, use of Predator drones and U-2s to monitor Republican Guard divisions and collect signals intelligence, and airstrikes against Iraqi artillery located within range of American and British troops in Kuwait.[133] Over the course of this secret campaign, U.S. pilots flew

21,736 sorties over southern Iraq, dropping 606 munitions on 391 targets.[134] Overall, Operation Southern Focus was a resounding military success: Operation Desert Storm in 1991 necessitated a six-week gap between the airwar and the ground campaign, but in 2003, by exploiting the southern NFZ, the air and ground components of Operation Iraqi Freedom could begin on the same day.

ASSESSMENT

This chapter is not intended to be an exhaustive history of the 140 months, 560 weeks, or nearly 4,000 days during which the Iraqi NFZs were maintained, but rather to understand their key twists and turns, and to analyze whether they achieved their primary political and military objectives. These NFZs are undoubtedly more difficult to evaluate than the other three DMOs assessed in this book. By their nature, DMOs are a temporary escalation of hostilities during an ongoing relationship with an adversary. By demonstrating a willingness to use force, the attacker attempts to achieve certain objectives, and to reestablish that relationship on terms more favorable to themselves. The NFZs, however, were a military operation intended and conducted to maintain the status quo. The United States had settled on a policy of containing Saddam Hussein's regime, and utilized the NFZs as the key component of that policy.

In regard to the NFZs, it is difficult to assess whether senior civilian officials are more likely to support the use of DMOs than the uniformed military, because they were far from a singular event. Nevertheless, from the time of their impromptu creation, they were generally supported by senior civilian officials and opposed by senior military officials, including the military commanders who led their enforcement. The NFZs began in early 1991, with the goal of ending Iraqi Air Force attacks against Shias in the south while protecting U.S. and UN soldiers in northern Iraq who were supporting the broader humanitarian assistance plan for displaced Kurds. While there was strong civilian support for the announced NFZs from James Baker and the George H.W. Bush White House, General Norman Schwarzkopf only once followed through on his threat by authorizing the shoot-down of an Iraqi fighter jet flying outside of the proscribed airspace. On many other occasions, General Schwarzkopf did not employ the substantial U.S. air assets in the region to more strictly enforce the NFZs, as he wanted to avoid mission-creep beyond the UN-sponsored mandate.

Throughout the mid-1990s, likewise, civilian officials within the Clinton administration never seriously considered ending the NFZs because they were believed to be an important tool in containing Iraq. Before September 11, 2001, some George W. Bush administration civilians—particularly Donald Rumsfeld—believed that the NFZs were no longer keeping Saddam Hussein "in the box."[135] Their support for ending or curtailing the NFZs, however, was based on the premise that a more comprehensive military solution—that is, regime change—was required to permanently resolve the threat Iraq posed to the region. At the same time, the commanders responsible for the NFZs— Generals Tommy Franks and Joseph Ralston—argued for either a sharp reduction in the enforcement patrols or a conclusion to both OSW and ONW. Until the Bush administration was committed to resolving the United States' adversarial relationship with Iraq through regime change, however, there was never a decision-forcing debate about the NFZs, so they simply continued the status quo that had been in effect for over a decade.

Note that the reasons provided by Clinton and George W. Bush civilian officials for continuing the NFZs match those proposed herewith—senior officials are more likely to favor DMOs because they believe they are militarily and politically effective, controllable, have little to no domestic political costs, and demonstrate resolve. First, until the summer of 2002, civilian officials overwhelmingly supported the policy of containing Iraq, and they believed that the NFZs were an important and effective tool in accomplishing this.[136] Second, a key reason that civilians supported the NFZs was that they were controllable given the size of the proscribed Iraqi airspace, duration of the patrols, and lethality of the response options. In 1996, the Clinton administration expanded the northern edge of OSW from the 32nd to the 33rd parallel, as punishment for Iraq's ground offensive against the Kurds. Three years later, administration officials gave Zinni "blank check" authority to respond, as he saw fit, to Iraqi air-defense threats to planes patrolling OSW.[137] Later, when the Bush administration decided to overthrow Saddam Hussein, the NFZs were utilized in Operation Southern Focus—which escalated attacks on Iraqi regime assets far beyond those related to its air-defense capabilities. Third, though civilians consistently worried about a downed U.S. pilot being taken hostage by Iraq, there were no adverse domestic political consequences for NFZ operations that went wrong. These include the tragic 1994 accidental shoot-down by two U.S. Air Force F-15s of two U.S. Army Black Hawk helicopters, which led to twenty-six American and coalition deaths, as well as hundreds of Iraqi civilian casualties that resulted from either targeting or weapons failures of the patrolling planes.[138] Finally, an important component of enforcing the NFZs was to demonstrate the resolve of the United States to its allies in the Persian Gulf. By placing U.S. pilots at risk, Clinton and Bush administration officials believed that they were undermining regional support for Saddam Hussein and ensuring the international community's support for the containment policy.

Did the no-fly zones achieve their intended military objective of preventing the Iraqi Air Force from flying above the proscribed territory? Yes. Before the NFZs were ever declared and enforced by the United States and its allies, the IrAF was already weakened by two factors: Saddam Hussein's decision to send over 120 IrAF combat aircraft to Iran during the First Gulf War—where they remained—and coalition airstrikes and air-to-air engagements during that war that decimated the bulk of the regime's capable air power.[139] Throughout the 1990s, the NFZs and sanctions had the cumulative effect of further deteriorating the already limited capabilities and combat readiness of the IrAF. By the start of the Second Gulf War, the IrAF was so ineffective that it did not attempt even one short-range attack against U.S. or British ground forces in Kuwait or Iraq.[140]

Did the no-fly zones achieve their intended political objectives of protecting vulnerable Kurdish and Shia populations, and preventing Iraq from threatening its neighbors? In this regard, the NFZs were a mixed success. While Saddam Hussein's regime refrained from using airpower against its enemies residing within the NFZs, it was not deterred from deploying its ground forces in conventional military and counterinsurgency operations. The Kurds and Shias were protected in the skies, but not on the ground. Hussein's regime, however, was effectively contained from using its air or ground forces, or ballistic missile arsenal, against its regional adversaries of Kuwait, Saudi Arabia, or Israel. In October 1994, when Hussein dispatched 70,000 troops and 1,000 tanks toward the Kuwaiti border, the Clinton administration responded by deploying 36,000 troops to the Persian Gulf and also secured an additional Security Council resolution, banning Iraq from augmenting its ground capabilities south of the 32nd parallel. In this test, and throughout the 1990s, the NFZs played a crucial role in the U.S. containment strategy.

While no-fly zones are useful for containing states, there are limits to using them as a tool for humanitarian operations. Policymakers and nongovernmental organizations have repeatedly called for implementing an NFZ over the Darfur region of Sudan to prevent government aircraft from bombing the villages of Darfurians.[141] There are two dilemmas that a hypothetical

Darfur NFZ would face. First, the political will required to actually enforce an NFZ is much greater than is needed to declare one. In the case of Bosnia, NATO officials aspired to prevent Serb aircraft from flying over Bosnian Muslims, but refused to provide NATO pilots with the rules of engagement that allowed this aspiration to become operational. The pilots enforcing a Darfur NFZ would need the ability to distinguish in real time between civilian and military aircraft, and the authority to attack suspected violators in air-to-air engagements or after they have landed. Furthermore, as the ingenious and tireless efforts of the Iraqi air-defense operators and pilots demonstrated, the Sudanese government can be expected to consistently push the limits of what they are prohibited from doing, thus further stressing the life-or-death decisions that the NFZ pilots are forced to make. After inevitable mistakes, it is unlikely that the international body that sanctioned a Darfur NFZ would continue supporting its robust enforcement.

Second, protecting vulnerable populations from one tactic of oppression while allowing equally destructive attacks on the ground is ultimately a counterproductive and demoralizing strategy. Aggressors prevented from using coercive airpower against their adversaries will redirect their attention and resources to cause damage by other means. In Darfur, preventing the use of airpower by the Sudanese government will have no lasting effect since Janjaweed militiamen already employ horses and camels on the ground to terrorize and displace villagers. If the goal of the international community is to stabilize the security situation on the ground to prevent further killings and to allow the more than two million displaced Darfurians to return home and live in peace, they will need a comprehensive political, economic, and military strategy. Denying the Sudanese government sovereignty in the airspace over Darfur could be one component of that strategy, but it should by no means be the primary one.

4 SUDAN AND AFGHANISTAN: AUGUST 20, 1998

OSAMA BIN LADEN expected an American retaliation for Al Qaeda's near-simultaneous bombings of the U.S. Embassies in Nairobi, Kenya, and Dar es Salaam, Tanzania, on August 7, 1998. Days before the bombings, Bin Laden, his personal bodyguard, Abu Jandal, and three other guards abandoned the Tarnak Farms compound, on the outskirts of the Kandahar Airfield in Afghanistan. They drove north from Tarnak Farms for over two hundred miles and reached a fork in the road: one route leading to the Zhawar Kili training complex at Khost ninety miles southeast of Kabul and the other straight through to the Afghan capital. Bin Laden turned to his guards and asked, "What do you think? Khost or Kabul?" "Let's just visit Kabul," replied the guards. Bin Laden agreed, "OK. Kabul."[1] The next evening, at 10:00 P.M. Afghan time, sixty-six American cruise missiles struck the Zhawar Kili complex at Khost. Soon after, Bin Laden's voice was heard crackling over a radio transmission: "By the grace of Allah, I am alive!"[2]

The August 20, 1998, cruise missile strikes against the Al Qaeda complex in Khost, Afghanistan, and the El-Shifa pharmaceutical plant in Khartoum, Sudan, had several unique characteristics among U.S. Discrete Military Operations (DMOs). First, they marked America's military entry into the global war on terrorism, through use of force against two countries that the United States was not then at war with to demonstrate resolve against Al Qaeda, a non-state terrorist organization. Second, to this author's best determination, it was the first time the United States—within one DMO campaign—used limited force simultaneously against targets in two different countries. Third, it was a prescient demonstration of the limits of using DMOs against targets generated solely by human and technical intelligence. The human intelligence that claimed Osama Bin Laden would be attending an Al Qaeda leadership conference in Khost was simply incorrect. The technical intelligence that identified the El-Shifa pharmaceutical plant as a possible chemical weapons factory was later openly questioned in the press, and other key information about the plant, such as who owned it and what it had been used for since its construction, was overlooked. Finally, and most important, both of the DMOs failed at achieving either of their intended political objectives, while only the Khartoum strike achieved its military objectives. The lasting effect of these political and military failures is that they deterred the Bill Clinton and George W. Bush administrations from using limited force against Al Qaeda again until after the attacks of 9/11.

This chapter contains six sections. First, it presents the strategic setting that characterized U.S. interests in Sudan and Afghanistan before the cruise missile strikes. Second, it describes the plot and aftermath of Al Qaeda's bombing of the two U.S. embassies, which were the justification for America's limited military retaliation. Third, it provides an unprecedented look—based on interviews with many of the key players—at the debate over the selection of targets within the Clinton administration's "Small Group" of senior civilian and military officials that planned the response. Fourth, it briefly describes the tactics and outcomes of the cruise missile strikes on Afghanistan and Sudan. Fifth, it describes the aftermath of the strikes. Finally, it assesses whether the strikes met their intended military objectives (yes for Sudan, no for Afghanistan) and political objectives (no in both cases), and analyzes the enduring impact on U.S. counterterrorism policy.

THE STRATEGIC SETTING AND AMERICA'S INTERESTS

Sudan

As the Cold War and the Soviet Union's influence in Africa ended, without a competitor, the already-marginal strategic interests of the United States in Sudan further declined. Throughout the 1990s, America's primary concern with Sudan would be the ruling Islamic regime's efforts to export terrorism and Islamic extremism throughout North Africa and beyond. The National Islamic Front (NIF) came to power in June 1989, when sympathizers in the army and security services overthrew the democratically elected—though corrupt and ineffective—government of Sadiq al-Mahdi. The NIF was led by Hassan al-Turabi, who effectively ruled Sudan, even as Brigadier General Omar al-Bashir was the country's titular president.[3] Turabi, who espoused a vision of revolutionary Islam, stated that "Most of the democracies, dictatorships or monarchies that call themselves Islamic are in total contradiction with Islam and must be overthrown."[4] To further that goal, Sudan provided assistance with training camps and logistical support to Hezbollah, Hamas, Palestinian Islamic Jihad, the Palestinian Front for the Liberation of Palestine, and Islamic Jihad of Egypt.[5] The regime in Khartoum also hosted and armed Islamic militants attempting to topple Western-friendly governments in Egypt, Algeria, Tunisia, Eritrea, Uganda, and Saudi Arabia.[6]

In the wake of the February 1993 World Trade Center bombing—and related plots to blow up New York City bridges, tunnels, and public buildings—the Clinton administration took an increasingly aggressive stance toward Sudan. Federal Bureau of Investigation agents determined that five of the fifteen men arrested in the attack were Sudanese nationals who had extensive contacts with Sudanese diplomats at the United Nations.[7] Three of the other fifteen traveled to the United States on Sudanese passports, as did the blind Egyptian Sheikh Omar Abdul-Rahman, who was among those convicted of "seditious conspiracy" for the World Trade Center attack.[8] In light of this evidence, and Khartoum's refusal to expel terrorist groups despite repeated requests by the American ambassador, Sudan was designated as a state sponsor of terrorism by the U.S. State Department in August 1993.[9] This label required that the United States impose sanctions on Sudan in the form of a ban on arms-related exports, most forms of economic assistance, and loans and aid from international financial institutions.[10]

Viewed in the context of Khartoum's sympathies and support for Islamic extremist groups, it was not unusual that Bin Laden and Al Qaeda decided to establish a base of operations in Sudan in 1991. Bankrupted from fighting an ongoing civil war with southern Christian rebels, Khartoum embraced Bin Laden's multi-million-dollar investments in Sudan's agriculture, trade, and construction industries, as well as his financial aid to resettle 480 Arab mujahideen veterans in Sudan.[11] According to the 9/11 Commission, soon after Al Qaeda was entrenched in Sudan, its "finance officers and top operatives used their position in Bin Laden's businesses to acquire weapons, explosives, and technical equipment for terrorist purpose[s]"; in short time, "Bin Laden now had a vision of himself as head of an international jihad confederation."[12] From Sudan, Bin Laden provided funding and technical support to terrorist groups ranging from the Abu Sayyaf Group in the Philippines to Somali rebels attacking U.S. troops in Mogadishu to Bosnian Muslims fighting in the former Yugoslavia.[13] As Daniel Benjamin and Steven Simon, counterterrorism officials in the Clinton White House, later noted, in the early 1990s, "There was hardly a battle anywhere involving Islamic radicals in which al-Qaeda was not involved."[14]

After the June 1995 assassination attempt on Egyptian president Hosni Mubarak in Addis Ababa, Ethiopia, Khartoum's support for Bin Laden decreased. Three of the would-be killers, members of Egypt's Islamic Jihad, had received assistance from Al Qaeda and were provided refuge in Sudan after the assassination attempt.[15] When the suspects were not extradited to Ethiopia for trial, the UN Security Council passed two resolutions—1054 and 1070—that called on all member states to expel Sudanese diplomats, further limit their travel, and ban the flight of state-controlled aircraft. Though the sanctions were intended to alter Sudan's behavior, few states bothered to implement them.[16]

However, international pressure that stifled foreign investment in Sudan's fledgling oil industry along with the threat of war with the Egyptian military succeeded in compelling Khartoum to consider washing its hands of Bin Laden.[17] Khartoum had earlier rid itself of an international terrorist in August 1994 when it handed over Ilich Ramirez Sanchez—"Carlos the Jackal"—to French authorities. Attempting to replay this venture, in March 1996, Sudan Minister of State for Defense Major General Elfaith Erwa met secretly with U.S. officials in Rosslyn, Virginia, where Erwa reportedly offered to have Bin Laden arrested and handed over to Saudi Arabia.[18] The Saudis refused, having earlier renounced Bin Laden's Saudi citizenship. American intelligence officials quietly approached Jordan and Egypt to see if they would detain Bin Laden, but they also declined. The U.S. intra-agency Counterterrorism Security Group (CSG) discussed bringing Bin Laden to the United States, but the Justice Department believed that there was no basis to detain him absent an indictment, which was impossible given the current evidence.[19] According to Erwa, U.S. officials told him to "Just ask him to leave the country. Just don't let him go to Somalia." Erwa replied, "He will go to Afghanistan," to which the U.S. officials stated, "Let him."[20] Leaving behind operatives to mind his business interests in Sudan, on May 19, 1996, Bin Laden boarded an Ariana Afghan jet, which refueled in Doha, Qatar, before reaching its destination, Jalalabad, Afghanistan.[21]

During the period between Bin Laden's fleeing Sudan and the U.S. cruise missile strikes in August 1998, relations between Washington and Khartoum continued to deteriorate, for three reasons. First, at a time when the Clinton administration rhetorically strongly supported human rights, the regime in Khartoum had one of the world's worst records in this field, terrorizing animist and Christian groups in the south and allowing slavery in certain parts of the country.[22] Second, the Sudanese government continued to harbor and aid terrorist organizations that threatened regional and international security, including Al Qaeda and insurgent groups that destabilized their home governments throughout central Africa. Third, elements connected to the regime aggressively conducted surveillance on and attempted attacks against CIA officials and contractors operating out of the U.S. Embassy, leading to a pull-out of all American intelligence officers and diplomats by February 1996, and reportedly considered assassinating U.S. National Security Advisor Anthony Lake, a harsh critic of Sudan.[23] The combined result of these actions was very poor diplomatic relations, and, despite half-hearted attempts at opening a dialogue on fighting terrorism, virtually no counterterrorism cooperation.[24]

Afghanistan

With the breakup of the Soviet Union, the reunification of Germany, and the events leading to the 1991 Gulf War at the forefront of U.S. foreign policy-making, after the last Soviet troops pulled out of Afghanistan in February 1989, America's strategic interests there were minor. The focus of the United States' limited objectives in Afghanistan was to drive the communist regime of President Muhammad Najibullah from power and to help create a politically stable climate in the country. The CIA and Pakistan's Inter-Services Intelligence directorate (ISI) collaborated to provide money and Iraqi heavy weaponry, captured after the Gulf War, to warlord factions fighting the Najibullah regime.[25] In 1992, Moscow and Washington ended most of their covert aid to Afghanistan, and Najibullah was soon thereafter forced to cede power to a UN-sponsored multiparty interim government.[26] During this period, a senior CIA official mentioned in passing to President George H.W. Bush the Agency's minor efforts to aid friendly factions in Afghanistan. As if to underscore how unimportant the efforts and the country were to senior policymakers, President Bush asked in earnest, "Is that thing still going on?"[27] Over the next three years, control over Kabul changed hands several times, while the countryside fragmented into personal fiefdoms characterized by ethnic or tribal identities, and financed by the heroin trade and the intelligence agencies of neighboring states.[28]

By March 1995, one of these warring factions, the Taliban, controlled the lower third of Afghanistan. The Taliban—translated literally as "the students"—was a mysterious Pashtun movement espousing a strict vision of Islamic practice and owed its existence to massive assistance from various government agencies and religious movements within Pakistan.[29] With no diplomatic representatives in Afghanistan, American officials operating out of the U.S. Embassy in Islamabad, Pakistan, did not have a clear picture of the Taliban's leadership, interests, and capabilities. Nevertheless, the United States initially had aspirations for the Taliban, because it was believed, incorrectly, that they would discourage heroin production, and that, in the words of a senior NSC official, it was "a force that could bring order to chaos."[30] Indeed, to many war-weary Afghans in the south, the Taliban's harsh implementation of *sharia* law was a tolerable price to pay for stability.[31] When the Taliban overran Kabul in September 1996, partly with the help of $3 million from Bin Laden used to pay off contending warlords, the U.S. State Department accepted the new Afghan government. In a September 28 classified instructions cable to American embassies in the region, the State Department provided talking points to U.S. diplomats who encountered Taliban representatives. At the end of the detailed guidance, the final question to be posed was "Do you know the location of ex-Saudi financier and radical Islamist Osama Bin Laden?" Taliban leaders phoned the U.S. Embassy in Islamabad to falsely claim that they had no idea of Bin Laden's whereabouts.[32]

The Taliban soon opened Afghanistan's borders to several regionally based militant and terrorist organizations. Included among these groups was Al Qaeda, which by early 1997 had openly entered into a resilient and collaborative, albeit sometimes contentious, relationship with the Taliban. From the Taliban, Bin Laden received a safe haven to spread his call for a jihad against the House of Saud and the United States through interviews with international media; cement working relationships with previously unconnected terrorist groups; purchase and import weaponry; train and indoctrinate between 10,000 and 20,000 Al Qaeda operatives and Kashmiri insurgents; and plan operations.[33] In return, Al Qaeda provided the Taliban with thousands of battle-hardened mujahideen veterans to assist in conquering the rest of Afghanistan; weapons and vehicles; and tens of millions of dollars per year from Bin Laden's dwindling personal fortune.[34]

By early 1998, believing that Osama Bin Laden was now indictable in a federal court, the United States wanted him captured, by either force or diplomacy.[35] The deployment of U.S. Special Operations forces or CIA covert operatives to attempt to detain Bin Laden was not considered at this time. A CIA operation to use thirty Pashtun tribesmen to snatch the Al Qaeda leader from his Tarnak Farms complex was halted by the Agency's own Directorate of Operations when the plan was deemed costly and unworkable; CIA director George Tenet also worried that if Bin Laden were killed, the CIA would be accused of conducting an assassination.[36] Diplomatic initiatives proved equally ineffective. In April, the U.S. ambassador to the UN, Bill Richardson, flew to Kabul to request that the Taliban hand over Bin Laden. Taliban officials claimed that the Saudi was their guest and that he would not resort to terrorism while living there, and assured Richardson that Bin Laden did not have the religious authority to issue fatwas calling on Muslims to kill Americans—whether military or civilian—anywhere in the world.[37] The Taliban refused the American appeal to hand over Bin Laden. In June 1998, Prince Turki Al-Faisal, the Saudi intelligence chief, received a promise from the Taliban leader Mullah Omar to turn Bin Laden over to Saudi Arabia to face treason charges, but the Taliban never followed through.[38]

Before the cruise missile strikes in August 1998, the United States-Afghanistan relationship was characterized by quiet hostility, and not only zero counterterrorism cooperation but a Taliban regime that openly supported radical terrorist groups that threatened American national interests and its people.

AL QAEDA'S PLOT AND THE AFRICAN U.S. EMBASSY BOMBINGS

When the first U.S. troops entered Somalia in December 1992 as part of a UN peacekeeping mission, Al Qaeda's leadership in Sudan believed that this was merely America's first step to spread its domination beyond the Persian Gulf and into Africa.[39] These Al Qaeda leaders issued a fatwa that described the American presence in Somalia as the "head of the snake," and declared that "we have to cut off the head of the snake and stop them."[40] To funnel support to rebel groups in Somalia, a command center of Al Qaeda's Military Committee was set up in Nairobi, Kenya.[41] Scores of trainers were sent from Sudan, through Nairobi, to instruct Somali Islamic militants from the Al-Itthad al-Islamiya group in how properly to fire rocket-propelled grenades to shoot down helicopters.[42]

While providing aid and training for the Somali rebel groups, Bin Laden looked for other American targets in Africa. In late 1993, he dispatched Ali Mohamed, a former U.S. Army Sergeant, to Nairobi to reconnoiter the American Embassy, the French Embassy, and British and Israeli targets. When Mohamed met Bin Laden in Khartoum, the Saudi pointed out the best place for a suicide truck bomb to enter the U.S. embassy compound.[43] To prepare for an eventual attack, the Nairobi cell was maintained by Wadi al Hage—Bin

Laden's personal secretary and a naturalized American citizen—and a second cell in Kenya was created in the coastal city of Mombasa by Mohamed Odeh and a half-dozen other Al Qaeda operatives.[44] In early 1998, when Al Qaeda decided to militarize the operation, a third cell in Dar es Salaam, Tanzania, was activated and controlled by Khalfan Khamis Mohamed. With these teams in place, the embassy bombing plans were initiated and given the code names Operation Holy Kaaba for Nairobi and Operation al-Aqsa for Dar es Salaam.[45] The total cost of planning and conducting both operations—including material, personnel, communication systems, safe houses, and travel—was estimated to be a mere $100,000.[46]

On August 7, 1998, at 10:30 A.M., a Toyota Dyna truck bomb exploded at the rear of the U.S. Embassy in Nairobi, Kenya, killing 213 people—including 12 Americans—and injuring more than 4,000 others. Nine minutes later, a 1987 Nissan Atlas refrigeration truck bomb exploded thirty-five feet outside of the U.S. Embassy in Dar es Salaam, Tanzania, killing 11 people—none of whom were Americans—and injuring 85 more. Both terrorist attacks would have been substantially more lethal were it not for the courageous acts of security guards who denied the trucks direct access to the embassies. Both truck bombs were made in Kenya by the same man, Egyptian explosives expert Mushin Musa Matwalli Atwah.[47] Atwah utilized a complex design using detonators consisting of RDX and blasting caps, fifteen tanks that held oxygen and acetylene, and over 2,000 pounds of explosive—an FBI expert later testified that the chemical composition of the truck used in Tanzania was as if it had been "dipped . . . in TNT."[48] The bombings, of which the CIA had had no tactical warning, were described with admiration by an Agency official as "on a scale of 1 to 10 [with one being the highest], that's a 1."[49]

THE SMALL GROUP PLANS A RESPONSE

Within four hours of the embassy bombings, the CIA made an initial finding, based upon its year-long monitoring of the Nairobi cell, that the attack had been perpetrated by Al Qaeda.[50] The following day, a "Small Group" within the National Security Council—consisting of the principals and a handful of other relevant senior officials—was formed by National Security Advisor Samuel Berger.[51] This group was intentionally composed of the fewest possible number of participants, who maintained their routine schedules, to prevent the leak of any planned retaliatory responses.[52] On August 8, at the first Small Group meeting, Director of Central Intelligence George

Tenet presented unusually specific evidence that perhaps two hundred to three hundred militants and Al Qaeda leaders, including some arriving from Pakistan, were planning to gather at the Zhawar Kili training complex in Khost, Afghanistan, to plan future terrorist attacks.[53] The intelligence supporting Tenet's presentation was based on communications intercepts and a CIA source inside Afghanistan who reported that Bin Laden had ordered the meeting to be held on August 20.[54] Some officials recalled that Tenet predicted Bin Laden would be at the meeting; others predicted the opposite.[55] Bruce Riedel, Senior Director for Near East and South Asian Affairs, recalled that with the intelligence of the upcoming Al Qaeda meeting in hand, "You got the Christmas tree effect—what else do you want to go after?"[56] Thus, at this August 8 meeting, the Joint Staff and the CIA were tasked to develop a list of other sites connected to Bin Laden that could also be targeted.[57]

On August 14, the Small Group reconvened. Tenet provided the CIA's formal determination that Bin Laden and his senior Egyptian aides were responsible for the embassy bombings—"This one is a slam dunk, Mr. President," the director stated.[58] Another participant later recalled that "there was a high degree of confidence" of Bin Laden's guilt based on the evidence presented.[59] In debating military responses, Chairman of the Joint Chiefs of Staff General Hugh Shelton presented a range of options, including using ground or airborne forces against the Taliban and Al Qaeda. The Small Group, however, agreed that neither America's allies in the region nor the Republican-controlled Congress would support a ground invasion against the Taliban.[60] The senior officials also discounted Pentagon options to conduct a smaller Special Operations forces raid into Afghanistan when Shelton noted the size of the force required, the possible delays in assembling and deploying the troops, and the absence of good targets.[61] Cruise missiles were soon decided on as the best military option, and the Small Group agreed to attack the Al Qaeda gathering with the intended purpose of killing Bin Laden and as many of his top lieutenants as possible.[62] There was widespread support for the Khost bombing, with the lone dissenter being Attorney General Janet Reno. Reno questioned whether the cruise missile strikes would meet the standard for a self-defense attack under Article 51 of the UN Charter, and sought a delay to give the FBI more time to assemble evidence against Bin Laden.[63]

In planning the U.S. response, the CIA, CENTCOM planners, and the Joint Staff produced an additional twenty targets in three countries: Afghanistan, Sudan, and another unnamed state (probably Yemen). That target list—

debated by the Small Group in its face-to-face meetings and secure phone conferences—was in constant flux: targets were added, then debated, then removed, and then re-added.[64] At one point, the CIA put forth five targets in Khartoum, Sudan, that were connected to Al Qaeda's business interests. According to General Anthony Zinni, who as commander in chief of CENT-COM oversaw the cruise missile strikes, "I hadn't seen any of those [five targets] before." Three of the five targets provided by the CIA were eliminated by CENTCOM planners out of concerns about collateral damage.[65]

Two Khartoum targets that stuck were the El-Shifa Pharmaceuticals Industries Company factory and the Khartoum Tannery Company, which Bin Laden had received from the Sudanese government as partial payment for building a 450-mile road linking the capital with the Red Sea.[66] In the weeks prior to the embassy bombings, the CIA had presented intelligence to the White House about Al Qaeda's recent efforts to acquire WMD.[67] In December 1997, an Egyptian agent working for the CIA collected a soil sample sixty feet in front of the main entrance to the El-Shifa factory. The clump of soil was analyzed, and found to contain two and one-half times the normal trace of O-ethyl methylphosphonothioic acid, or Empta, a chemical precursor used in the production of VX nerve gas.[68] Two CIA analytical reports, produced on July 28 and August 4, concluded that El-Shifa, on the basis of the soil sample, satellite imagery, and other intelligence, was connected to Bin Laden through the Sudan government-owned Military Industrial Corporation.[69] One of the reports, however, warned that while the presence of Empta made it a near certainty that the plant had something to do with chemical weapons, it did not guarantee the plant manufactured VX or was merely a warehouse or transshipment point for the nerve gas.[70] Tenet also told the Small Group that the CIA had evidence that Bin Laden had sought to test poisonous gases in Sudan to use against U.S. forces stationed in Saudi Arabia.[71] Tenet's assessment, combined with the fact that the factory was well guarded, and, according to U.S. officials, did not produce any commercial pharmaceuticals, placed El-Shifa on the target list, along with the Khartoum Tannery Company, because of its role in Al Qaeda's financial network, and the Khost training complex.

Before El-Shifa was destroyed by a barrage of cruise missiles, much of the U.S. intelligence community disagreed with Tenet's assessment of a link between El-Shifa and Bin Laden. The standard of proof the Small Group developed for any potential military responses to the embassy bombings was "Would George Tenet be willing to go before Congress, raise his right hand, and say the intelligence supported striking these targets?"[72] Most members of the Small Group accepted Tenet's word, but were largely unaware of the dissension between intelligence analysts in different government agencies. For example, analysts from the State Department's Bureau of Intelligence and Research argued in an August 6 memo that the CIA's claims of a connection between Bin Laden and chemical weapons and the factory were weak.[73] Mary McCarthy, the NSC senior director for intelligence programs, warned Berger in an August 11 memo that the "bottom line" was that "we will need much better intelligence on this facility before we seriously consider any options."[74] An anonymous senior military intelligence official was also unhappy that El-Shifa was on the target list, believing that it was chosen not because of its potential for producing nerve gas but for undefined political reasons.[75] Even within the CIA, there was considerable debate. Before Tenet gave his final briefing at the White House about Bin Laden's connections to El-Shifa, a group of senior CIA officials met with Tenet at the Agency headquarters in Langley, Virginia. According to Paul Pillar, National Intelligence Officer for the Near East and South Asia, who attended the meeting, a straw poll was held about whether the United States should attack El-Shifa. The majority of the senior CIA officials said, "Don't do it."[76]

On August 19, the Small Group reconvened to go over the three targets one last time. Tenet admitted that there were "gaps" in the intelligence linking Bin Laden to El-Shifa, and that the CIA was working to "close the intelligence gaps on this target."[77] According to Sandy Berger, there was little debate among the participants about the evidence regarding the factory, but more about whether it made "geopolitical" sense to bomb Sudan when Bin Laden no longer lived there.[78] One senior military participant, however, was strongly opposed to striking El-Shifa because he "didn't think it was a very good idea," adding, "Why destroy a penicillin plant, which will only lead to you getting more grief?"[79] Others, most vocally Richard Clarke, the senior White House counterterrorism official, strongly supported attacking the factory even though the evidence of Bin Laden's connections was not definitive.[80] Berger ended whatever debate there was that day by highlighting that the Clinton administration would be pilloried if the United States bypassed bombing El-Shifa and Bin Laden went ahead with future chemical attacks.[81] Furthermore, President Clinton, who was not at the August 19 meeting, had earlier "embraced [El-Shifa]" because he had consistently worried about the possibility of terrorists acquiring WMD since the March 1995 sarin nerve gas attacks by Aum Shinrikyo on the Tokyo subway system.[82]

The final target list submitted to President Clinton consisted of the Khost training complex, the El-Shifa factory, and the Khartoum Tannery. Later that afternoon, General Shelton and other members of the Joint Chiefs—who were never told about the attack until the day before it was scheduled—pressured the White House to remove the tannery from the target set because of concerns about civilian casualties and its absence of any connection to Bin Laden's purported WMD aspirations.[83] On August 20 at midnight, from a previously scheduled vacation in Martha's Vineyard, according to his autobiography, President Clinton "took the tannery off the list because it had no military value to al Qaeda and I wanted to minimize civilian casualties."[84] One-and-one-half hours later Clinton called Tenet to ask if there was any new intelligence that he should know about. Tenet told him there was not. According to Clinton, he was "trying to make absolutely sure that at that chemical plant there was no night shift. . . . I didn't want some person, who was a no-body to me but who may have a family to feed and a life to live and probably had no earthly idea what else was going on there, to die needlessly."[85] Clinton called Berger three hours later to give his formal approval for the cruise missile strikes.[86] At 8:30 A.M., Lieutenant General Donald Kerrick, Deputy National Security Advisor to the President, walked from the staff house to the main house at Martha's Vineyard to alert the president, "If you want to turn off this operation, you have thirty minutes before the cruise missiles fire." The president asked once again, "Is there any new intelligence?" Assured that there was none, Clinton ordered the attack to proceed, and Kerrick relayed the order back to Washington via a secure phone.[87]

THE CRUISE MISSILE ATTACKS

The cruise missile strikes—named Operation Infinite Reach—were the very model of precise execution of American limited military force. At 7:30 P.M. local time in Sudan, more than an hour after sundown, two U.S. Navy warships in the Red Sea fired thirteen BGM-109 Tomahawk Land Attack Missiles (TLAMs) at the El-Shifa factory in Khartoum. Although General Zinni was unaware of it, El-Shifa had actually been in the Pentagon's target portfolio for several years.[88] Pentagon planners ran computer models to calculate the risk of the possible release of a chemical plume from the attack. After assessing the suspected chemicals produced in the factory, the building's structure and properties, and weather forecasts, it was determined there would be minimal harmful effects.[89] To ensure that any toxins would be incinerated, extra Tomahawks were added to the strike package with the goal of burning the factory to the ground.[90] El-Shifa was destroyed, its night watchman was killed, and a watchman in a sugar factory next door was horribly injured.[91]

At 10:00 P.M. in Afghanistan, four Navy ships in the Arabian Sea off the coast of Pakistan launched sixty-six TLAMs against six sites within the Zhawar Kili complex at Khost—a base camp, support facility, and four training camps (see Exhibit 1).[92] After his planners war-gamed the attack, General Zinni pointed out that Pakistan's naval or coastal radars might mistake the American Tomahawks as an Indian nuclear strike.[93] The cruise missiles, in fact, were programmed to fly over a suspected Pakistani nuclear weapons site.[94] To deal with this issue, on the evening of the attack, Vice Chairman of the Joint Chiefs of Staff General Joseph Ralston arranged to meet with Pakistan's Army Chief of Staff General Jehangir Karamat for a friendly dinner

Exhibit 1. Zhawar Kili complex before it was bombed
SOURCE: Department of Defense

in Islamabad. As the cruise missiles flew above Pakistani airspace, Ralston watched to see if anyone burst into the room to alert Karamat that Pakistan was under attack from India. After the Tomahawks would have made impact on the Khost training complex, General Ralston informed his counterpart that "we did it," as a retaliation against Bin Laden for the embassy bombings.[95] Some senior U.S. officials believe that Pakistan's ISI somehow relayed a warning about the slow-flying cruise missiles to Al Qaeda in time for the group to flee the camp.[96] Others strongly disagree, noting that there has never been any documented evidence presented to support this assertion, and asking why the ISI would warn Al Qaeda but not its own agents, some of whom were killed in the attack.[97] According to Tenet, the CIA was never able to determine if Bin Laden had been tipped off to the attack.[98]

With no concern about collateral damage to innocent civilians, the bombing of the Khost complex sought to inflict the maximum number of casualties. To accomplish this, Pentagon planners prepared a tactic that deployed cruise missiles in two waves. The first began with several C-model unitary warhead Tomahawks that hit the complex to lure the assembled group outside to find out what was happening.[99] The follow-up wave consisted of a saturation of D-model Tomahawks armed with 166 soda-can-sized bomblets that burst several hundred feet above the target and blanket an area roughly eight hundred by four hundred feet with shards of shrapnel.[100] Some of the TLAMs failed to explode, and according to intercepted communications from a Milan-based Al Qaeda cell and Russian intelligence, Chinese officials visited Khost after the attack to study and purchase the intact Tomahawks.[101] Reportedly, between twenty and sixty people at Zhawar Kili were killed, including Pakistani ISI officers training militants to fight in Kashmir.[102] Osama Bin Laden, his second-in-command, Ayman al-Zawahiri, Mohammed Atta—ringleader of the 9/11 attacks—and other key Al Qaeda leaders were not killed.

THE AFTERMATH OF OPERATION INFINITE REACH

The Clinton administration announced that Operation Infinite Reach would be the opening phase in a long-term fight against Al Qaeda.[103] One senior White House official described the cruise missile strikes as the start of "a real war against terrorism," adding that "this is not a one-shot deal here."[104] On the afternoon of the attacks, President Clinton met with top advisors to discuss the next steps, and General Shelton issued a planning order—named Operation Infinite Resolve—to plan for a follow-on military campaign against Al

Qaeda facilities.[105] In the proceeding weeks and months, at the White House's request, the Pentagon produced a range of expansive military options: firing a fresh batch of cruise missiles or using an AC-130 gunship against Al Qaeda headquarters in Kandahar; using a "phased campaign concept" with a wide range of airstrikes on Taliban targets and no fixed end date; deploying special operations teams into Afghanistan to kill or capture terrorists; and allying with non-Taliban tribal elements to capture Bin Laden.[106] Although the Clinton administration started a few minor intelligence, diplomatic, and economic initiatives after Operation Infinite Reach, it took no further military actions against Al Qaeda, because neither the CIA nor the military could develop timely intelligence on Bin Laden's location, the options were deemed too risky for American soldiers, or the potential operation could result in civilian casualties.[107]

Many civilian officials, and even some senior military officers, were deeply troubled by what they believed was an unwillingness of the military to comprehend the threat represented by the Al Qaeda network and to develop innovative and feasible options to attack it. Samuel Berger summarized this opinion of the Joint Chiefs and General Shelton, stating, "They didn't want to do it [attack Al Qaeda]. . . . There was just no enthusiasm and creativity."[108] Berger's deputy, James Steinberg, recalled that civilian members of Clinton's National Security Council "were not at all happy with the military's options for going after Bin Laden."[109] Lieutenant General Kerrick, a personal military advisor to President Clinton, echoed this sentiment: "The military were reluctant warriors in the war against terrorism to take on Al Qaeda." Even after the *U.S.S. Cole* bombing in 1999, "the military was happy to just send the FBI."[110] According to Kerrick, after Operation Infinite Reach, whenever President Clinton would ask Shelton about the possible use of American ground forces to attack Bin Laden or Al Qaeda facilities in Afghanistan, the Joint Chiefs chairman would tell him flatly, "there are none."[111]

In fact, however, at the tasking of the NSC, there were a range of limited ground options developed and refined by CENTCOM planners for going after Bin Laden. General David Petraeus, then an executive assistant to General Shelton, recalled that despite the impressions of some, the Chairman of the Joint Chiefs actually "made a good faith effort to deliver the options" requested by civilian leadership.[112] But as Vice Admiral Scott Fry, who as the Joint Staff's director of operations from 1998 to 2000 managed the iterative back-and-forth between the CENTCOM planning staff and frustrated civilians at the NSC, noted, "We could never impress upon the civilians in the NSC how far Afghanistan was from a staging base or carrier group."[113] This failed hunt for Bin Laden before 9/11 was a real-life and tragic instance in which the divergent perspectives, characterized by the Surgical Strike School for civilians and Functional Force School for the military, resulted in a decidedly suboptimal outcome whereby neither group was satisfied with the process by which the military options were developed.

While there is evidence that General Shelton and other uniformed officers were reluctant before 9/11 to use limited bombing, Special Forces, or overwhelming ground forces in Afghanistan, all of the senior civilian and military officials interviewed remarked that if President Clinton had made it perfectly clear that military force would be used against Al Qaeda, then the Joint Staff would have developed options marrying the available capabilities with mission objectives. In early March 2000, when Clinton received a memo listing all of the U.S. direct action efforts against Bin Laden, he returned it with a note in the margin, "We've got to do better than this. This is unsatisfactory."[114] While President Clinton's impatience was funneled through the NSC and back to the relevant military and counterterrorism agencies, it did not lead to the specific and concrete actions, on the fastest possible timetable, that would have been necessary to capture or kill as elusive a figure as Bin Laden. Considering that the president did use his authority as the commander in chief to force Shelton to create these options, and that many senior military officials consistently provided a list of professional objections to using military force, there is ample blame to be shared between civilian decisionmakers and senior military officials for not attacking Al Qaeda or its Taliban hosts after Operation Infinite Reach during the remainder of the Clinton administration. The fault of the senior civilians was in not following up on Clinton's demands for better options, while senior military officials can be blamed for their opposition to most of the options they helped develop.

Senior military officials who served during the Clinton administration recognized the depth of frustration of their civilian counterparts about the lack of practical military options. Nevertheless, these same generals and admirals believed that their civilian counterparts—and moreso their staffs—held a dangerously naïve and simplistic view about how military operations are developed and implemented. According to Lieutenant General Gregory Newbold, who also served as the director of operations at the Joint Staff, much of the divergence between civilians and the military over the acceptable risk and relative ease of using force stemmed from how each arrived at their jobs. Military officers undergo several levels of very similar education in military doctrine, tactics, operations, and national strategy at the War Colleges and the Command and General Staff College. Furthermore, they have either experienced combat directly or participated in the past in decisions to use force. Civilian officials, by comparison, are "beamed into" administration positions through political connections or dumb luck. For these civilians "very infrequently have they made the study of strategy and operations a way of their life."[115] Newbold, and many other military officials, believed that this absence of shared education or experiences compelled civilians to migrate toward the easiest and most responsive tool at hand to attack Al Qaeda—military force. Senior civilians in the Clinton administration, these military officials believed, were reacting to a specific event—the embassy bombings—rather than crafting a comprehensive national strategy to achieve the objective of defeating international terrorist networks.

ASSESSING OPERATION INFINITE REACH

In this instance, assessing the evidence for the proposition that senior civilian officials are more likely to support the use of DMOs than are the uniformed military is difficult, because the proposals were only debated among a very small number of civilian and military officials. For example, the Joint Chiefs of Staff were not informed about the cruise missile retaliation until the day before the missiles struck Afghanistan and Sudan. While they backed the attack against the Zhawar Kili training complex at Khost—as did almost all informed military and civilian officials—the Joint Chiefs and General Zinni opposed the two Sudan targets, the Khartoum Tannery and the El-Shifa pharmaceutical factory, the former because it had no clear connection to Al Qaeda's suspected WMD efforts and the later because of inconclusive intelligence linking it to the production of VX nerve gas. In addition, the El-Shifa factory was a CIA-generated target, which the CENTCOM planning staff and Zinni had never seen, thus lessening its value as a legitimate military target among some senior military officials. As one general recalled, in his gut, he just "didn't think [El-Shifa] was a very good idea."[116] Therefore, the available evidence shows that the military was opposed to two of the three targets initially selected to be bombed in retaliation for the African Embassy bombings.

The senior civilian officials involved in the Small Group debates, on the other hand, generally favored striking all three of the proposed targets, and have defended this position ever since. (The only exception was Reno, who questioned the operation's legality and sought more time for the FBI to gather evidence to indict Bin Laden.) Tenet, Berger, and Albright all told the 9/11 Commission that, even given what they knew six years after the fact, they still supported their recommendation to President Clinton to strike El-Shifa. William Cohen testified that "[El-Shifa] was the right thing to do then. I believe—I would do it again."[117] Steinberg recalled that the Small Group "made the judgment that the probability the plant was connected to WMD was high enough, and collateral damage was low enough, that it was worth doing. I don't feel uncomfortable with the target."[118]

Their reasons for supporting Operation Infinite Reach match those set forth in this work's other proposition—civilian officials are more likely to favor DMOs because they believe they are militarily and politically effective, controllable, have low domestic political costs, and demonstrate resolve. First, with the exception of Janet Reno, all of the civilian officials involved believed that the cruise missile strikes would be militarily effective and would achieve their intended political objective (punishment) and secondary political objective (deterring future Al Qaeda operations).[119] Second, for President Clinton, the precise and controllable nature of cruise missiles made them the optimal means of retaliation. According to a senior military official, told of this account by General Shelton himself, when the chairman of the Joint Chiefs presented Clinton with six different retaliation operations, the President "went right to the cruise missile option."[120] Alongside the logistical concerns of deploying a small ground team into Afghanistan, Clinton preferred cruise missiles because he was persistently concerned about possible civilian casualties resulting from U.S. military operations.[121] A cruise missile strike against the El-Shifa factory, in the middle of the night, would best keep civilian casualties at a minimum. Third, although Clinton was embroiled in the Monica Lewinsky scandal by August 1998 and White House relations with the Republican-controlled Congress were increasingly dismal, according to the participants, and in the unanimous opinion of the 9/11 Commission, domestic political concerns played no role in the debates or plans behind Operation Infinite Reach. Finally, demonstrating resolve was a key justification provided for the cruise missile strikes. As President Clinton stated in his public address soon afterward, "But of this, I am also sure. The risks from inaction to America and the world would be far greater than action. For that would embolden our enemies, leaving their ability and their willingness to strike us intact."[122] In addition, the simultaneous bombing of Afghanistan and Sudan was intended to demonstrate that just as Al Qaeda had "global reach" to bomb embassies in two countries, so did the United States.[123]

Did the DMOs against Afghanistan and Sudan achieve their military objectives of killing Osama Bin Laden and destroying the El-Shifa pharmaceutical factory? No for Bin Laden and yes for El-Shifa, but ultimately the operation was a failure. El-Shifa was totally destroyed—an underwhelming accomplishment given the facility was not obscured, was above ground, and sat on flat terrain. As General Zinni sarcastically noted, "it was a success. We sprayed aspirin all over Khartoum."[124] The primary stated military goal, however, was to take revenge against the masterminds behind the African Embassy bombings. Yet neither Bin Laden nor his compatriots were ever in danger because he was not in Khost at the time of the missile strikes.

However, that is not to suggest that the attack on Khost was a mistake. According to the civilian and military officials involved in the decisionmaking process, many of whom had been desperately searching for an opportunity to kill or capture Osama Bin Laden, the intelligence about the gathering of Al Qaeda officials on August 20 was the most specific they would ever receive. The CIA did not have confidence in the ability of Pashtun tribal forces to get Bin Laden, and senior military officials were uncomfortable deploying U.S. forces to Afghanistan given the logistical demands and the dearth of actionable intelligence. A bombing campaign with U.S. airplanes could have caused collateral damage and resulted in Afghan civilian casualties. Cruise missiles, therefore, were the only remaining military option. Using them required knowing where Bin Laden would be in the next four to six hours: the amount of time between obtaining presidential authorization, programming the missiles, and flying them to the target.[125] As Tenet wrote of his frustration at providing the intelligence that could justify another missile strike: "My job was to assess objectively whether the data we had . . . could ever get policymakers above a 50 or 60 percent confidence level so they could launch cruise missiles in the next thirty minutes. It never did."[126] In fact, it was only in this one instance in mid-August 1998, with Al Qaeda's fingerprints on the African embassy bombings, that the CIA had more than one week's warning about the location of Bin Laden and his senior lieutenants. The Clinton administration would have been irresponsible if it had decided to bypass this unprecedented opportunity.

Did the DMOs achieve their primary political objectives of further disrupting Al Qaeda attacks against the United States or its interests, and denying terrorists safe havens in Sudan and Afghanistan? Here, both of the DMOs failed to meet their political goals.

The embassy bombings caused the United States to undertake greater precautions to prevent terrorist attacks on American diplomatic installations abroad. American intelligence officers and Albanian law enforcement foiled an effort by five members of Egyptian Islamic Jihad to use a truck bomb against the U.S. Embassy in Tirana.[127] Greater security in the short term was also provided to embassies that were reportedly threatened in Malaysia, Yemen, Egypt, and Uganda.[128] At the time, Secretary of State Madeline Albright claimed that it was "very likely something would have happened had we not [bombed Afghanistan and Sudan]."[129] It is doubtful, however, that the cruise missile strikes played any role in disrupting these potential terrorist attacks. They were more likely disrupted by an increased awareness of Al Qaeda threats to American diplomatic institutions and the providing of tactical intelligence to local law enforcement officials. Meanwhile, the U.S. bombs did nothing to disrupt Al Qaeda plots or attacks. As George Tenet warned in Senate testimony six months after Operation Infinite Reach, "we are concerned that one or more of Bin Laden's attacks could occur at any time."[130] In the near future, this would be proven by the foiled plots to bomb the Los Angeles International Airport and tourist sites in Jordan, and the successful terrorist attacks against the U.S.S. Cole, the Limburg—a French oil tanker—and the World Trade Center and Pentagon.

The cruise missile strikes also failed to compel Sudan and Afghanistan to deny terrorists from using their territories as a safe haven. The State Department issued formal warnings to the Taliban and the Sudanese government that they would be held responsible for any attack on Americans by Al Qaeda if they continued to provide it sanctuary.[131] Yet Sudan remained on the State Department's state sponsors of terrorism list, continued to allow senior Al Qaeda operatives to visit Khartoum, and even released two suspects involved in the embassy bombings after the U.S. cruise missile strikes.[132] As Paul Pillar, a senior CIA official who opposed the bombing of El-Shifa, put it succinctly, "It is hard to identify any offsetting benefit from destroying the plant."[133] In Afghanistan, the Tomahawks had the opposite effect from was intended: they transformed what was, at times, a rocky relationship between the Taliban and Al Qaeda into a symbiotic team effort that succeeded in conquering the rest of Afghanistan, growing opium for export, and manufacturing fundamentalist Islamic terrorists.[134] Furthermore, Bin Laden's survival from an overwhelming American bombing transformed him from a lesser-known international terrorist financier to the embodiment of resistance for anti-Western Islamists around the world. As a senior U.S. counterterrorism official noted of Bin Laden six months after the attacks intended to kill him, "I don't think he's isolated, incommunicado or out of money. And I don't think anything we've done has changed the minds of his true believers."[135]

Finally, the unsuccessful attempt at killing Bin Laden and the embarrassing aftermath of the El-Shifa bombing had another noteworthy political effect: it deterred the Clinton administration in its remaining months, and the George W. Bush administration before 9/11, from using limited military force against Al Qaeda. If the United States had launched Tomahawks or deployed a Special Operations unit to kill or capture Bin Laden, and the mission failed, it would have elevated the opinion of Al Qaeda and its leader while making the United States look impotent. As James Steinberg recalled, "There was a strategic concern that it would be damaging to [America's] reputation regarding Al Qaeda if we kept flinging missiles and missed."[136] This sentiment was, if anything, more pronounced in the early months of the Bush administration. Even while campaigning for the presidency in 2000, Governor Bush derided the "pinprick strikes" in retaliation for suspected Al Qaeda terror attacks. National Security Advisor Condoleezza Rice also described how Bush was "tired of swatting at flies"—meaning a tit-for-tat retaliation to terrorist attacks—and wanted a comprehensive plan that went beyond military options to try to eliminate Al Qaeda.[137] That plan, which was expected to take three years to take effect, was approved by the Principals Committee of the NSC on September 4, 2001—one week before 9/11.[138]

5 YEMEN: NOVEMBER 3, 2002

IN THE CLIMACTIC SCENE from the 2005 cinematic thriller *Syriana*, a nationalist prince from an unnamed Persian Gulf emirate speeds along a desert highway among a convoy of SUVs. A shadowy cabal of CIA employees operating from a task force center is alerted as to which truck the prince is riding in by a traitorous bodyguard. As the CIA tracks the prince's convoy with an unmanned Predator aerial drone loitering four miles above, a rogue former Agency officer drives alongside the convoy, frantically signaling for it to halt in an apparent effort to warn the prince of this imminent danger. The convoy slows to a halt. As he walks toward the Prince's SUV, the former CIA operative begins to speak, when, in a flash, the SUV, the Prince, and the rogue ex-agent are all incinerated by a Hellfire missile fired from the Predator overhead.[1]

The real-life inspiration for the *Syriana* scenario occurred three years earlier on a desert highway one hundred miles east of Sana'a, the capital of Yemen. On November 3, 2002, a Predator drone bombed an SUV carrying Abu Ali al-Harithi, a suspected operational planner of the attack on the *U.S.S. Cole*, and five other suspected terrorists. This Predator strike represented a turning point in the U.S. uses of DMOs. First, it was the first post-9/11 DMO, and the first overt use of force outside of Afghanistan in what was then already being labeled as the "Global War on Terrorism" (GWOT). After DNA tests concluded that the Predator attack had killed the correct person, senior U.S. officials bragged of its demonstrative effect in deterring terrorists everywhere. Second, it was the first acknowledged targeted killing by the United States government, outside of a battlefield, since political assassinations were prohibited by President Gerald Ford in 1976. Third, it was a military operation conducted on the territory of a sovereign state that the United States was not at war with, nor even hostile toward. Fourth, the operation was conducted with the full knowledge and consent of the Yemeni government, after its own security forces had failed at capturing al-Harithi. Finally, it was a DMO that was strongly supported by both civilian and military officials in the George W. Bush administration.

This chapter contains five sections. First, it presents the strategic setting in the 1990s that characterized U.S. interests in Yemen, including Yemen's sup- port for international terrorism and threats to Americans. Second, it describes the post-9/11 counterterrorism demands made by the Bush administration on Yemen for it to reform its domestic security, enhance intelligence coopera- tion, and provide greater assistance in capturing or killing Al Qaeda members. Third, it assesses America's role in peacetime targeted killings—or assassina- tions—and the debate among senior U.S. officials both before and after 9/11 about their use as a tool of counterterrorism policy. Fourth, it presents a detailed re-creation, based on the best possible publicly available information, of the No- vember 2002 Predator attack. Finally, it describes the aftermath of the strike, and assesses whether it met its intended military objective of killing al-Harithi (yes) and its political objectives of deterring future Al Qaeda attacks and com- pelling more consistent counterterrorism cooperation from Yemen (no).

STRATEGIC SETTING AND AMERICAN INTERESTS

Yemen's Geostrategic Location

A 1978 Joint Chiefs of Staff policy statement articulated what has historically been America's key goal in the Persian Gulf: "To assure continuous access to petroleum resources."[2] Since then, the Persian Gulf has remained a reliable source of oil—providing 10 percent of America's imported oil, 25 percent of Western Europe's, and 60 percent of Japan's.[3] Yemen is located on the heel of the Arabian Peninsula, south of Saudi Arabia along the Arabian Gulf and the Bab-el-Mandeb—the narrow straits linking the Red Sea and the Gulf of Aden (see Map 2). Petroleum heading westward out of the Persian Gulf must pass through the Bab-el-Mandeb, and since the 1980s it has serviced around three billion barrels of oil per year. Identified by the Department of Energy as a significant "world oil transit chokepoint," if the Bab-el-Mandeb were closed it would effectively keep oil tankers from reaching the Suez Canal and the Sumed Pipeline complex, which traverses through Egypt to link the Red Sea with the Mediterranean Sea. Such a blockade would divert oil tankers around the southern tip of Africa, tying up tanker capacity, delaying delivery times, and increasing costs for consumers and industry.[4]

America's limited diplomatic engagement with Yemen during the 1980s and 1990s focused on preventing political or civil instability from within the fractured state from infecting Saudi Arabia—the world's largest source of proven oil reserves.[5] Through this strategy, known as the Reagan Corollary to the Carter Doctrine, the United States was committed to protecting Saudi Arabia from external, regional, or internal threats.[6] During a brief civil war between Northern Yemen and Southern Yemen in 1994, the United States used its diplomatic leverage to attempt to broker a deal between the warring parties to keep it from destabilizing Saudi Arabia—which openly financed and armed the Southern Yemen secessionist movement because Iraq was providing military support to the north.[7] Washington also tried to resolve the historical dispute between Yemen and Saudi Arabia over control of the six-hundred-mile oil-rich border shared by the states.[8] After Yemen held the first ever multi-party elections on the Arabian Peninsula in 1993, the United States welcomed the event but warned against any attempts to threaten the ruling House of Saud by exporting democracy. As Assistant Secretary of State David Mack proclaimed

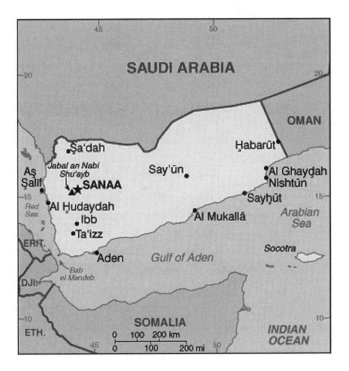

Map 2. Yemen, *CIA World Factbook*
SOURCE: Central Intelligence Agency

upon visiting Sana'a at the time, "It is important to remember that no country has a blueprint for democracy in another country . . . So I don't think you should look on what you do here as a model for anyone else to follow."[9]

Owing to its location astride the major Saudi oil fields, Yemen was a minor player in the field of international energy during the 1990s. A non-OPEC member, Yemen saw its oil exploration stifled by its unsettled political situation, its inability to attract Arab investment after it aligned with Saddam Hussein during the first Gulf War, and its underdeveloped transportation infrastructure. Soon after the country's civil war ended in 1994, Yemen's oil blocks were opened up for partnership agreements with international firms. As a consequence, between 1990 and 2000, oil production increased from 10,000 to 400,000 barrels per day, placing Yemen around twenty-fifth among all nations in global oil exports.[10] Starting in the mid-1990s, Yemen also signed international agreements to develop and export its significant natural gas resources.[11]

Support for International Terrorism
After the international mujahideen successfully expelled the Soviet Red Army from Afghanistan, many battle-hardened Arabs came back to the Arabian Peninsula. In Yemen alone, estimates vary, but perhaps tens of thousands of men returned from Afghanistan with an evolving and dedicated commitment to global jihad and working relations with Al Qaeda affiliates throughout the Middle East.[12] Mujahideen veterans settled in the Islamic northern portion of Yemen, spreading a fundamentalist Islam and fighting alongside the central government against the breakaway Marxist southern region.[13] The Saudi leader of Al Qaeda, Osama Bin Laden, financed terrorist training camps for Afghan Arabs in northern and southern provinces and traveled throughout the country campaigning against the Marxists.[14] According to the Yemeni government, "Yemeni Afghan groups executed several socialist figures and mounted 158 operations . . . between 1990 and 1994 on the strength of fatwas issued by Osama bin Laden."[15]

The central government made sporadic attempts to crack down on terrorist groups after its officials were assassinated or Westerners were kidnapped, but for several reasons it was consistently unwilling to make fighting terrorism a national priority. First, Yemen is a tribal society, and the central government had to defer its law enforcement activities to the fiercely independent tribes in areas outside of the capital and along its borders.[16] Second, Yemen has more small arms per capita than any other state in the world—four guns for each person—and the government was simply outmanned and outgunned by tribal militias that counted as many as 50,000 dedicated fighters.[17] Third, the Arab Afghan fighters had played a crucial role in the government's defeat of South Yemen during the civil war.[18] Afterward, the central government provided them with powerful state jobs and the relative freedom to operate provided they did not directly threaten the state.[19] As the U.S. Department of State's 1996 *Patterns of Global Terrorism* listing for Yemen stated clearly, "Lax implementation of security measures and poor central government control over remote areas continued to make Yemen an attractive safe haven for terrorists."[20]

While Osama Bin Laden moved his personal headquarters to Sudan in 1992, Yemen emerged as a central hub for Al Qaeda recruitment and operations. Bin Laden took a personal interest in the presence of his network there: of the 1,100 intercepted phone calls originating from Bin Laden's satellite phone in the mid-1990s, 221 were made to Yemen.[21] Attempted or successful terrorist attacks either conducted inside of Yemen or originating from Yemen targeted American, British, and German diplomatic missions; Western oil workers; hotels frequented by Westerners; an Anglican church; Atef Sidqi, the Egyptian prime minister, in Cairo; American military barracks in Saudi Arabia; U.S. Embassies in Khartoum and Jakarta; and the *Limburg,* a French oil tanker.[22] Senior Al Qaeda leaders rotated through the country spreading their jihadist ideology, recruiting operatives, running safe houses, and raising funds from business fronts and wealthy sympathizers.[23] Even as late as August 2001, Al Qaeda's number two official, Ayman al-Zawahiri, was receiving medical treatment in a hospital in Sana'a.[24]

In 1996, after Bin Laden relocated from Sudan to southern Afghanistan, Yemenis followed him in large numbers back to the birthplace of Al Qaeda.[25] Interviews with Yemenis captured by the anti-Taliban Northern Alliance suggested that they entered Afghanistan with the intention of furthering their expertise of how to plan and conduct terrorist operations before returning home to implement them.[26] Under American interrogation, the head of Al Qaeda operations, Khalid Sheikh Mohammed, later revealed that roughly 20 percent of the men in Afghan terror camps were Yemenis—an assertion supported by the fact that approximately a hundred of the more than five hundred detainees in Guantanamo captured in Afghanistan were Yemeni.[27]

Americans Threatened in Yemen

Given Yemen's essential role in Al Qaeda's global network, and its harboring of tens of thousands of terrorist sympathizers, it was inevitable that

American military and civilian personnel would be threatened in Yemen. In fact, Al Qaeda's first terrorist attack outside of its home base of Afghanistan was against U.S. soldiers residing in Yemen.[28] On December 29, 1992, bombs exploded at two hotels in Aden with the intention of killing one hundred U.S. airmen en route to Somalia to support UN peacekeeping operations. (Osama Bin Laden argued that "the U.S. tried to make a base under the UN umbrella so that it could capture Sudan and Yemen.") The bomb missed the U.S. soldiers, who were evacuated after being tipped off by Yemeni security, but killed an Australian tourist and a hotel employee.[29] Within days, all of the American troops were shipped out of Yemen for Somalia on schedule.[30] Though the hotel bombings went largely unnoticed at the time, Bin Laden later boasted that the American withdrawal was "the first al Qaeda victory scored against the Crusaders."[31]

In response to the Bill Clinton administration's cruise missile strike against a gathering of Al Qaeda officials in Khost, Afghanistan, in August 1998, Osama Bin Laden sought again to attack Americans in Yemen. In late 1998, Abd al Rahim al-Nashiri—a Saudi mujahideen veteran, and Al Qaeda's chief of operations for the Persian Gulf—proposed to Bin Laden that they should target U.S. warships in Yemen.[32] The Al Qaeda chief agreed, and suggested warships refueling at Aden as targets, provided money for the operation, and personally selected the suicide operatives.[33] Al-Nashiri assembled a terrorist cell comprising sixteen people, eleven of whom were Yemeni.[34] On January 3, 2000, as part of what was supposed to be simultaneous attacks against infidel symbols coinciding with the millennium, Al Qaeda operatives attempted a waterborne suicide attack on the refueling U.S.S. The Sullivans. The attack failed when the small boat, overloaded with explosives, sunk shortly after it was launched.[35] The U.S. Navy, unaware of the failed operation, continued using Aden for refueling because it suited the service's specific requirements and it enhanced military-to-military cooperation with Yemen.[36] Al-Nashiri's cell regrouped and ten months later attacked the 505-foot naval destroyer U.S.S. Cole with a sturdier speedboat that was laden with a six-hundred-pound shape-charged RDX explosive.[37] This suicide attack killed seventeen sailors, wounded thirty-nine others, and caused a quarter-billion dollars worth of damage to the ship. Planning and carrying out the bombing cost al-Nashiri's terror cell around $5,000.[38] With slightly better execution it could have killed up to three hundred sailors and sunk the destroyer.[39]

THE BUSH ADMINISTRATION'S DEMANDS AFTER 9/11

After the Taliban government in Afghanistan fell in December 2001, the Bush administration sought to expand the GWOT to target other states suspected of harboring international terrorists. In a clear post-Taliban articulation of U.S. counterterrorism strategy, Deputy Secretary of Defense Paul Wolfowitz warned that fragile states—the Philippines, Indonesia, Somalia, and Yemen—unwilling or unable to enforce law and order within their borders could be targeted for imminent military action. Wolfowitz noted specifically, "There are very significant back regions of Yemen. That's a case of an ungoverned piece of a country."[40] Two weeks earlier, Defense Secretary Donald Rumsfeld had also pointed out that "there are, obviously, a number of countries that have active al Qaeda cells, and Yemen is one."[41] The Pentagon's concerns about Yemen were well founded, as former Taliban and Al Qaeda members needed a new territory from which to recover and regroup. As a central hub in the global jihadist movement since the early 1990s, Yemen was considered as a potential fallback safe haven for Al Qaeda. Conflicting intelligence reports even named Yemen's Hadramawt region, Osama Bin Laden's ancestral homeland, as his likely hiding place.[42]

Ali Abdullah Saleh, Yemen's president since 1978, was appropriately worried that his country could be attacked by the American military. Even as the Bush administration made unspecific threats toward Yemen, however, Saleh had already made the strategic decision to cooperate with the United States. Two days after 9/11 he gathered his country's politicians at a military base outside of Sana'a and announced that he would side with the Bush administration.[43] Saleh had aligned himself with Saddam Hussein during the first Persian Gulf War, and suffered hostile relationships with his neighbors and the United States throughout the 1990s as a result. According to an NSC official in the Clinton White House, when the United States tried to reach out to Sana'a by providing economic and military assistance, in exchange for a promise from Saleh to "talk nice about Iraq, and indicate some support for the Arab-Israeli peace process," the Yemeni president would make inflammatory statements against the United States and its allies. The NSC official, who was part of the pro-engagement crowd, recalled in frustration that "although some Yemenis wanted to be on the right side of history," in general, "they were impossible."[44] Determined not to repeat his strategic mistakes, after 9/11, Saleh dispatched a key senior advisor to Washington to ask what was required of Yemen.[45] The issue for President Saleh, in 2001, was to what degree he could cooperate in the GWOT while not upsetting a population sympathetic toward some of Al Qaeda's positions and hostile toward America's Middle East policies.[46]

In late 2001, the Bush administration considered Yemen to be among the most important countries in the emerging global campaign to defeat Al Qaeda and sought to elicit more consistent counterterrorism cooperation.[47] Pleased with Saleh's initial enthusiasm to align its policies more closely with the United States, the Bush administration made three sets of counterterrorism demands on Yemen. The first focused on six unilateral initiatives that the central government was to undertake to improve security within its borders. First, it had to prevent Muslim leaders from describing the resistance to America's war against the Taliban as another jihad. Second, it had to seal its borders to prevent militants from fighting in Afghanistan and then returning to Yemen, as they had twenty years earlier. Third, it had to require that Arab citizens flying into Yemen enter from their home country, to prevent Yemen from becoming a terrorist refuge. Fourth, it had to institute mandatory background checks for anyone applying for a Yemeni visa. Fifth, it had to deport hundreds of veterans from the Afghan mujahideen, as well as most of the foreign students from al-Iman University—a reputed terrorist training center. Finally, it had to freeze the assets of honey shops that the United States claimed were used to funnel money to Al Qaeda.[48]

The second set of demands was for more in-depth intelligence cooperation. Heading this agenda was the request that Yemen allow Federal Bureau of Investigation (FBI) and CIA investigators to revive their ongoing inquiry into the *U.S.S. Cole* bombing, which had been stalled by the persistent interference of the central government.[49] For the first time, Yemen allowed the FBI and the CIA to view key documents related to the case, analyze evidence in the United States, and directly interview detained suspects—a long-standing American demand that President Saleh had repeatedly denied, including just six days prior to 9/11. Yemen also delayed the start of a trial against two suspected members of the *U.S.S. Cole* cell in order to search for connections to Al Qaeda.[50] In short time, the American investigators found clear links between the *Cole* attack, the East Africa U.S. Embassy bombings, and September 11.[51]

The enhanced intelligence cooperation also included exchanging information on the identity and locale of suspected terrorists in Yemen. To facilitate this, Yemeni and American security officials set up a joint counterterrorist operations center, which included occasional Saudi participation.[52] The National Security Agency (NSA)—which already had a burgeoning presence in Yemen before 9/11—deployed a Cryptologic Support Group with sophisticated surveillance equipment into Yemen to collect, process, and analyze signals intelligence.[53] The U.S. Air Force was allowed to fly U-2 surveillance planes through Yemeni airspace.[54] Yemenis also provided the CIA with the phone records and dossiers on suspected Al Qaeda members in country.[55] In turn, the CIA handed over the names of suspected terrorists to be apprehended for questioning, dozens of whom were held without trial in Yemen.[56] In exchange for its closer intelligence cooperation, the CIA began providing hundreds of millions of dollars of assistance to President Saleh.[57]

The final set of Bush administration demands on Yemen was for greater support in uprooting and killing Al Qaeda members operating within the country. Prior to 9/11, substantive U.S.-Yemeni security cooperation had been active for only four years, and was limited to groups of U.S. Special Forces A Teams—each consisting of twelve soldiers—providing basic counterterrorism training to the president's Republican Guards.[58] The U.S.-Yemeni training efforts were a component of the security cooperation relationships that U.S. Central Command (CENTCOM) sought to develop with each state located within its area of operations.[59] Coinciding with several official and unofficial visits by Director of Central Intelligence George Tenet, and one visit by Vice President Richard Cheney, in March 2002, Yemen also agreed to allow up to a hundred U.S. Special Forces and affiliated intelligence analysts to train, advise, and assist Republican Guard troops in offensive counterterror operations in country.[60] On April 10, Yemen was formally designated a combat zone in support of Operation Enduring Freedom by the United States, which allowed the Special Forces trainers to be deployed.[61] By July the first class of Yemeni Republican Guard soldiers had completed training in marksmanship, maneuver techniques, explosives, and assault.[62]

One specific request made by Tenet to President Saleh was to allow the CIA to fly armed Predator drones over Yemeni airspace.[63] The MQ-1 Predator is a twenty-seven-foot-long propeller-driven unmanned aircraft that can fly three miles above a battlefield for up to twenty-four hours. It can track both people and vehicles on the ground with radar, infrared sensors, and a color video camera, and fire anti-tank AGM-114 Hellfire missiles at self-generated targets. In 2002, the Predator was under the operational control of the Agency's Directorate of Operations' Special Activities Division—though actually flown by Air Force controllers after take-off—in close collaboration with military officials in the theater.[64] In Afghanistan, where the Predator was first used in offensive military operations, the Pentagon claimed that the drone had a nearly "100 percent record of hits" in several dozen attacks against Al Qaeda and Taliban figures, including the killing of Al Qaeda's military commander, Mohammed Atef, in November 2001.[65] President Saleh agreed to Tenet's request to fly Predators above Yemen, but initially placed restrictions on how it could be used, which infuriated President Bush.[66] In time, Saleh allowed the Predators greater freedom of movement, and they began flying over Yemen from secret warehouses located just across the border in Saudi Arabia, and from Camp Lemonier in Djibouti—a French Air Force base, and the headquarters of U.S. Central Command's Combined Joint Task Force-Horn of Africa.[67]

THE BUSH ADMINISTRATION DEBATE
AND AMERICA'S ROLE IN TARGETED KILLINGS

Throughout the Cold War, the United States either directly or through foreign agents participated in targeted killing plots against the leaders of perceived allies of the Soviet Union. An eighteen-month U.S. Senate Select Committee investigation, led by Senator Frank Church, implicated the United States in assassination plots—all either unsuccessful or unimplemented—against several foreign leaders, including at least eight separate plans to kill the Cuban president, Fidel Castro.[68] In response to the Church Committee's revelations, in 1976, President Gerald Ford issued Executive Order 11905, which declared, "No employee of the United States Government shall engage in, or conspire to engage in, political assassination."[69] President Ford's proclamation was renewed by all subsequent presidents.[70] For the quarter-century after 1976, as a general proposition, the ban on peacetime targeted killings was strongly supported by all senior U.S. national security policymakers. For the most part, whenever mid-level staffers or foreign intelligence agents recommended assassinating leaders of states that were enemies of the United States, the plots died within the bureaucracy, were denied funding by the relevant congressional oversight committees, or were vetoed outright by senior officials.[71]

There were several reasons why, among all types of Discrete Military Operations, targeted killings were opposed by most U.S. senior civilian and military officials before 9/11. First, U.S. presidents still made exceptions to the assassination ban by allowing the use of lethal military force against the leadership of command and control networks of adversaries, which included heads of state, such as the 1986 bombing of the Azizihhah Barracks compound in Tripoli, where the Libyan leader Muammar Qadhafi was known to be, or the 1999 missile strikes into the bedroom of Serbian president Slobodan Milosevic's personal residence in Belgrade.[72] Second, assassinations ran counter to well-established international norms, and were prohibited under both treaty and customary international law. Third, weakening the international norm against assassinations could result in retaliatory killings of American leaders, who are more vulnerable as a consequence of living in a relatively open society. Fourth, the targeted killing of suspected terrorists or political leaders was generally considered an ineffective foreign policy tool. An assassination attempt that failed could be counterproductive, in that it would create more legal and diplomatic problems than it was worth. An attempt that succeeded, meanwhile, would likely do little to diminish the long-term threat from an enemy state or group. Finally, the secretive and treacherous aspect of targeted killings was considered antithetical to the moral and ethical precepts of the United States.[73]

Prior to 9/11, neither the Bill Clinton nor the George W. Bush administrations considered formally rescinding the ban against assassination. Both presidents did, however, permit the killing of international terrorists, specifically Al Qaeda members, as acts of self-defense. In the wake of the African Embassy Bombings in 1998, President Clinton issued three top secret Memoranda of Understanding that authorized the CIA to kill Bin Laden and several of his key lieutenants—fewer than ten—and only if in an attempt to capture them they resisted. While Clinton and his senior aides recalled that it was clear that the president wanted Bin Laden and his cohorts dead, the CIA interpreted the Memoranda as insufficient in permitting the use of lethal force.[74] As George Tenet later noted, "Almost every authority granted to CIA prior to 9/11 made it clear that just going out and assassinating [Bin Laden] would not have been permissible or acceptable."[75] During the first eight months of the Bush administration, as the relevant agencies labored to develop a comprehensive plan to defeat Al Qaeda, the Deputies Committee of the National Security Council concurred with the Clinton administration's legal opinion that permitted the CIA to kill Bin Laden or his deputies, but did not seek greater authorities for lethal covert actions from President Bush.[76]

After 9/11, among senior civilian and military officials a new consensus opinion emerged that supported the peacetime targeted killing of members of the Al Qaeda network, but only on a limited basis, and only if the suspected terrorists could not be captured for interrogation. One senior U.S. official admitted that although killing individual terrorists would only be the equivalent of "clipping toenails," since the dead could be quickly replaced, it was worth doing since "we should use all the weapons at our disposal."[77] On September 17, 2001, Bush formalized this judgment in a Memorandum of Notification that authorized the CIA to kill, without further presidential approval, members of Al Qaeda or other global terrorist networks—including American citizens—that appeared on a "high-value target list," which initially consisted of some two dozen terrorist leaders.[78] This finding was considered by CIA officials to be more expansive and unambiguous than any of the previous presidential Memoranda that provided limited exceptions to the assassination ban.[79] Along with providing the legal protection for targeted killings, it directed the CIA to develop paramilitary teams to hunt down and kill individuals on the high-value target list.[80] As one senior Bush administration official explained, "The president has given the [CIA] the green light to do whatever is necessary. Lethal operations that were unthinkable pre-September 11 are now underway."[81] Included on the high-value target list of most-wanted Al Qaeda terrorists was Abu Ali al-Harithi, an operational planner in al-Nashiri's cell that attacked the *U.S.S. Cole* and one of the "key cogs in the machine that make the Al Qaeda mechanism work," according to Edmund Hull, then the U.S. Ambassador to Yemen.[82]

THE HUNT FOR ABU ALI AL-HARITHI

Abu Ali al-Harithi also appeared at the top of another list, consisting of the names of the roughly three dozen terror suspects demanded by the Bush administration from Yemen.[83] The central government's concerted efforts for capturing al-Harithi were closely followed by the Yemeni press, with analysts speculating on his location, the number of his dedicated followers, and whether or not he was being hosted by tribal sheiks.[84] In early December 2001, Yemeni security forces laid siege to the house of al-Harithi, but he was able to escape during negotiations over the terms of his surrender. A week later, on December 18, President Saleh ordered Republican Guard troops—supported by armor and airpower—to capture al-Harithi, believed to be cornered again, in the village of al-Husun. During an inspection of one of the houses, a jet fighter broke the sound barrier directly above the village, alerting al-Harithi and sympathetic local tribesman.[85] In the ensuing firefight, nineteen Republican Guard soldiers—including the commanding officer—were killed, and al-Harithi again escaped.[86]

Before the failed raid at al-Husun, Yemen had assumed the primary responsibility to pursue the Al Qaeda operative, but afterward President Saleh agreed to allow the United States to pursue al-Harithi more aggressively inside of Yemen.[87] Most important, it was after al-Husun that Saleh finally allowed the CIA's Predator drones to make surveillance flights over the vast, unpopulated Marib region.[88] Those within the U.S. government that were reportedly involved in the pursuit of al-Harithi included FBI agents, Special Operations teams from CENTCOM, the U.S. Army's covert "Gray Fox" surveillance unit, the CIA, the NSA, and State Department diplomats.[89] The key diplomat was Ambassador Hull, the former State Department counterterrorism chief and fluent Arabic speaker, who made repeated trips to the isolated Marib region to meet with local tribesmen. During these "diplomatic journeys," which upset the political leadership in Sana'a, Hull developed intelligence about al-Harithi's location and movement from the tribes in exchange for money, clinics, and schools.[90]

While Hull developed Yemeni sources on the ground, U.S. intelligence caught the lucky break that eventually led to al-Harithi's death. In February 2002, Moroccan intelligence agents were allowed by the United States for the first time to interrogate seventeen Moroccan nationals captured in Afghanistan and detained at Guantanamo Bay, Cuba. One Moroccan identified a former Saudi bodyguard of Bin Laden, Zouhair Hilal Mohamed Tabiti, handler of a cell in Morocco that was plotting strikes on U.S. and British warships in the Straits of Gibraltar. In May, Tabiti was detained in Casablanca while attempting to board a flight to Saudi Arabia. Under questioning, Tabiti admitted to receiving operational instructions and $5,000 in seed money from al-Nashiri—the *U.S.S. Cole* bombing mastermind—to fund the proposed maritime attacks. Information from Tabiti led to al-Nashiri's arrest in the United Arab Emirates in late October. Before entering the CIA's rendition program, where he was tortured, al-Nashiri allowed his interrogators to listen into phone calls he made to associates, including al-Harithi.[91]

At the time, al-Harithi and his bodyguards were living in tents in the Marib region near the Saudi border, using different vehicles and moving every few days without the support of local tribes. Yemeni security forces, U.S. Special Operations teams, U-2 planes, and Predators had been combing the unpopulated region for months, but were unable to unearth al-Harithi. On at least one occasion, a Predator was about to strike a pickup truck with a mounted heavy machine gun, but Yemeni forces on the ground determined it was driven by innocent Bedouins.[92] Al-Harithi had five mobile phones on him, and was constantly changing the chips and numbers for them.[93] The NSA had a partial

NSA   SigInt (handwritten)

list of al-Harithi's phone numbers, and had created an alarm that would alert analysts if any of them were used.[94] His final phone call was reportedly made to a number in the United Arab Emirates, probably al-Nashiri's.[95]

American Special Operations forces on the ground, supported by a Predator circling above, found and were monitoring al-Harithi's group when they left a compound in the Marib in two Toyota SUVs.[96] All of the men were in one vehicle, the women in another. According to an unnamed U.S. official, "If the women hadn't gotten into another car, we wouldn't have fired."[97] The NSA alarm sounded when a phone number al-Harithi had not used for some time was activated. The person speaking on the phone was unfamiliar, but an NSA analyst—having listened to the hunted terrorist's voice for years—instantly recognized al-Harithi talking in the background, giving directions to the driver. A second NSA analyst concurred that it was al-Harithi's voice.[98] The picture from the SUVs was watched simultaneously by George Tenet at the CIA's Counter-Terrorist Center in Langley, Virginia, and Lieutenant General Michael DeLong, the deputy commander of CENTCOM, at the command's headquarters in Tampa, Florida.[99] The two men agreed on the intelligence that indicated al-Harithi was in the targeted SUV, and Tenet, who had received the authority from President Bush after 9/11 to authorize targeted killings, ordered the Predator to fire.[100] The Predator climbed into position, maneuvered its nose downward, and fired one Hellfire missile, destroying the SUV and killing al-Harithi, four other Yemenis, and Ahmed Hijazi, a naturalized U.S. citizen and ringleader of an alleged terrorist sleeper cell in Lackawanna, New York.[101] After-action video of the blast site showed that the only identifiable item was the SUV's oil pan.[102]

AFTERMATH AND ASSESSMENT

It is inherent that all covert action programs are politically controversial, potentially embarrassing if discovered, and often ethically questionable. As such, they are developed and implemented so that both the sponsoring government and any foreign clients can plausibly deny them. The November 3, 2002, Predator strike in Yemen was just such a covert operation: a targeted killing by the CIA in a country whose population was hostile toward the United States and its Middle East policies. Ambassador Richard Armitage, Deputy Secretary of State, recalled of the strike that "the deniability was an important component of the mission."[103] Prior to the attack, Tenet and President Saleh had agreed to keep America's involvement in the operation secret.[104] It could plausibly be asserted that the SUV had blown up when a propane tank or explosives it was carrying had accidentally detonated, or that it had hit a landmine. In fact, immediate reports from international and Yemeni media, citing unnamed tribal or government sources, made just such claims.[105] Somebody in the United States or Yemen, however, soon leaked that a missile fired from a CIA Predator had destroyed al-Harithi's SUV.[106] Acting on the instruction of Secretary Rumsfeld, Paul Wolfowitz appeared on CNN to confirm America's involvement and to boast that it had been "a very successful tactical operation," which had "gotten rid of somebody dangerous."[107]

President Saleh and other senior Yemeni leaders were furious with the leak, in part because they were still tracking down other fugitives affiliated with al-Harithi.[108] Brigadier General Yahya M. al-Mutawakel, a senior official for the ruling People's Congress party, broke Yemen's official silence, stating, "This is why it is so difficult to make deals with the United States. . . . They don't consider the internal circumstances in Yemen. In security matters, you don't want to alert the enemy."[109] The CIA, which had operational command of the mission and had cultivated Saleh as a client for years, was also angry that its cover was blown.[110] A covert operation that could have been plausibly disavowed by Sana'a and Washington was demonstrated to have involved the United States in providing both the technical support to track al-Harithi and the weapons system that killed him. Having learned from the embarrassing aftermath of the Yemen strike, after similar CIA Predator attacks against Al Qaeda leaders in northwest Pakistan since May 2005, nobody from the U.S. government has confirmed them on the record.[111]

For this case, assessing the evidence for the proposition that senior civilian officials are more likely to support the use of DMOs than the uniformed military is very difficult, since it was a covert operation. In published news articles and interviews, senior civilian and military officials have been very reluctant to discuss the Yemen operation in detail. Nevertheless, as a general proposition, military officials are much more reluctant than civilians to support the targeted killing of adversaries of the United States. Targeted killings are a short-term, tactical response to a specific foreign policy problem. Senior military officials prefer the development and implementation of a comprehensive national strategy—using non-military and military means—to resolve the long-term problems posed by the group or state to which the targeted individual belongs. As one senior military official noted about the targeted killings of Al Qaeda and Taliban suspects in Pakistan, "We'll get these one-off flukes once every eight months or so, but that's still not a strategy—it's not a plan. Every now and then something will come together. What that serves to do [is] it tamps down discussion about whether there is a better way to do it."[112] In addition, given the choice, military officials generally support capturing suspected terrorists to develop further sources and intelligence over attempting to kill them.[113] Finally, given the inherent difficulties, military officials are also less likely than civilian officials to believe that targeted killings will succeed militarily.[114]

In addition, a close reading of the dozen or so off-the-record comments by Bush administration civilian officials about the Predator strike shows that they were overwhelmingly supportive. One administration official declared, "We've got new authorities, new tools and a new willingness to do it wherever it has to be done."[115] Another civilian, described as a senior law enforcement official, stated more bluntly, "I'm ecstatic."[116] Perhaps because the Predator was controlled and operated by the CIA, no military officials commented on the DMO off the record. Although there are limited data about the planning and debates, it is possible to say that, in this case, senior civilian officials are more likely to favor DMOs because they believe they are militarily and politically effective, are controllable, have low domestic political costs, and demonstrate resolve.

Did the DMO in Yemen achieve its intended military objective to kill Abu Ali al-Harithi? Unquestionably. A loyal Al Qaeda member for over a decade, who was implicated in the unsuccessful plot against *The Sullivans* and responsible for overseeing the bombing of the *U.S.S. Cole*, was assassinated. This fact was reportedly determined by a DNA sample taken from al-Harithi's remains and analyzed in a military laboratory in the United States.[117] That the operation was conducted with no collateral damage, and no casualties of American or Yemeni troops, was a demonstration of the remarkable advances in American remote-sensing, stand-off, precise military power.

Did the DMO achieve its intended political objectives to deter Al Qaeda members from committing future terrorist attacks against the United States and its allies, and compel more consistent counterterrorism cooperation from Yemen? For both political objectives, the answer is no. According to Armitage, "The goal of the strike was to make Al Qaeda feel frightened, so that they knew we could reach out and hit them without them knowing."[118] While there was some evidence from captured signals intelligence of Al Qaeda that they were shocked by the Predator strike, the killing of al-Harithi and his cohorts in no way deterred the international terrorist organization from conducting future attacks.[119] This was demonstrated by the steady number of Al Qaeda–sponsored terrorist bombings in Tunisia, Istanbul, London, Malindi, Kenya, and elsewhere.[120] Furthermore, it is unlikely that the Predator strike disrupted any terrorist plots that were in the final stages, since al-Harithi had likely been too occupied hiding from the American-Yemeni manhunt to plan or conduct operations.

The Predator DMO also failed in its other political objective of encouraging better counterterrorism cooperation from Yemen. The central government made a more determined effort at fighting terrorism within its borders, which greatly reduced the ability of non-governmental organization and sympathetic tribal elements to openly support foreign jihadist groups.[121] The allegiance of Yemen's security forces at all levels, however, remained mixed, as demonstrated by the February 2006 prison escape of twenty-three suspected members of Al Qaeda, who received assistance from sympathetic guards.[122] Since 2002, Yemen has also worked more closely with the United States in terms of sharing intelligence, but the cooperation had been limited and halting until late 2009, when President Saleh embraced enhanced and more overt U.S. assistance.[123] In 2006, senior civilian and military officials at CENTCOM believed that Yemen was essentially a failed state, and that the Saleh regime remained in power only with its financial and diplomatic support from the United States.[124] Furthermore, as a Bush administration official who worked on the Middle East stated, "Yemen is a tough client. We have to hold their feet to the fire to carry through on anything."[125] As a result of Yemen's on-again-off-again counterterrorism efforts, Al Qaeda terrorists have not been deterred from operating in Yemen since November 2002.[126] In fact, as was apparent after the failed bombing of a Detroit-bound Northwest Airlines flight on Christmas Day 2009 by Umar Farouk Abdulmutallab, Yemeni-based Al Qaeda operatives had made "a quantum leap to being the [Al Qaeda] affiliate that wants to carry out attacks against the United States and its allies," according to Daniel Benjamin, the State Department's Coordinator for Terrorism.[127]

The targeted killing of a suspected terrorist outside of a battlefield setting was possible only because of the confluence of four factors: the 9/11 attacks, more expansive legal authority from President Bush to the CIA, innovative military capabilities with the armed Predator drone that had been flying for only one year, and the political will of the Bush administration to end the long-standing taboo against assassinations. The military success of the DMO was both quietly and publicly celebrated by military and civilian officials.

President Bush himself was said to be elated by the results, telling a senior advisor, "We're talking to them in a way they can understand."[128] The inability of the Predator attack to clearly achieve both of its political objectives, however, speaks to the limited effect of targeted killings in fighting terrorism. Defeating a highly capable international terrorist organization, and helping to develop the security and governance capacity of underdeveloped countries, requires a sustained collaboration with the ruling regimes of countries where terrorists operate and a willingness of those regimes to reciprocate. In Yemen, despite the best intentions of Washington and Sana'a, this type of deep cooperation had not begun to occur until late 2009.[129] What is more, despite the increased threat warnings emanating from the country, there was no comprehensive military campaign plan for Yemen until it was developed and approved by Gen. David Petraeus, commander of Central Command, in late April 2009.[130] Furthermore, the manner in which the intelligence to kill al-Harithi was slowly cultivated—through lengthy interrogations, technical surveillance, and close cooperation with foreign intelligence agencies—suggests that every possible effort should be made to detain high-value Al Qaeda terrorists. The intelligence that American investigators have obtained about the organization's personnel, methods, and targets through interrogations has been more valuable in ongoing counterterrorism operations than the short-term gains from targeted killings.[131]

6 KHURMAL, IRAQ: SUMMER 2002

IN THE AFTERMATH of the September 11, 2001, terrorist attacks, President George W. Bush's declared national security policy focused on two central premises: the United States would "pursue nations that provide aid or safe haven to terrorism" and prevent terrorist groups from acquiring weapons of mass destruction (WMD) that could be used to attack or coerce America or its allies.[1] The reasoning behind this conceptual framework was that without state sponsorship, terrorist organizations are less effective in recruiting new members and planning large-scale operations, and given the commitment of groups such as Al Qaeda to create mass casualties, it was likely that they were seeking to obtain WMD. In the face of threats from reckless state leaders and terrorists who employed suicide tactics, long-term strategies of containment or deterrence could not be counted upon. The Bush administration's national security framework justified the use of preemptive force to attack state sponsors of terrorism and defeat the catastrophic threat of WMD before it was fully formed.

Six months after this national security framework was first articulated, an unprecedented opportunity emerged for the United States to use preemptive force to attack a terrorist organization operating in a country that was labeled a state sponsor of terrorism by the U.S. State Department and was reportedly developing WMD to use against America, or its allies in Western Europe. In the Zagros Mountains of Iraqi Kurdistan, a Kurdish terrorist organization—Ansar al-Islam—was running a training camp near the city of Khurmal, where it reportedly was producing cyanide gas, toxic poisons, and ricin for terrorist attacks by its affiliated cells in Britain, Germany, France, and Italy.[2] The U.S. military developed a combined air-ground operation option that anticipated striking the camp on July 4, 2002. That option was unanimously supported by the Joint Chiefs of Staff and proposed to the White House. According to General Richard Myers, Chairman of the Joint Chiefs, the planned operation to destroy Khurmal "would have been challenging, but doable."[3] General Jack Keane, the Army's representative on the Joint Chiefs, recalled the proposed option as "very doable from a military perspective."[4] If there ever was a clear instance for the Bush administration to execute its post-9/11 national security policy, this was it. Yet despite the alleged threat from Ansar al-Islam, and a reliable option to use preemptive force to defeat it, President Bush chose not to utilize a Discrete Military Operation (DMO).

While there have been a few passing news media references, this chapter tells the complete story of the negative case of Khurmal for the first time. It contains six sections. First, it sketches the emergence of Islamic fundamentalism in Iraqi Kurdistan, the founding of Ansar al-Islam, and its links to terrorist operative Abu Musab al-Zarqawi. Second, it follows the early debate among senior officials about the threat posed by Ansar al-Islam and what the United States should do, if anything, to counter it. Third, it details the two DMOs to strike the Ansar training camp near the Kurdish village of Khurmal that were developed by the military, one of which was unanimously approved by the Joint Chiefs of Staff. Fourth, it offers and evaluates four plausible explanations for why President Bush ultimately decided against implementing either operation: the threat was not great enough, there was no actionable intelligence, the political costs of failure were too high, and the main goal of regime change could be disrupted. This section concludes that the last explanation—President Bush did not want to undertake any actions that could have derailed the option of regime change in Iraq—is the most powerful reason Khurmal was not attacked. Fifth, it discusses the costs and consequences to American interests of the decision to leave Ansar al-Islam and al-Zarqawi untouched. Finally, this chapter analyzes five lessons that this case can tell us about the non-uses of DMOs.

THE RISE OF ANSAR AL-ISLAM

Influenced by the Iranian revolution in 1979, proselytizing of the Muslim Brotherhood, and return of battle-hardened Kurds who fought alongside the mujahideen in Afghanistan against the Soviet army, Islamic fundamentalism emerged as a minor political force in northern Iraq in the late 1980s. This was reflected in 1992 by the first democratic elections in northern Iraq for the regional parliament. The main Islamist party, the Islamic Movement of Iraqi Kurdistan (IMK), received 6 percent of the vote, far trailing the two dominant secular Kurdish factions: the Kurdish Democratic Party (KDP) with 46 percent and the Patriotic Union of Kurdistan (PUK) with 45 percent. Throughout the early 1990s, Kurdistan flourished via oil-smuggling revenues and the armed protection of the American-led no-fly zone north of the 36th parallel—within which Iraqi security services were forbidden from flying fixed-wing aircraft. In short time, the Kurds established a court system, armed an internal security force, built schools and clinics, and installed an elected parliament in the provincial capital of Irbil.[5] The IMK utilized this safe haven to expand its ranks by recruiting young urban men disillusioned by the encroaching secular and Western influences into northern Iraq. Between 1994 and 1996, the tentative coalition between the KDP and PUK unraveled over a disagreement regarding the division of oil-smuggling profits.[6] After intermittent fighting, a settlement was reached in which Kurdistan was evenly split, with the KDP controlling the northern and western portions bordering Turkey, and the PUK the south and east. In May 1997, through a diplomatic agreement brokered by Tehran, the IMK was able to carve out a fifteen-square-mile area of its own within the PUK's territory that bordered Iran.[7] Of the sixteen villages in this small mountainous terrain, the largest was named Khurmal.[8]

Ten days before the September 11 attacks, a breakaway faction of the IMK aligned with other Islamist Kurdish groups and was reconstituted as *Ansar al-Islam*—Arabic for "Supporters of Islam." Ansar issued a fatwa, or religious edict, which declared war against the two secular Kurdish parties and welcomed fellow jihadists to join the fight by infiltrating their enclave via the porous border with Iran. Backed by financing from Osama Bin Laden and Saudi Arabia, and with modest security assistance from Iran, Ansar established a Taliban-style social order within its territory: drinking, smoking, and satellite televisions were strictly forbidden; women were prohibited from education or employment; and men were required to pray five times daily at their village mosque.[9] Kurds within the enclave who did not adhere to Ansar's strict decrees were threatened, forcibly displaced, or tortured.[10] Islamist Kurds and small numbers of Arab fighters were trained in small arms tactics, explosives, suicide bombings, and assassinations. Armed skirmishes between Ansar and the secular Kurdish militias were videotaped and posted on a website (www.ansarislam.com) or circulated throughout the Muslim world for recruitment purposes.[11] Estimates of Ansar al-Islam's members in Iraqi Kurdistan ranged from 600 to 1,000 armed and dedicated militants within a civilian population of 4,000.[12] They were a violent and dedicated terrorist organization, though largely contained, but not defeated, by the approximately 10,000 PUK fighters surrounding them in the region.[13]

While the existence of an armed Islamic fundamentalist movement in northern Iraq was a concern acknowledged by U.S. officials, it did not threaten American interests until it formally merged with Al Qaeda members and affiliates fleeing Afghanistan after the fall of the Taliban.[14] Foremost among these exiled operatives was Abu Musab al-Zarqawi, the Jordanian terrorist, who oversaw a string of spectacular and gruesome attacks throughout Iraq between July 2003 and June 2006, when he was killed by an American airstrike. From early 2000 to October of the following year, al-Zarqawi managed the Al-Matar training facility in the western Afghanistan town of Herat, which contained around 2,000 fighters and their families. His group, *Jund al-Sham*—Arabic for "Soldiers of the Levant"—was dedicated to overthrowing the Jordanian monarchy. In December 2001, al-Zarqawi and three hundred of his fighters left the Afghan safe haven for northern Iran. Over the next fourteen months, al-Zarqawi traveled to southern Lebanon, Syria, and northern Iraq, expanding his terrorist network. In March 2002, either on his own accord or at Tehran's insistence, al-Zarqawi and his followers left Iran to live and train in the Ansar enclave in Iraqi Kurdistan.[15] The arrival of al-Zarqawi and his affiliates had an impact on the capabilities and character of Ansar al-Islam in two important ways. First, it meant the arrival of what one U.S. Special Forces officer—who later investigated Khurmal—referred to as the "Al Qaeda mobile curriculum" that had been developed and refined in the training camps of Afghanistan.[16] Second, it catalyzed Ansar to adopt even bloodier tactics against innocent Kurdish civilians and secular political leaders.[17]

THE CIVILIAN DEBATE ON IRAQ

Within ten days of assuming office, President Bush convened his first meeting of the Principals Committee of the NSC, with the only topic being "Mideast Policy." The consensus of the senior officials was that Saddam Hussein's regime was destabilizing the region and most likely developing proscribed WMD and ballistic missiles. President Bush tasked the heads of the State Department, the Pentagon, and the CIA to review America's diplomatic and military approach toward Iraq.[18] On September 11, the Bush administration's Iraq review, though overdue, remained unfinished. A few months later, the review was restarted with a series of secret informal gatherings of the Deputies Committee (DC) of the NSC, known as non-DC meetings, or "Deputies Lunches."[19] The meetings were chaired by Deputy National Security Advisor Stephen Hadley and included key senior officials heavily involved in Iraq war planning: Deputy Secretary of Defense Paul Wolfowitz and Undersecretary of Defense for Policy Douglas Feith, from the Pentagon; Deputy Secretary of State Richard Armitage and Undersecretary for Political Affairs Marc Grossman, from the State Department; Vice Chairman of the Joint Chiefs General Peter Pace; Deputy Director of Central Intelligence John McLaughlin; NSC regional specialist Zalmay Khalilzad; and Scooter Libby or John Hannah from the Office of the Vice President.[20] This group of second- and third-ranking foreign policy officials decided early on that the policy of containment had failed and that Saddam Hussein would have to be removed from power.[21] Though the decision to invade Iraq had not been made by early 2002, the Deputies considered the checklist of all requirements should the president decided on regime change, from selecting a post-Hussein governing structure to refurbishing the aging electrical grid to developing and distributing a new currency.[22] The Deputies also debated several schemes to overthrow Hussein, including establishing an independent enclave in southern Iraq, arming Iraqi exile groups, fomenting a coup from within the Iraqi Army, and using unilateral American military force.[23]

As the Deputies Lunches continued, in early spring 2002 *New Yorker* reporter Jeffrey Goldberg toured Iraqi Kurdistan to investigate the lives of the Kurdish victims of Hussein's Anfal Campaign in 1987 and 1988, a genocidal effort that featured mustard and nerve gas attacks against civilians in at least sixty villages.[24] In the course of his interviews, Goldberg visited a prison in Sulaimaniya run by the intelligence service of the Patriotic Union of Kurdistan. Three of the prisoners provided evidence of connections between the Iraqi regime and Al Qaeda: Qassem Hussein Muhammad, an Iraqi intelligence officer who alleged that another Mukhabarat employee was "the actual decision-maker" of Ansar al-Islam; Haqi Ismail, an Iraqi Arab who was alleged, by his Kurdish captors, to have connections to the Mukhabarat, and who admitted to working in the Taliban Foreign Ministry; and Muhammad Mansour Shahab, an Arab-Iranian who claimed to have smuggled explosives, small arms, and several dozen refrigerator motors that each contained an unidentified liquid canister between the Iraqi Mukhabarat and Al Qaeda in Afghanistan.[25]

The essential findings from these interviews were a series of damning allegations:

> That Ansar al-Islam has received funds directly from Al Qaeda; that the intelligence service of Saddam Hussein has joint control, with Al Qaeda operatives, over

Ansar al-Islam; that Saddam Hussein hosted a senior leader of Al Qaeda in Baghdad in 1992; that a number of Al Qaeda members fleeing Afghanistan have been secretly brought into territory controlled by Ansar al-Islam; and that Iraqi intelligence agents smuggled conventional weapons, and possibly even chemical and biological weapons, into Afghanistan."[26]

Goldberg's article, titled "The Great Terror," made an immediate impact on the emerging national debate about whether or not to confront Iraq. Political leaders from both parties, Director of Central Intelligence George Tenet, and serving and retired government officials commented on what was characterized by Vice President Dick Cheney as a "devastating story."[27] If it were true that Saddam Hussein was harboring Al Qaeda members ousted from Afghanistan, and that his intelligence operatives were cooperating with Al Qaeda over the production of weapons of mass destruction, then Iraq would clearly meet the threshold for using preventive force as articulated by President Bush after September 11. Appearing on talk shows to promote his article, Goldberg was careful not to oversell the validity of his allegation, noting that while he "understands that all intelligence is colored by motivation," he felt the prisoners' "stories were credible enough to warrant reporting."[28] Furthermore, perhaps Goldberg's most damning allegation was that no American government employees—either from the diplomatic, military, or intelligence services—had questioned the prisoners, despite repeated pleas from PUK officials. Commenting on this assertion, former Director of Central Intelligence James Woolsey proclaimed, "It would be a real shame if the C.I.A.'s substantial institutional hostility to Iraqi democratic resistance groups was keeping it from learning about Saddam's ties to Al Qaeda in northern Iraq."[29]

Goldberg's article catalyzed ongoing and divisive inter-agency discussions about possible links between Al Qaeda and Iraq. A front-page *Washington Post* story on the *New Yorker* article quoted an unnamed senior administration official "disposed toward U.S. military confrontation with Iraq" as stating, "[the piece] doesn't strike me as incredible, and may fill in gaps in our knowledge. I'll be interested in what our intelligence people say."[30] At the first Deputies Lunch after Goldberg's article was published, on March 25, discussion turned toward his allegations, as well as the claim that the CIA had made no effort to interrogate the PUK's prisoners. At one point, Stephen Hadley turned to John McLaughlin and asked, "What is going on here?"—meaning: "Why hasn't the CIA investigated this?"[31] At each meeting over the subsequent weeks, the Pentagon's representatives, Wolfowitz and Feith, would press McLaughlin on the status of whether the lead American intelligence agency charged with collecting human intelligence abroad would enter Iraqi Kurdistan to follow up on Goldberg's charges. It would not be until June 27, three months after the initial allegations surfaced, that McLaughlin would consent to allowing CIA teams to interview the PUK's prisoners, but only on the condition that the Principals Committee of the NSC approved.[32] In the second week of July, an eight-person CIA team—the Northern Iraq Liaison Element—finally crossed into northern Iraq from Turkey to investigate the threat from Ansar al-Islam. The intelligence operatives interviewed the Ansar detainees, verifying that three had trained at camps in Afghanistan but failing to obtain any physical evidence that poisons were being produced at Khurmal.[33]

MILITARY OPTIONS AND JOINT CHIEFS OF STAFF APPROVAL

Months before the CIA was investigating Ansar al-Islam, the Pentagon was collecting intelligence about the group, compiling detailed targeting information, and drawing up military options to strike Khurmal. Military planning began at the regional command level, which included both U.S. Central Command (CENTCOM), the command that included Iraq, and U.S. European Command (EUCOM), the command whose Special Operations assets would have led the mission. The plans were then submitted to the Joint Chiefs of Staff, consisting of the service chiefs of the Army, Navy, Air Force, and Marines, and the Chiefs' vice chairman and chairman—the principal military advisor to the president, NSC, and secretary of defense. The six Chiefs and their staffs meet once or twice a week in "The Tank"—a secure conference room in the Pentagon used for official meetings.[34] During a Tank gathering over the Memorial Day weekend in 2002 the Joint Chiefs received their first formal briefing about the intelligence on Khurmal, or "Khurma" as it was also described in internal Pentagon papers.[35] The Chiefs were informed that Ansar al-Islam, an organization distinct from Al Qaeda, was preparing toxins that could be used against targets in Europe or the United States.[36] According to Lieutenant General Gregory Newbold, the Joint Staff's director of operations at the time, the information was based on "extremely good intelligence."[37] General Jack Keane, the Army's vice chief of staff, agreed, concluding that, given all of the intelligence he saw in early summer 2002, "there was no doubt about the target [Khurmal] in my mind."[38]

Military operations officers at the regional commands, supported by the Joint Staff, immediately worked up detailed plans to go after Khurmal. The plans were based upon the best intelligence, U.S. strike capabilities stationed in the region, and political sensitivities of the countries in which the participating aircraft and helicopters would have to be based, or flown over. While there were many versions as they were constantly updated and refined, the operations officers developed two broad options for striking the camp: an air-only option, and an air-ground combination.[39] Since the specific military plans remain classified, the following analysis of options is based upon all of the publicly available information, discussions with informed civilian and military officials, an understanding of recent American uses of limited force, and an examination of the eventual destruction of Khurmal by the U.S. Army Special Forces and Kurdish militias in March 2003, after the start of Operation Iraqi Freedom.

The air-only option could have been conducted through two means. The first was with a barrage of sea-launched Tomahawk Land Attack Missiles (TLAMs) from U.S. Navy assets in the Persian Gulf. The upsides for using cruise missiles is that they almost always impact targets with pinpoint accuracy, making them the ideal weapon for attacking above-ground and well-exposed facilities such as the Ansar camp at Khurmal. The downside with cruise missiles is that they cannot penetrate deep enough into the earth to destroy hardened underground bunkers and command centers. Furthermore, the conventional warhead mounted on a TLAM does not burn at a hot enough temperature to reliably incinerate biological or chemical agents, and the Joint Chiefs believed that chemical testing was happening at Khurmal. Therefore, if Ansar al-Islam had indeed developed WMD stockpiles and buried them deep enough, a cruise missile attack would have destroyed the buildings but left the threatening weapons untouched.

The second air-only method could have been to drop conventional bombs on the target from manned U.S. aircraft. One positive element with air-dropped bombs is that they burrow deeper and contain more explosive power than TLAMs, so that they provide more certainty that any stocks of buried WMD would be destroyed. The key problem with a bombing mission, however, would have been that Khurmal was located outside of the northern no-fly zone (NFZ) patrolled by American and British aircraft flying out of the Incirlik Air Base in Turkey. The Ansar camp was fifty-five miles south of the 36th parallel, which served as the southern boundary to the northern NFZ.

Since the creation of the northern NFZ in 1991, the Turkish government had severely proscribed the rules of engagement and number of sorties per week for the aircraft patrolling it.[40] As Marc Grossman, U.S. ambassador to Turkey in the mid-1990s, recalled, these restrictions "were all designed to remind us that we should not allow an independent Kurdish state in Northern Iraq."[41] Given such concerns, and that American officials were concurrently pressing Ankara for permission to use its territory to serve as a staging area for a U.S. ground invasion into Iraq, it is highly unlikely that Turkish officials would have approved a strike on Khurmal using its ground facilities or airspace.[42]

The other three possible flight paths to Khurmal also made them an unlikely avenue for a bombing attack. One would have been to fly eighty miles north through Iran, and then west into Iraq. Although Iran allowed U.S. pilots to drift into its airspace in the 2001–2002 war against the Taliban in Afghanistan, it is highly doubtful that American planes would have been given overflight rights to bomb Khurmal, especially since Tehran was a minor patron of Ansar al-Islam. Therefore, a strike package flying over Iran would likely have encountered air-defense and air-to-air attacks, which would have placed American pilots unnecessarily at risk.[43] A second alternative flight path would have been to fly north through Iraq from the Persian Gulf or Kuwait. This route would have required flying through the well-maintained integrated air-defense system in central Iraq, between the southern and northern no-fly zones.[44] A final route would have been to take off from a friendly state in Central or Eastern Europe, traverse through Israel and Jordan, and then across central Iraq. Again, the size of the flight package required for such a bombing operation, and a pathway through the most lethal area of the Iraqi air-defense system, would have unnecessarily threatened the pilots and planes. The logistical and political hurdles with each possible flight path to Khurmal would have made the manned bombing option severely unlikely. Therefore, a barrage of a few dozen TLAMs from U.S. Navy assets in the northern Persian Gulf would have been the most probable air-only option to strike the targeted training camp.

The other option developed by the military for striking the target was with a combined air-ground attack.[45] The goal of this option would have been to saturate the training camp with bombs; insert ground forces via helicopter to survey the damage; capture or kill any survivors; and conduct sensitive site exploitation to gather any physical evidence of WMD production, intelligence about the group, and/or propaganda material that would have been useful in justifying the attack. The ground forces component of this option was to have been led by U.S. Special Operation Forces (SOF) teams, with support from the Kurdish PUK militias.[46] The SOF teams would have been covertly transported by helicopters from the 352nd Special Operations Group based in Mildenhall, United Kingdom, under darkness from a base either in Constanta, Romania, or Akrotiri, Cyprus, through Turkey to Khurmal.[47] According to a U.S. Air Force colonel who was involved in planning the operation, a tactical concern with the mission was that Khurmal was situated at a high altitude and protected by mountain ridges on all sides: "We weren't worried about getting to the target, we were worried about getting out."[48] Despite the difficult geographic features, and persistent worry of a dust storm that could have blinded helicopter pilots, the Air Force colonel believed that the Khurmal operation was "doable, but challenging."[49] Officials from the U.S. Special Operations Command (SOCOM) initially informed the Joint Chiefs that it would take months for their teams to be prepared, since they would have to first build a replica of the camp to practice against. Though SOCOM routinely requested extra time to plan and prepare for operations, the Chiefs told them that requesting such a delay for Khurmal was "unsat"—unsatisfactory—and SOCOM officials accelerated their planning process to meet the required timelines.[50]

In the last week of June, the Joint Chiefs submitted their plans for striking Khurmal to the White House, recommending that the combined air-ground operation occur on Thursday, July 4.[51] Though no formal vote was taken, there was strong and unanimous support among all six of the Joint Chiefs to attack.[52] What is remarkable about their position regarding Khurmal is that during the same time the Chiefs sought to avoid a war with Iraq, believing that the adequate ground forces and logistical support were not available for another war so soon after Afghanistan. As Thomas Ricks, defense correspondent for the *Washington Post*, wrote in late May, "The Joint Chiefs of Staff have waged a determined behind-the-scenes campaign to persuade the Bush administration to reconsider an aggressive posture toward Iraq in which war was regarded as all but inevitable."[53]

ASSESSING EXPLANATIONS FOR WHY KHURMAL WAS NOT ATTACKED

According to knowledgeable senior officials, the inter-agency debates over Khurmal were among the most contentious—though least publicized—within the Bush administration's policy toward Iraq in 2002. Senior civilians from the Pentagon and the Office of the Vice President, as well as counterterrorism officials in the NSC, argued strongly in favor of an attack. Many civilian officials from the other national security agencies were opposed.[54] The final decision by President Bush was "no." None of the officials interviewed about Khurmal have a clear explanation why the president made the decision he did. General Myers, who personally followed the potential WMD threat from Khurmal in early 2002, recalled that it "was a mystery to me" why civilian officials at the highest levels of the U.S. government did not support a limited operation against Ansar al-Islam.[55]

The key question is, since it was the consensus professional opinion of the Joint Chiefs of Staff and its chairman—the principal military advisor to the president—to employ limited force to eliminate the Khurmal camp, why did the president ultimately choose to reject that counsel? Given interviews with officials who were closely involved in national security policymaking at the time, statements by government officials, and contemporary news accounts, there are four plausible explanations. While each influenced the decision somewhat, the primary explanation why the president deferred attacking Khurmal was over concerns that it could possibly disrupt what was the White House's goal from the first meeting of the Principal's Committee of the NSC—regime change in Iraq.

The Threat Was Not Great Enough

Some news accounts contend that Bush administration officials believed that the Khurmal camp was so "small and crude," and not a direct threat to the United States, that attacking it was unnecessary.[56] This explanation, however, is belied by the fact that the WMD threat from Khurmal and al-Zarqawi was believed to be real and growing by the majority of the civilian and military officials at the time. George Tenet, who spent much of the pre-war period disproving some of the wilder allegations about the Osama Bin Laden-Saddam Hussein connection, described Zarqawi as a "senior associate and collaborator" of Al Qaeda who oversaw the operations at Khurmal and had terrorist cells in more than thirty countries.[57] Tenet writes in his memoirs, "One of the camps run by [Ansar al-Islam], known as Kurmal [*sic*], engaged in production and training in the use of low-level poisons such as cyanide. We had intelligence telling us that Zarqawi's men had tested these poisons on animals and, in at least one case, on one of their own associates. . . . Our efforts to track activities emanating from Kurmal resulted in the arrest of nearly one hundred Zarqawi operatives in Western Europe."[58]

Secretary Powell's February 2003 presentation to the UN Security Council to detail "what the United States knows about Iraq's weapons of mass destruction as well as Iraq's involvement in terrorism" contained much of the CIA intelligence referred to by Tenet. Powell declared that al-Zarqawi was connected to Bin Laden and regime elements in Baghdad, and highlighted that one of his specialties was producing poisons. An accompanying slide of the facility was titled "Terrorist Poison and Explosives Factory, Khurmal" (see Exhibit 2). Utilizing uncharacteristically vivid and threatening language, Powell made clear the potentially lethal threat from Khurmal: "Let me remind you how ricin works. . . . Less than a pinch of ricin, eating just this amount in your food, would cause shock, followed by circulatory failure. Death comes within 72 hours and there is no antidote. There is no cure. It is fatal."[59] Underscoring that threat, two weeks after Powell's presentation, the State Department formally designated Ansar al-Islam as a Foreign Terrorist Organization for "its close links and support for al-Qaida."[60]

While it was later shown that certain elements of the pre-war intelligence

Exhibit 2. Ansar al-Islam facility
SOURCE: Department of State

on Iraq was wrong, from mid-2002 to early 2003 the specific threats from Ansar al-Islam as a potential producer of WMD and al-Zarqawi as an Al Qaeda affiliate were believed by the Pentagon, the CIA, the White House, and the State Department, and widely accepted by most of the key decisionmakers that managed these agencies. Furthermore, the threats were believed by the Joint Chiefs to be credible enough that they were considered important targets to attack and destroy. That the White House exploited the threat from Ansar al-Islam and al-Zarqawi—and exaggerated their connections to Hussein's regime in Baghdad—to build support for the war is irrelevant to the fact that on their own they were considered to be a clear threat to American interests in mid-2002. What is more, under the Bush administration's post-9/11 national security framework, which focused on denying terrorist safe havens and preventing terrorists from acquiring WMD, attacking what was probably the largest international terrorist training camp—"a hub for Al-Qaeda operations" according to Tenet—should have been a logical decision.[61]

There Was No Actionable Intelligence

Another explanation, offered by an NSC spokesman, was that "because there was never any real-time, actionable intelligence that placed al-Zarqawi at Khurmal, action taken against the facility would have been ineffective."[62] This assertion overlooks two key issues. First, while it is impossible to know if al-Zarqawi was, or was not, at Khurmal at any specific moment in 2002, there is evidence he was there. Michael Scheuer, then a special advisor to the chief of the CIA's Bin Laden Unit, wrote that "over the summer and fall of 2002 the quality of the intelligence on al-Zarqawi remained high, and the targeters came to the point of being routinely and reliably able to fix al-Zarqawi's location."[63] According to NSC's Director for Combating Terrorism Lisa Gordon-Hagerty, who was also a participant in the administration's working group that reviewed the military options to strike the camp, "[Khurmal] was definitely a stronghold, and we knew that certain individuals were there *including Zarqawi*."[64] An anonymous U.S. intelligence official involved in planning the attack claimed that "[al-Zarqawi] was up there, we knew where he was, and we couldn't get anybody to move on it."[65] Kurdish intelligence officials also placed al-Zarqawi at the camp.[66]

Second, the proposed use of limited force was intended to eliminate a terrorist group with international connections that was reportedly developing WMD, not to kill one specific terrorist. In August 2002, there was clear actionable intelligence to strike and destroy the threat from Ansar al-Islam at Khurmal. Along with Lieutenant General Newbold's earlier statement that the plans were based on "very good intelligence," the Joint Chief's director of operations also recalled that during his tenure, "[Khurmal] was the best target we ever had against a terrorist camp."[67]

This unprecedented opportunity to attack the Ansar camp ended as rumors of a possible strike began leaking. In late July or early August, an article appeared in the Turkish press that hinted at an American-led raid.[68] In early August, Turkish government officials also learned of the plans to strike Khurmal and recalled their intelligence officers that were in northern Iraq.[69] Finally, on the evening of August 19, ABC News reported that Al Qaeda operatives under the protection of Ansar al-Islam "had been experimenting with both poisonous gas and various toxic chemicals, killing various barnyard animals and, sources say, at least one human." The broadcast revealed that the CIA and Pentagon had been planning a covert operation against "what appeared to be a budding chemical weapons laboratory."[70] The following morning, CNN corroborated the report, adding that although President Bush had been briefed on the potential target, according to an unnamed official, "any plan for an attack has now been called off."[71] With satellite dishes prevalent in the region, this information would have circulated throughout Iraqi Kurdistan; Ansar members remaining at the targeted training camp would have fled. It is likely no coincidence that it was around this time in August that al-Zarqawi temporarily fled Iraq, disappearing from the radar screens of American and Jordanian intelligence officials for months.[72]

The inter-administration debates over Khurmal continued until the story was finally leaked in the American press and beyond. As late as July 30, 2002, Secretary of Defense Donald Rumsfeld and General Tommy Franks, Commander of CENTCOM, were holding meetings in the Pentagon to discuss the goals and options of an attack.[73] The SOF teams that had planned and trained for the Khurmal operation remained on a high state of alert, believing that they could be deployed at any moment. "Intelligence and tactics officers were constantly updating the plan to the last minute," recalled the Air Force colonel.[74] By mid-to-late August of 2002, however, with the element of surprise eliminated, the window of opportunity to strike Ansar al-Islam was effectively closed. Congressional members, as well as military and intelligence officers, persistently questioned Bush administration officials for a definitive answer about attacking Khurmal.[75] In January 2003, the debate briefly re-emerged when the Office of the Undersecretary of Defense for Policy developed an "options briefing" memo that listed three possible goals for striking Khurmal: eliminate potential WMD and conventional military threats to the United States, Turkey, and the PUK; establish a staging area for bigger U.S. combat operations against Baghdad; and apply additional pressure on Saddam Hussein.[76] The issue of attacking Khurmal did not gain any traction in inter-agency meetings for reasons that are detailed further on. It was not until weeks before the ground war began in March 2003 that the White House formally rejected the military option proposed and endorsed by the Joint Chiefs of Staff nine months earlier.[77]

The Political Costs of Failure Were Too High

A third plausible explanation is that the White House believed that the political fallout from a failed operation was too great to risk it. There were three types of failure that concerned administration officials: American soldiers could be killed in action, the attack could result in civilian casualties, or the military objectives could be unmet.[78] Although these potential problems and others are found in most instances of American non-uses of limited force, none would have been a deal-breaker in a hypothetical operation against Khurmal in 2002. While American or Iraqi civilian casualties might have caused some temporary political damage for the Bush administration, they would have been downplayed when the rationales for the mission were clarified after the fact. As is true of all uses of force, while the military was planning for Khurmal, the CIA and State Department were drafting papers for release to outline the intelligence justifying the attack, and to address any questions of international legality.[79]

Support from the American people for attacking Khurmal would have been a near certainty, since after the attacks of 9/11, public opinion overwhelmingly supported military operations against international terrorist organizations, especially those with an interest in producing or using WMD.[80] Eight in ten Americans agreed with how the Bush administration was handling the war on terrorism, and the president was personally enjoying 70 percent approval ratings.[81] Furthermore, even before the White House's public relations campaign to justify regime change in Iraq, the majority of Americans favored using force to topple Saddam Hussein.[82] Thus a limited military strike against a terrorist group, with alleged connections to Al Qaeda and operating from within Iraq, would have almost certainly been endorsed by the American public in 2002.

As for the concerns of an unsuccessful mission, as was noted with the examples in the introduction to this book, there have been many American uses of limited force that failed militarily with little domestic or international impact on the White House specifically, or the reputation of the United States more generally. If a raid against Khurmal had failed, it is likely that the domestic and international environment would have accepted the operation.

What is more puzzling in President Bush's decision to bypass striking Khurmal is that just three months later he approved a use of limited force in Yemen, when a CIA-operated Predator aerial drone fired one Hellfire missile into an SUV carrying Abu Ali al-Harithi, a suspected operational planner of the *U.S.S. Cole* bombing, four other Yemenis, and Ahmed Hijazi, a naturalized U.S. citizen. Though the Predator strike was a covert operation and supposed to remain a secret, American involvement was acknowledged by Deputy Secretary of Defense Paul Wolfowitz. The reaction from the international community to this well-publicized attack was one of general acceptance. The domestic political response, meanwhile, ranged from quiet approval to overt praise, with the hope that similar strikes against Al Qaeda members operating elsewhere were soon to come. (This operation is described more fully in Chapter 5.)

Attacking Khurmal Could Have Disrupted or Accelerated the Option of Toppling Saddam Hussein

While the three preceding explanations may have played some minor role, the final and most powerful reason for why the Bush administration did not strike Khurmal was that by August 2002 an informal decision had been made, if not to remove Saddam Hussein from power, then to take no actions that could either derail the option of regime change or initiate a war with Iraq ahead of schedule.[83] Evidence for this assertion is found in several sources. First, in April 2002, President Bush declared flatly, "I made up my mind that Saddam needs to go. . . . The policy of my government is that he goes."[84] Second, on the eve of the Second Gulf War,, a senior administration official reflecting on the opaque decisionmaking process recalled that while "[i]n the immediate aftermath of [September] the eleventh . . . the focus was on Afghanistan, Osama bin Laden, Al Qaeda. . . . It's somewhere in the first half of 2002 all this changed. The President internalized the idea of making regime change in Iraq a priority."[85] Third, according to Ambassador Richard Haass, State Department Director for Policy Planning, when he asked National Security Advisor Condoleezza Rice in early July about whether the Bush administration wanted to invade Iraq at the expense of the global war on terrorism, Rice replied, "That decision's been made, don't waste your breath."[86] Finally, the timing of Haass's assertion is consistent with the "Downing Street Memo"—the minutes of a July 23 gathering of top British national security officials with Prime Minister Tony Blair. The Memo detailed "recent talks in Washington" by Richard Dearlove, head of MI6, Britain's foreign intelligence service, with senior U.S. officials. Dearlove reported "a perceptible shift in attitude. Military action was now seen as inevitable. Bush wanted to remove Saddam, through military action," and "*the intelligence and facts were being fixed around the policy.*" At that same meeting, Defense Minister Geoffrey Hoon noted that while "no decisions had been taken . . . he thought the most likely timing in U.S. minds for military action to begin was January."[87] According to Douglas Feith, the Pentagon's number three official and a proponent within the administration for removing Saddam Hussein from power: "If you end up with empty hands [no WMD at Khurmal] you could conceivably derail a much larger project [regime change]."[88]

The other concern about attacking Khurmal, relating to the ultimate goal of regime change, was that it could escalate into a full-scale war before the political, diplomatic, and military planning was completed. By early August 2002, there were still many logistical and political tasks to finish before D-Day: the administration still sought a congressional resolution authorizing the use of force; President Bush had yet to choose between the "Running Start" and "Generated Start" warplans offered by General Franks; American diplomats were still working to secure diplomatic, economic, and military assistance from the largest number of countries possible; and the Pentagon needed to initiate planning for the post-war stabilization and reconstruction of Iraq.[89] There was a concern among senior civilian and military officials that striking Khurmal could compel Baghdad to trigger a war with the United States before the full range of tasks—between 150 and 200 interagency responsibilities coordinated by the NSC's Executive Steering Group—were finished.[90] CENT-COM's intelligence analysts, for example, worried that Iraq could initiate a war prematurely by launching a ground invasion into Kuwait, flooding the Mesopotamian Valley, igniting the southern oilfields, instigating a conflict with the Kurds, or using WMD.[91]

Statements corroborating the proposition that a military operation on Khurmal could have led to a full-scale war with Iraq prematurely are found from a range of senior policymakers within the Bush administration. Ambassador Marc Grossman, Undersecretary of State for Political Affairs, recalled, "At the bosses' level, there was a concern that [attacking Khurmal] could start a war before having decided to do so."[92] Ambassador Richard Armitage, the State Department's number two official, concurred, noting that a raid on the camp "could have gotten us rolling in a fight with Saddam Hussein before we were ready to go."[93] From the Pentagon, Douglas Feith remembered, "If we did this Khurmal thing as a one-off thing prematurely, it could set off a chain of events before we were ready to handle them."[94] Yet another senior administration official noted that after August, "with a fair amount of planning going on for the larger war, there was considerable hesitation with attacking Khurmal."[95] Whenever General Keane asked administration officials about striking Khurmal in the fall of 2002 and spring of 2003, he was informed that "it was getting too close to the invasion date, and we didn't want to flag our hand."[96]

AFTERMATH AND ASSESSMENT

As the Joint Chiefs predicted in the summer of 2002, destroying Khurmal would prove to be a "very doable" mission for the U.S. military and its Kurdish allies. On the second day of the war, March 21, 2003, Operation Viking Hammer commenced, during which sixty-four Tomahawk cruise missiles razed the camp and its surrounding fortifications. After a week-long logistics delay, on March 28, several thousand lightly armed PUK fighters, supported by the Army Special Forces 3rd Battalion, marched on the remaining Ansar al-Islam militants. After four days of intense fighting, the Ansar enclave was successfully eliminated and secured. Although two dozen Kurdish militiamen were killed, not one U.S. soldier was even wounded in the battle. However, several hundred Ansar members who survived the cruise missiles and ground fighting fled over the border into Iran, many returning later to join up with the Iraqi Sunni insurgency.[97]

Although largely overlooked or forgotten, the Bush administration's claims in 2002 that WMD were being produced at Khurmal turned out to be highly accurate. An American sensitive site exploitation team deployed to Khurmal uncovered chemical hazard suits, atropine injectors, and Arabic-language manuals on how to make chemical munitions. Tests also revealed traces of cyanide salts, ricin, and potassium chloride, all deadly toxins.[98] An investigative report by the *Los Angeles Times*, which both examined documents and computer files seized at Khurmal and was informed by interviews with U.S.

and Kurdish intelligence operatives, found no evidence that Ansar al-Islam was connected to Hussein's regime, but was able to prove that the group "was partly funded and armed from abroad; was experimenting with chemicals, including toxic agents and a cyanide-based body lotion; and had international aspirations."[99] According to Tenet, after the U.S. invasion of Iraq, "[the CIA] obtained reliable human intelligence reporting and forensic samples confirming that poisons and toxins had been produced at [Khurmal]."[100] While administration officials later opined about whether Hussein's unaccounted-for arsenal and mobile weapons labs had been buried, dismantled, or hidden in Syria or Iran, Khurmal is the only place in Iraq where the United States discovered that WMD were actively being produced, albeit in small quantities, before the war.

The Bush administration's decision not to use a DMO against the Ansar al-Islam camp in Kurdistan in the summer of 2002 was one of many tactical mistakes that contributed to the strategic disaster that America faced in Iraq. Soon after the United States missed its best opportunity to attack Ansar al-Islam at Khurmal and potentially to kill Abu Musab al-Zarqawi, the Jordanian terrorist and his associates organized what became the Sunni insurgency's most violent wing in order to resist what they believed would be the inevitable American occupation of Iraq and to foment sectarian conflict between Sunnis and Shias.[101] An intelligence assessment by the British Joint Intelligence Committee on the eve of the war accurately forewarned that "reporting since (February [2002]) suggests that senior Al Qaida associate Abu Musab al Zarqawi has established sleeper cells in Baghdad, to be activated during a U.S. occupation of the city. These cells apparently intend to attack U.S. targets using car bombs and other weapons. . . . Al Qaida-associated terrorists continued to arrive in Baghdad in early March."[102] Seven months into the American occupation, Lieutenant General Norton Schwartz, the Joint Chiefs' director of operations after Newbold, labeled Ansar al-Islam as "our principal organized terrorist adversary in Iraq right now."[103]

The United States and Osama Bin Laden—in significantly different ways—both acknowledged the growing importance of al-Zarqawi as a terrorist leader. In October 2002, the U.S. State Department placed a $5 million bounty on al-Zarqawi's head, doubling that amount in February 2004 and finally increasing it to $25 million four months later, the very same amount offered as a reward for information leading to the capture or death of Bin Laden himself. By 2006, the U.S. military unit—the Joint Special Operations

Command (JSOC)—responsible for tracking down both terrorist leaders would recognize that finding al-Zarqawi was a higher priority than finding either Bin Laden or his deputy Ayman al-Zawahiri.[104]

In December 2004, what had been speculated for over three years—the existence of a formal relationship between Al Qaeda and al-Zarqawi—became a reality when Bin Laden dubbed the Jordanian terrorist the "Emir" of Al Qaeda in Iraq—the Sunni terrorist group that had merged with Ansar al-Islam. In a letter to Bin Laden, al-Zarqawi proclaimed it his goal "to drag the Shi'a into the battle because this is the only way to prolong the fighting between us and the infidels."[105] According to intelligence selectively declassified by President Bush, in January 2005, Bin Laden tasked al-Zarqawi to form a cell for planning operations outside Iraq, noting that America should be the primary focus of foreign attacks.[106]

Though Bin Laden's efforts to form such a cell apparently failed when an Al Qaeda official sent to brief al-Zarqawi was detained in Turkey en route to Iraq, the Jordanian terrorist had already activated his extensive international networks to plan and conduct terrorist attacks outside of Iraq after August 2002.[107] These began with his orchestration of the October 2002 shooting death of the U.S. Agency for International Development official James Foley in Amman, Jordan. Later, in early 2003, British police dismantled a jihadist cell in London—linked directly to al-Zarqawi—that was planning attacks using ricin on the city's subway system.[108] Additional cells were uncovered in France, Germany, Italy, Jordan, Norway, Saudi Arabia, Spain, and Turkey that were formed to plan terrorist operations in those countries, as well as recruit, fund, and funnel European Muslim jihadists to join the Iraqi insurgency.[109] The most spectacular attack outside of Iraq that was attributable to al-Zarqawi was the near simultaneous bombings of three hotels in Amman in November 2005, which killed sixty civilians, including those attending a wedding party. These attacks prompted the government of Jordan to substantially increase its intelligence sharing with the United States, which helped lead to the June 7, 2006, F-16 airstrikes that killed Abu Musab al-Zarqawi while he hid in a house forty miles northeast of Baghdad.[110]

Since the action regarding Khurmal is a negative case, it is only possible to assess the evidence for the proposition that senior civilian officials are more likely to support the use of DMOs than the uniformed military. As the preceding case study demonstrates, senior military support for the Khurmal DMO was overwhelming. Senior civilian officials in the Bush administration, on the other hand, were opposed to attacking Khurmal, but only because they did not want to do anything that could either derail the option of regime change or initiate a war with Iraq ahead of their carefully scripted schedule. The same senior military officials who backed the DMO for Khurmal were arguing behind the scenes against what they believed would be a preventive, mostly unilateral, invasion of another country to remove a sitting leader from power. This case brings forth an important caveat to the declaratory proposition: senior military officials will generally support a DMO in lieu of larger and more lethal military operations that have more ambitious but less well-defined political objectives. DMOs when compared to conventional military invasions have more clearly defined political objectives, are less likely to escalate beyond the initial military objectives, have less risk of mission failure, and will likely result in fewer military and civilian casualties. In confronting a hypothetical foreign policy problem, senior military officials will stress the necessity for developing a comprehensive national strategy that emphasizes both non-military and military means. If, however, senior civilian officials have already decided upon a military solution to the hypothetical problem, then military officials will work within the inter-agency debate process to limit and clearly delineate the military and political objectives behind the use of force ultimately selected.

KHURMAL AND NEGATIVE CASES

What lessons derived from the decision not to attack Khurmal could be applied to other negative cases of American DMOs? First, and most important, when deciding not to use limited force, policymakers should carefully weigh the potential risks and benefits of taking action versus not taking action. Senior civilian officials opposed to striking Khurmal had internalized a Murphy's Law mind-set about the proposed operation: that which could go wrong, would go wrong. Overemphasizing the possible failures, however, inherently discounts the potential gains. In short, policymakers must accept that choosing not to use limited force is as much an active decision as choosing to use force. Psychologically though, from the perspective of attempting to avoid blame or criticism—in other words, "covering your ass"—policymakers are held accountable for actions much more than non-actions.

Second, bypassing a DMO in the hope that the conditions for a larger operation will emerge could preclude any opportunity for using military force against an adversary. For example, the primary reason the Bush administration chose not to attack Khurmal was that it could have prematurely triggered a full-scale war with Iraq, which had already been decided upon. However, if Saddam Hussein had accounted for the history and status of his proscribed WMD and ballistic missile programs, and fully complied with the UN Security Council Resolution 1441, most Bush administration officials believe that the war would have been avoided. Then, as the international crisis passed, Hussein would have been verifiably disarmed while still remaining in power, but the threat from Khurmal would have persisted, because it was never inspected by the UN inspection teams.[111] This would have had the effect of leading to a worst-case scenario: a verifiably disarmed country that retained some capability to produce WMD within its borders.

Third, one missed opportunity to use limited force against a target should not set a precedent inhibiting future actions against that same target. The best opportunity to strike Khurmal was in August 2002, before the camp was vacated by the rumor of a possible U.S. military operation. Later in 2002 and early 2003, however, Bush administration officials noted that Khurmal's population ebbed and flowed as various Ansar members came while others left. Although there were further inter-agency discussions about Khurmal in January 2003, with the planning for the invasion of Iraq consuming the administration these discussions never moved beyond the conceptual stage. As one senior administration official noted of the possibility of attacking Khurmal in January 2003, there was a sense among policymakers that "we'd already had that debate."[112]

Fourth, a recent unsuccessful use of a DMO should not be the reason for not using force in the future. Policymakers, like everyone else, misapply and overextend historical analogies when deciding a course of action.[113] In the Bush administration debates in 2002, several officials raised the militarily successful, but politically unwise, bombing of the El-Shifa pharmaceutical plant in Khartoum, Sudan, in 1998 as one reason not to strike Khurmal. The lesson learned from the mistake over El-Shifa was that faulty intelligence—specifically, that generated by the CIA—had betrayed the Clinton White House. The key factor that contributed to the intelligence failure of El-Shifa, however, was that the decisionmaking process was constrained to a small group of senior officials, and they were largely unaware of dissenting voices from the wider intelligence community.[114] Thus Bush administration officials remembered the embarrassing results of El-Shifa but forgot the flawed policymaking process that contributed to the outcome.

Fifth, policymakers should not be paralyzed by the possibility of "gradu-alism." Some senior officials, primarily military officers, believe that limited force is rarely applied in a clean and controllable manner. These officials con-tend that limited force intended to achieve a limited effect could possibly fail, and that failure could compel a military escalation to definitively destroy the target, achieve the desired political effect, or recover any loss in reputation. In 2002, Bush administration officials worried specifically about American casualties or hostages, or being dragged into a conflict between Ansar al-Islam and the PUK, who controlled the territory that surrounded the Khurmal en-clave. But by avoiding a relatively limited problem in 2002, the United States was forced to risk the lives of many more American troops against a much bigger problem years later. The Khurmal option merely consisted of a short bombing campaign and the temporary infiltration of Special Operations Forces to assess and verify the destruction. The hunt for al-Zarqawi alone, on the other hand, demanded using thousands of troops over more than two years to capture the person that the JSOC considered to be the most wanted terrorist in the world. While military officials are prudent to worry about gradual escalation as a result of limited uses of force, they must acknowledge that if no actions are taken, the problem itself can escalate uncontrollably and exponentially.

7 CONCLUSION AND POLICY RECOMMENDATIONS

"War is not about killing people and blowing things up. It is purposeful violence to achieve a political goal. The death and destruction, though the most deplorable aspect of war, are of secondary importance. The pursuit of the political objective is all, in fact, that separates killing in war from murder."[1]

Frederick W. Kagan, military historian

"The President has to make a decision: will the application of military force in this circumstance meet the broader national-security goals of the United States?"[2]

Barack Obama, 44th U.S. president

"The military's impressive, isn't it?"[3]

William Clinton, 42nd U.S. president

GIVEN THEIR LIMITED political and military objectives, do Discrete Military Operations (DMOs) work? The answer—based on the previous in-depth case studies, bolstered by the cases presented in Appendix I—is that in general they do not.

First, it is very difficult for DMOs to achieve all of their intended political goals. Policymakers use limited force in an effort to deal with a specific foreign policy problem, and often with low expectations. What is apparent, however, is that these expectations should be lowered even further to take into account the usually minor political gains achieved by DMOs. In spite of their negligible political returns, civilian policymakers remain attracted to them because failed DMOs have few political costs, even though successful DMOs bring few political gains. An important lesson from recent U.S. foreign policy history is that the use of one sole instrument of national power will rarely succeed at fully achieving its intended political objective on its own, and limited military force is no different.

Second, despite the unparalleled technological capabilities of the U.S.

armed forces, DMOs achieve all of their intended military objectives only about one-half of the time. Political constraints, weapons failures, inclement weather, inaccurate targeting intelligence, human error, and other unforeseen hurdles all contribute to the consistent underperformance of limited military operations. Nevertheless, despite all of their inherent limitations, DMOs continue to be utilized because civilian officials believe they can achieve their limited objectives.

ACHIEVING POLITICAL OBJECTIVES WITH DMOs IS HARD

In the days following a non-covert DMO, administration officials, speaking from prepared talking points agreed to by the relevant national security agencies, will often explain and defend the intended political objectives of the attack.[4] For the purposes of analytical evaluation, these can be distilled into three primary types: *punishment,* or revenge, for an adversary's past behavior with no intention of altering its future behavior; *deterrence,* to attempt to maintain the status quo by discouraging an adversary from initiating a specific new action; and *coercion,* to attempt to compel a change in the future behavior of an adversary. DMOs with the primary goal of punishment are attempted in conjunction with either deterrence or coercion. For punishment to succeed, however, the military objective must be met by imposing a cost on an adversary. Even when punishment DMOs succeed—destroying a target or killing someone—their secondary political goals of deterrence or coercion are almost never met—though the talking points often claim otherwise.

Determining whether any of these intended political objectives of a DMO have been met is a difficult analytical undertaking. Establishing a clear causal link between a military strike and a targeted adversary's behavioral change is difficult, given the range of institutional, social, and psychological factors that influence human decisionmaking. Sound policy evaluation is a combination of art and social science. Such caveats aside, of thirty-six U.S. DMOs since 1991, fewer than 6 percent were outright political successes (two cases), and 69 percent were mixed successes (twenty-five).

Notably, in both of the two clear successes, the targeted adversary was an autocratic ruling regime. One had the primary political objective of compellence: the 1995 on-again-off-again bombing campaign against the Serbian Army—*Operation Deliberate Force*—compelling the Serbian political leadership to negotiate an end to the Yugoslavian wars. The other had the primary goal of punishment, with a secondary objective of deterrence: the June 1993 cruise missile strikes on Iraqi intelligence headquarters in Baghdad, which destroyed the targeted buildings and deterred Iraq from sponsoring future terrorist attacks against Americans. In each case the decision to comply was made primarily by one individual, Slobodan Milosevic in Serbia and Saddam Hussein in Iraq. While additional intervening variables may have affected their decisionmaking, both leaders would not have changed their state's behavior but for the attacks. Yet other limited attacks against autocratic regimes—including additional ones against Iraq and Serbia—clearly failed to achieve their political objectives.

The twenty-five mixed successes fell short of their political objectives for a number of reasons. Some were unnecessarily limited in their scope, lethality, and target selection by *political constraints*. The most glaring example of such a reason was the "dual key" command and control arrangement that required both UN and NATO political authorization for U.S.-led NATO airstrikes against Serbian Army and regime assets in 1994 and 1995.[5] Another example occurred during the 1996 and 1998 bombing of Iraq, during which Clinton administration officials allowed Central Command planners to utilize only U.S. military assets already in the region in an effort to avoid upsetting U.S. regional allies.[6] The four-day December 1998 bombing campaign was scripted to end before the Muslim holy month of Ramadan to try to avoid adverse political consequences.[7] One Pentagon official closely involved in the bombing campaign recalled the extent of this political sensitivity: "We all became experts on when Ramadan would start," knowing that "different Muslim prelates declared different beginnings to the holy month."[8]

Other political mixed successes occurred because of a clear *design failure* of the DMO itself, when the level of force used against the targeted adversary was incorrectly drawn up or insufficient to achieve the political intent. This was the case of the Iraqi no-fly zones, which effectively kept Iraq's Air Force grounded but did little or nothing to protect the Kurds in northern Iraq and the Shias in the south because they were simply attacked by Saddam Hussein's ground forces.

A final and consistent reason for political mixed successes was because, simply put, a DMO was designed with clearly *unattainable political objectives*. Frequent examples of such DMOs concern the U.S. strategy of targeted killings of suspected Al Qaeda operatives living within countries that the United States is not at war with, namely, Yemen, Somalia, and Pakistan. In the instance of Pakistan, between 2005 and June 1, 2009, the United States has used at least seventy DMOs against suspected Al Qaeda or Taliban leaders located in the Federally Administered Tribal Areas (FATA) in the northwest region of the country.[9] While the core political objective of these strikes was punishment, the Bush administration also hoped to deter the avowed enemies of the United States—and the government of Pakistan, whose territory Al Qaeda operates from—from using the FATA as a safe haven to plan terrorist attacks. Although the sought-after operatives have been killed more than half the time, the DMOs have done little to deter Al Qaeda from operating there. According to U.S. intelligence and military officials, throughout 2008, the terrorist network had protected and regenerated its core operational capabilities required to strike America from within the FATA.[10] As of early 2010, the unrelenting campaign of unmanned U.S. drone strikes in the FATA—significantly enhanced by closer Pakistani intelligence cooperation—had reportedly succeeded at killing scores of mid-level Al Qaeda and Taliban operatives. In response, these targeted groups simply adapted defensive countermeasures by killing suspected informants, destroying communications towers, dispersing into smaller cells, and moving to heavily populated cities, from Quetta to Karachi.[11] In addition, according to Daniel Benjamin, Department of State Coordinator for Counterterrorism, as of early 2010, "I would still say that the FATA is the beating heart of Al Qaeda."[12]

The targeted-killing DMOs did not achieve their secondary goals in Pakistan—or Somalia and Yemen, for that matter—because they are in no way connected to the lives of the people living on the ground who ultimately decide if they will support, remain neutral, or resist international terrorist groups from operating among them. In the case of Pakistan, American officials acknowledged that the FATA needs massive economic and infrastructure developmental assistance, and that Pakistani counterinsurgency forces must be better trained and armed to provide security for the bulk of the population, which actually has little sympathy for Al Qaeda.[13] There is no coordination between the essential foreign aid and development strategy, and the ongoing middle-of-the-night missile strikes. An April 2008 Government Accountability Office report summarized America's inadequate strategy after September 11 with the unusually alarming title "The United States Lacks [a] Comprehensive Plan to Destroy the Terrorist Threat and Close the Safe Haven in Pakistan's Federally Administered Tribal Areas."[14] A U.S. government-wide Afghanistan and Pakistan strategy was finally produced by December 2009, but it is unlikely that the increased DMOs in Pakistan were coordinated or prioritized within that strategy.[15] Given the facts on the ground, it is clear that the targeted-killing

DMOs against Al Qaeda and Taliban operatives in Pakistan can only be one component of an overall strategy but not a substitute for it. The same is true of Yemen and Somalia, where international terrorist networks continue to operate with the tacit support, or indifference, of the local political authority.

MILITARY OBJECTIVES ARE NOT GUARANTEED

The U.S. military has made enormous advances in its target acquisitions, instantaneous communications, and precision-strike warfare capabilities over the past quarter-century.[16] In addition, soldiers tasked with carrying out the type of limited operations described herein are better trained and equipped to conduct fast, stealthy, and lethal attacks. Pentagon and Combatant Command press conferences underscore and trumpet these advances and specialized soldiers, which helps to create the inaccurate impression that the military has nearly unlimited and infallible stand-off precision-strike capabilities. Through the selective and sporadic release of video, gun camera film, and after-action photographs of bomb and missile attacks, the general public can see the impressive results of a DMO within hours of the event. Consequently, policymakers assume that even if a limited strike achieves no political goals, it should at least find and eliminate a target. A study of recent U.S. DMOs, however, demonstrates that they achieve all of their military objectives only half of the time. Of thirty-six cases, in fact, sixteen succeeded, six enjoyed mixed success, five had indeterminate results (and are not counted among the DMOs for evaluating military objectives), while nine were outright failures.

The six mixed-success DMOs were against a combination of mobile and fixed targets, the latter of which are easier to acquire and destroy. Nevertheless, each fell short of their military objectives for reasons unique to each case. The January 13, 1993, raid against Iraqi air-defense targets resulted in only half of the aim-points being struck because cloud cover disrupted laser-guidance for some bombs and prevented pilots from seeing their targets. On August 5, 1994, a limited raid against Serb anti-tank weapons was a mixed success because of persistent cloud coverage. The September 3–4, 1996, strikes against components of the Iraqi air-defense system fell short in part because Central Command planners rushed the planning process, lacked the required expertise in cruise missiles, and were constrained by Pentagon officials in the number of missiles they could deploy. In December 1998, the four-day bombing campaign against Iraq's suspected WMD and ballistic missile programs—*Operation Desert Fox*—caused moderate, light, or no damage against more than half of the one hundred sites targeted: the suboptimal outcome re-sulted from limiting the strikes to four days when many CENTCOM planners wanted to pursue additional targets.[17] The February 2001 raid against Iraq's air-defense command and control system went awry due to high winds, and because someone programmed incorrect guidance data into the precision-guided munitions. Finally, the unprecedented Special Operations raid into Pakistan in September 2008 failed to kill or capture any high-value targets. What these cases show is that the friction inherent in warfare due to Mother Nature, technological glitches, inaccurate intelligence, or human error is also found in the most carefully planned and executed DMOs. Moreover, because of the limited duration and scope of DMOs, even the smallest mistakes or setbacks can render them entirely ineffective.

The nine DMOs that totally failed to meet their intended military objec-tives all had mobile assets or individuals as their targets. Consider two of the better-known examples. First, on August 20, 1998, in retaliation for the African Embassy bombings, the United States launched seventy-nine cruise missiles against a pharmaceutical factory in Khartoum, Sudan, and an Al Qaeda com-plex in southern Afghanistan. The primary military goal was to kill Osama Bin Laden and his top lieutenants. Director of Central Intelligence George Tenet presented evidence based on communications intercepts, and a source inside Afghanistan, that Bin Laden had ordered a meeting to be held on August 20. While driving to that meeting, Bin Laden's entourage opted instead to visit Kabul at the last minute, thus potentially sparing the Al Qaeda leader's life. In another example, in early 2006, U.S. and Pakistani intelligence tracked down Ayman al-Zawahiri, Al Qaeda's second in command, to a compound in a Paki-stani village just inside the Afghan border. According to Pakistani intelligence officials, al-Zawahiri ate dinner but did not spend the night at the compound, thus escaping the Hellfire missiles that killed eighteen civilians and perhaps four Al Qaeda militants. In both instances, the predictive intelligence capabili-ties of the United States and its allies could not account for the combination of luck and the adaptive behavior of humans who know they are targeted.

ASSESSING THE RESEARCH FINDINGS FOR THE CIVIL-MILITARY SPLIT

Senior civilian officials are more likely to favor DMOs because they believe they are militarily and politically effective, are controllable, have low domestic political costs, and demonstrate resolve. Support for this proposition comes from evidence gathered on the four actual, or proposed, DMOs examined in the case studies. The Iraq no-fly zones (NFZs) were generally supported by senior civilian officials but opposed by senior military officials. This split was consistent with the four reasons provided in the first chapter. First, civilian leaders within the Clinton administration had settled on a policy of containing Iraq, with the aspiration of Saddam Hussein being removed from power. They believed that the NFZs were a militarily and politically effective containment tool, since the Iraqi Air Force could not realistically challenge the ban on flying over two-thirds of its air space, and Turkey, Saudi Arabia, and Kuwait generally supported this open-ended enforcement. Second, because U.S. air assets in the region dominated Iraqi air space, the patrols and rules of engagement for the NFZs were highly malleable, dependent upon the desire to intensify or reduce tensions with Iraq. Third, there were no substantially adverse domestic political consequences to enforcement of the NFZs. Finally, civilian officials believed that the NFZs clearly demonstrated resolve and a commitment to the Iraq containment policy.

Although the 1998 cruise missile strike against a reported meeting of senior Al Qaeda officials in Afghanistan was supported by both civilian and military officials, the decision to simultaneously bomb the El-Shifa pharmaceutical factory in Sudan was opposed by many senior military officials. Here again, the split over the Sudan target is consistent with the four reasons provided in the evaluative proposition. First, the civilian officials strongly believed that the Tomahawk cruise missiles could be militarily effective in killing Osama Bin Laden and destroying El-Shifa, and achieving the political objectives of punishing Al Qaeda and deterring it from conducting future operations. Second, cruise missiles were selected among all the military options presented by the chairman of the Joint Chiefs to the civilians in the Small Group because they were precise in their delivery and thus highly controllable. Third, because the cruise missile strikes were meant to be a retaliation against Al Qaeda for its role in the African U.S. Embassy bombings, they were widely supported by the general public, as well as most politicians on both ends of the political spectrum. Finally, civilian officials noted in speeches and press briefings at the time that the goal of demonstrating resolve to Al Qaeda and other international terrorist organizations was a key justification for the DMO.

The November 2002 Predator strike in Yemen was impossible to assess since it was a covert operation, which most civilian and military officials have refused to acknowledge. Nevertheless, in general, it can be said that military officials are much more reluctant than civilians to support the targeted killing of adversaries of the United States. Senior military officials prefer comprehensive strategies to resolve the long-term problems posed by the group or state to which the targeted individual belongs, while civilian officials are willing to use force for the potential short-term gain of eliminating a threatening individual. In addition, military officials are also less likely than civilian officials to believe that targeted killings will succeed militarily.

As an important caveat to this finding, senior military officials generally will support a DMO in lieu of larger and more lethal military operations that have more ambitious, but less well-defined political objectives. As noted in the Khurmal case study, for the decision not to strike the Ansar al-Islam camp in the summer of 2002, it is only possible to assess whether senior civilian officials are more likely to support the use of DMOs than the uniformed military. Senior military officials overwhelmingly supported the Khurmal DMO. Senior civilian officials, however, refused to consider attacking Khurmal, because they did not want to do anything that could either derail the option of regime change or initiate a war with Iraq ahead of their carefully scripted schedule. In comparison with the plans in place to invade Iraq in the summer of 2002, the Khurmal DMO had more clearly defined political objectives, was less likely to escalate, had less risk of mission failure, and was less likely to result in military and civilian casualties. For all of those reasons, the Joint Chiefs of Staff and other senior military officials strongly supported striking Khurmal, while they simultaneously opposed the invasion of Iraq.

WHY DMOS CONTINUE TO BE USED

If DMOs have been so unsuccessful at achieving their intended political objectives, and only moderately successful at achieving their military objectives, why are they used so often?

First, and most important, DMOs are both low-cost—in terms of domestic political and diplomatic capital, financial cost, military capabilities, and U.S. or foreign casualties—and low-expectation events. They fail with few negative consequences, and thus civilian decisionmakers accurately perceive that there will be little political fallout for an unsuccessful DMO. In fact, most failed DMOs result in somewhat greater support from Congress, the media, and the public: these constituencies appear to accept and support the serving administration's rationale for "doing something." In addition, DMO failures are interspersed with successes, which decrease the likelihood that civilian decisionmakers will learn or correctly interpret the key causal factors behind prior mistakes.[18]

Second, senior civilian officials, who ultimately have the Constitutional authority to order their use, believe that DMOs can achieve their limited objectives and are the better policy response when compared either to doing nothing, using less-responsive instruments of national power, or going to full-scale war. In general, these civilians can be characterized as the *Surgical Strike School.* These officials have great—though often unrealistic—faith in the abilities of long-range precision attacks and believe that DMOs can achieve their limited political objectives in a low-cost and low-risk manner.

Third, senior military officials, who plan and execute military operations, generally oppose DMOs in the abstract. For example, throughout 2007, the Joint Chiefs of Staff reportedly pushed back against pressure from White House civilians to support a poorly defined military strike against Iran's suspected nuclear program and regime assets.[19] As was noted in Chapter 6, however, senior military officials will support DMOs in lieu of larger and more lethal military operations that have more ambitious but even less well-defined political objectives.

Fourth, successive administrations have sought to avoid the deployment of ground forces in conjunction with the use of limited force. This is due to the desire to avoid casualties, and the potential political fallout from putting U.S. boots on the ground in another sovereign country, as opposed to shooting missiles from sea or airborne platforms. Even limited raids or short-term deployments have historically received little support from civilian and military officials. For example, in September 2009, when the Obama White House was presented with the option of attempting to capture or kill the sought-after Saleh Ali Nabhan in Somalia—with the potential for another 1993 "Black Hawk Down" tragedy looming large—it authorized the latter option, concerned that U.S. ground troops would be vulnerable to attack. As an administration official noted, "The safety and security of U.S. military personnel is always something the president keeps at the highest level of his calculus."[20] Recent technological advances, such as precision-guided munitions and unmanned drones, are increasingly making the substitution of machines for manpower the norm.[21]

POLICY IMPLICATIONS AND RECOMMENDATIONS

The most important reason to study the efficacy of DMOs is to better inform civilian and military officials who will face near-term decisions about using them. It has never been a more important topic, because U.S. DMOs remain a growth industry. Along with the actual increase in limited uses of force since 2001, the Department of Defense has undertaken several studies, and begun investing in the capabilities to develop by 2018 what they loosely term *prompt global strike:* the ability to rapidly plan and conduct, within one hour, "limited-duration and extended-range attacks to achieve precision effects against highly valued adversary assets [anywhere in the world]."[22] Given the actual increase in DMOs over the past two decades, and such ongoing plans to develop them further in quantity, capability, and variety, there are several issues that policymakers and the general public should take into account.

More Military Options

Presidents of the United States and their senior civilian advisors often wish that they had more military options for confronting a specific foreign policy problem than those that are presented by the military.[23] To elicit a broader range of options, the president's civilian advisors must consistently listen to the concerns of their military counterparts, reframe their intended political objectives, adjust their desired end state, and, most important, argue repeatedly and with a unified voice for a greater quantity of options. In addition, senior civilian advisors must respectfully question whether the advice received reflects an institutional desire by senior military officials to simply avoid a particular fight. As the historian A.J.P. Taylor observed about larger uses of force, "Generals and admirals are confident of winning a war when they want to fight; they always find decisive arguments against a war which they regard as politically undesirable."[24] If senior civilian advisors think they have received biased advice from senior officers about one set of military options, but do not have the courage to question them, they will remain skeptical of the soundness of initial military options offered in the future.

When senior military officials perceive that civilian officials are not serious about effectively dealing with a problem, they will be less likely to develop more creative (and risky) options, which can result in the presentation of "over-sized options" that essentially render any use of force politically impossible. Such over-sized options are indicative of the worst-case assumptions inherent in military planning for force protection reasons and to better ensure victory. As one former director of operations for the Joint Staff described it, "War is not a game to be won six to five. You want to win twenty-one to zero."[25] Further, more creative options could be riskier in terms of mission success, potential loss of U.S. lives, collateral damage, and civilian casualties.

Therefore, when civilians decide to request a greater range of military options, they should carefully deliberate both to what extent the advice that senior military officials provide reflects their specialized expertise and not an aversion to using force for a particular problem, and whether the potential gains from using force are worth the increased risks.

Politically Aware Military Advice

Senior military officials do not present military options and corresponding professional advice in a political vacuum, even though they often contend that they do or make every effort to do so. To provide military options and advice that is most useful for civilian decisionmakers, military officials should be well informed about how policy is made in the administration that they are serving in, and aware of the likely range of military and non-military options that are relevant and applicable for a foreign policy problem. As a component of offering politically aware military advice, military leaders should not expect the type of precise guidance that political officials simply cannot provide: the promise of broad and deep domestic and international support, few operational constraints, and a clearly articulated desired end state.[26] Eliot Cohen aptly captures this concern of military officials: "It is one of the greatest sources of frustration for soldiers that their political masters find it difficult . . . to fully elaborate in advance the purposes for which they have invoked military action, or the conditions under which they intend to limit or terminate it."[27] The hard balance to strike for senior military officials is to be politically aware without adopting the preferences and policy mantle of the civilians they are serving.[28]

Military Power Does Not Equal "Military Options"

The United States spends more money on its armed forces than every other country combined, and possesses unparalleled military projection capabilities.[29] Senior civilian officials, however, should not conflate raw national military power with the realistic capabilities available for a specific foreign policy problem. The disregard of senior military officials for civilians' non-pragmatic expectations of what military power can accomplish is a characteristic revealed often in memoirs, histories of use of force decisions, and countless interviews. According to former Chairman of the Joint Chiefs of Staff General Richard Myers, as a customary matter, senior civilian officials "don't understand the complexities or the risk equation" of military operations.[30] Or in the blunt words of General Anthony Zinni, civilians' knowledge of the military is "almost non-existent."[31] Just as military officials should recognize the political realities that their civilian leaders are facing, it is the responsibility of key civilian decisionmakers to make every effort to overcome their lack of military expertise when requesting and debating the possibility of using force with senior uniformed officers.

Negative Cases

Negative cases are non-events, when an expected and relevant outcome of interest did not occur, but was a strong possibility.[32] For every DMO that is executed, there are many more that are planned and debated by senior civilian and military officials but ultimately rejected. The case study of the George W. Bush administration's decision not to strike the Ansar al-Islam camp in 2002 shows how a missed opportunity to attempt to eliminate a smaller problem then greatly expanded to exacerbate the U.S.-led campaign against the Sunni insurgency led by Ansar al-Islam operative Abu Musab al-Zarqawi. A list of similar, publicly available negative cases is presented in Appendix II. Khurmal and these other known cases show that policymakers must more carefully weigh the potential risks and benefits of both using a DMO and not using one.

Targeted Killings

International terrorist networks targeting the United States, its military forces, or its allies should be eliminated with all of the capabilities that can be brought to bear. As politically popular as they may be, however, targeted killings of suspected terrorists should be used sparingly, and only for those senior operatives who are clearly culpable for previous or likely future attacks against Americans, and then only in close coordination with an overall security strategy for the state in which they reside. Where possible, precedence should be given to capturing over killing suspected terrorists, to develop further sources and intelligence.[33] The fourteen such DMOs against Al Qaeda operatives or their affiliates demonstrate that while the group has seen its day-to-day activities disrupted, it has not been deterred from operating in any of the countries where targeted killings have been attempted. In addition, no clear evidence exists that sought-after Al Qaeda operatives have been compelled to abandon their strategic goals by these attempts. In short, policymakers who bomb terrorists with the goal of killing them should do so with great discretion and low expectations.

Unified Voice

Finally, the most important recommendation is for senior civilian and military officials to develop a much more unified agreement about what DMOs can realistically achieve. This is a crucial step, not only because of the divergent opinions about limited force, but also because of the unique planning process for DMOs as opposed to large wars. To maintain operational security against what are often time-sensitive targets, most DMOs are planned, proposed, and conducted in secret. Planners at the regional command level, the Joint Staff, and the Joint Chiefs develop operational concepts. Small numbers of senior civilian officials in the relevant agencies debate the plans and ask clarifying questions about the military options presented to them. The president then follows a similar procedure before finally authorizing or not authorizing a DMO. Often missing in this process, as opposed to during the run-up to wars, are the outside opinions of retired generals, elected officials, policy and military analysts, political pollsters, and concerned citizens. Usually, ranking majority and minority congressional members on relevant national security committees are neither asked for their opinions nor told of the DMO until the weaponry is already in the air. Operational secrecy requirements prevent a national debate from occurring over the wisdom of using or not using a DMO. There is rarely an external examination of the foreign policy problem; intended objectives; and type, scope, and intensity of force to be employed. This absence of transparency and outside inspection by neutral and disinterested third parties means that political and military officials must have a clear, open, and frank dialogue about exactly what the foreign policy problem is, what the operation is intended to accomplish, and to what degree (if any) force should be utilized.[34]

APPENDIX I
CODING CASES AND DESCRIPTIONS: U.S. DISCRETE MILITARY OPERATIONS, 1991 TO JUNE 1, 2009

Table 1. Coding cases and descriptions: U.S. Discrete Military Operations, 1991 to June 1, 2009

Country	Date	Political Objective	Military Objective	Political Evaluation	Military Evaluation
Iraq: No-fly zones	April 1991–April 2003	Deter attacks on Shias and Kurds, and contain Iraq from threatening its neighbors	Deny Iraq the ability to fly over two-thirds of its airspace	Mixed success	Success
Iraq	Jan. 13, 1993	Compel Iraq to move surface-to-air missiles from southern NFZ	Destroy four air-defense targets in southern NFZ	Failure	Mixed success
Iraq	Jan. 17, 1993	Compel Iraq to respect NFZ enforcement and cooperate with UN weapons inspectors	Destroy seven buildings at Zaafaraniyah industrial complex	Mixed success	Success
Iraq	June 27, 1993	Punish Iraq for attempt on President George H.W. Bush and deter Iraq from future terror attacks on Americans	Destroy one wing in the Iraqi intelligence headquarters in Baghdad	Success	Success
Bosnia-Herzegovina	Feb. 28, 1994	Deter Bosnian Serb flights in UN-mandated NFZ	Destroy Serb planes violating the NFZ	Mixed success	Success
Bosnia-Herzegovina	April 10–11, 1994	Compel Bosnian Serbs to stop threatening UN-safe haven Gorazde	Destroy Serb command post and armored vehicles	Failure	Success
Bosnia-Herzegovina	Aug. 5, 1994	Deter Bosnian Serbs from raiding UN-monitored arms depots	Destroy one Serb anti-tank weapon	Mixed success	Mixed Success

Country	Date	Political Objective	Military Objective	Political Evaluation	Military Evaluation
Bosnia-Herzegovina	Nov. 21, 1994	Deter Bosnian Serbs from violating NFZ and threatening Bihac	Destroy components of Serb airfield in Ubdina, Croatia	Failure	Success
Bosnia-Herzegovina	May 25–26, 1995	Compel Bosnian Serbs to return artillery from UN arms depot	Destroy eight Serb ammunition depots near Pale	Failure	Success
Bosnia-Herzegovina	Aug. 30–Sept. 14, 1995	Compel Bosnian Serbs to negotiate the terms that ended the war	Degrade Serbian Army's ability to conduct offensive operations	Success	Success
Iraq	Sept. 3–4, 1996	Compel Iraq to withdraw armored divisions from Kurdistan	Destroy eight surface-to-air missile sites and seven air-defense centers	Mixed success	Mixed success
Afghanistan and Sudan	Aug. 20, 1998	Punish Al Qaeda (AQ) and deter it from future terror attacks against the United States	Kill Osama Bin Laden and AQ officials and destroy Sudanese factory	Failure	Failure
Iraq	Dec. 16–19, 1998	Compel Iraq to cooperate with UN weapons inspection regime	Degrade Iraq's WMD and ballistic missile programs	Failure	Mixed success
Iraq	Feb. 16, 2001	Deter Iraq from threatening pilots patrolling the southern NFZ	Destroy Iraqi air-defense command and control centers	Mixed success	Mixed success
Yemen	Nov. 3, 2002	Punish and deter AQ from using Yemen as a safe haven	Kill Abu Ali al-Harithi, planner in U.S.S. Cole bombing	Failure	Success
Iraq	March 19, 2003	Decapitate Iraq's political leadership to compel surrender before the war	Kill Saddam Hussein	Failure	Failure
Pakistan	May 8, 2005	Punish and deter AQ from using Pakistan as a safe haven	Kill Haitham al-Yemeni, senior AQ official	Mixed success	Success
Pakistan	Nov. 5, 2005	Punish and deter AQ from using Pakistan as a safe haven	Kill Abu Hamza Rabia, senior AQ official	Mixed success	Failure
Pakistan	Dec. 1, 2005	Punish and deter AQ from using Pakistan as a safe haven	Kill Abu Hamza Rabia	Mixed success	Success
Pakistan	Jan. 7, 2006	Punish and deter AQ from using Pakistan as a safe haven	Kill unidentified AQ official	Mixed success	Failure
Pakistan	Jan. 13, 2006	Punish and deter AQ from using Pakistan as a safe haven	Kill Ayman al-Zawahiri	Mixed success	Failure

Country	Date	Political Objective	Military Objective	Political Evaluation	Military Evaluation
Somalia	Jan. 7, 2007	Punish and deter AQ from using Somalia as a safe haven	Kill any of three AQ officials	Mixed success	Failure
Pakistan	Jan. 16, 2007	Punish and deter AQ from using Pakistan as a safe haven	Kill unidentified AQ or Taliban operatives	Mixed success	Unknown
Somalia	Jan. 22, 2007	Punish and deter AQ from using Somalia as a safe haven	Kill Sheik Ahmed Madobe, leader of deposed Somali regime	Mixed success	Failure
Pakistan	April 27, 2007	Punish and deter AQ from using Pakistan as a safe haven	Kill unidentified AQ or Taliban operatives	Mixed success	Unknown
Somalia	June 1, 2007	Punish and deter AQ from using Somalia as a safe haven	Probably to kill Fazul Abdullah Mohammed, AQ operative	Mixed success	Failure
Pakistan	June 19, 2007	Punish and deter AQ from using Pakistan as a safe haven	Kill unidentified AQ or Taliban operatives	Mixed success	Unknown
Pakistan	Jan. 29, 2008	Punish and deter AQ from using Pakistan as a safe haven	Kill Abu Laith al-Libi	Mixed success	Success
Pakistan	Feb. 28, 2008	Punish and deter AQ from using Pakistan as a safe haven	Kill unidentified AQ or Taliban operatives	Mixed success	Unknown
Somalia	March 3, 2008	Punish and deter AQ from using Somalia as a safe haven	Kill Saleh Ali Saleh Nabhan	Mixed success	Failure
Pakistan	March 16, 2008	Punish and deter AQ from using Pakistan as a safe haven	Kill unidentified AQ or Taliban operatives	Mixed success	Unknown
Somalia	May 1, 2008	Punish and deter AQ from using Somalia as a safe haven	Kill Aden Hashi Ayro	Mixed success	Success
Pakistan	May 14, 2008	Punish and deter AQ from using Pakistan as a safe haven	Kill Abu Suleiman al Jaziery and other militants	Mixed success	Success
Pakistan	Sept. 3, 2008	Punish and deter AQ from using Pakistan as a safe haven	Kill unidentified AQ or Taliban operatives	Failure	Mixed success
Syria	Oct. 27, 2008	Punish and deter support for Iraqi insurgents	Kill Abu Ghadiyah	Mixed success	Success
Indian Ocean	April 12, 2009	Punish and deter Somali pirates	Kill three unnamed Somali pirates	Mixed success	Success

Iraqi No-Fly Zones, April 1991–April 2003
(Political mixed success; Military success)

See Chapter 3 for in-depth case study.

Iraq, January 13, 1993
(Political failure; Military mixed success)

On January 6, 1993, American, French, British, and Russian diplomats issued an ulti-matum to the Iraqi representative to the United Nations, demanding that Iraq remove its recently placed surface-to-air missiles (SAMs) and air-defense radars from the southern NFZ within forty-eight hours, or else they would respond "appropriately and decisively."[1] Iraq briefly complied in the south, but U.S. intelligence found evidence that Iraq had activated SAMs batteries within the northern NFZ. Subsequently, the Hussein regime violated other UN Security Council resolutions by placing restrictions on UN weapons inspectors and sending hundreds of soldiers into Kuwait to retrieve Silkworm anti-ship missiles and SAM systems. On January 11, after consulting with President-Elect Bill Clinton, President Bush "in principle decided something must be done," according to a Pentagon official; "It's just a matter of when to pull the trigger."[2]

On January 13, starting at 9:15 P.M. and ending a half-hour later, eighty attack and thirty support planes from the United States, Britain, and France conducted a thirty-minute raid on four permanent components of the Iraqi air-defense system, at Talill, Samarra, Najaf, and al-Amarah, and two mobile surface-to-air missile sites, near Basra and Talill.[3] Out of the 110 planes that participated in the operation, 38 U.S. and British planes actually dropped bombs.[4]

The political objective was to compel Iraq to remove SAMs from the southern NFZ: it failed. The SAMs and air-defense radars that were not destroyed or damaged in the January 13 attack remained, and Iraq continued firing missiles at U.S., British, and French planes patrolling the NFZs.

The military objective was to destroy four antiaircraft missile batteries and four air-defense command centers in the southern NFZ: it was a mixed success. Accord-ing to U.S. intelligence analysts, of the thirty-three aim-points targeted by U.S. and British bombers, between sixteen and twenty-one were hit.[5] Pentagon spokesman Pete Williams admitted that of the four fixed air-defense sites that were bombed, only one was destroyed—two were moved before the airstrikes, and one continued operating.[6] Persistent cloud cover led pilots to abort strikes on targets that they could not visually identify and also interfered with the laser guidance required for the precision-guided munitions. One F-117A stealth fighter pilot incorrectly bombed a Basra apartment building. The airstrike, initially ordered for January 12, was postponed because of bad weather at the last minute. The Pentagon had asked for another day's delay hoping for clearer skies, but the Bush administration decided to proceed on the 13th.[7]

Iraq, January 17, 1993
(Political mixed success; Military success)

In April 1991, the UN Security Council passed Resolution 687, which demanded that Iraq "accept the destruction, removal, or rendering harmless" of all WMD stockpiles and research, as well as any ballistic missiles with a range of more than ninety miles.[8] Iraq responded by hiding its WMD-related systems, lying about its earlier weapons and missile developments, and obstructing the UN Special Commission (UNSCOM) and International Atomic Energy Agency inspectors tasked with enforcing Resolution 687. Though it cooperated intermittently, by 1993, Iraq had reverted to a pattern of disruptive behavior termed "cheat and retreat."[9] Furthermore, after the January 13 bombing, the Baghdad regime maintained SAMs and air-defense radars in the NFZs, threatening U.S. and British pilots. As a consequence of Iraq's violation of the Security Council resolutions, on January 15, President Bush issued an ultimatum that UNSCOM aircraft must be cleared to enter Iraqi airspace within forty-eight hours. Iraq did not comply.[10]

On January 17, at 8:00 P.M., four U.S. Navy ships—the *U.S.S. Cowpens*, *U.S.S. Hewitt*, and *U.S.S. William H. Stump* in the Persian Gulf, and the *U.S.S. Caron* in the Red Sea—fired forty-five Tomahawk cruise missiles at seven specific buildings that sat among two dozen facilities at the Ministry of Industry and Militarization's Djilah Industrial Park at Zaafaraniyah, thirteen miles southeast of central Baghdad. The Zaafaraniyah facilities, selected as targets by the Joint Staff and the CIA, had reportedly been associated with Iraq's program to enrich uranium with electromagnetic isotope separation calutrons. The cruise missiles—arriving in two waves—began striking the complex at 9:15 P.M. One Tomahawk, apparently hit by anti-aircraft fire, crashed fifteen miles from Zaafaraniyah into Baghdad's Al Rashid hotel, killing two hotel employees.[11]

The political objective was to compel a change in Iraq's behavior: it was a mixed success. On January 18, Pentagon spokesman Pete Williams made four specific demands of Iraq: remove SAM sites from the no-fly zones, stop tracking U.S. planes enforcing the NFZs, stop shooting anti-aircraft artillery (AAA) at those planes, and cooperate with UN weapons inspectors.[12] Though Iraq improved cooperation with the inspectors for a short time, Hussein's regime continued using tracking radars and made AAA and SAM attacks against planes patrolling both NFZs.[13]

The military objective was to destroy the seven specific buildings at the Zaafaraniyah complex: it succeeded. According to the Pentagon, thirty-seven of forty-five Tomahawks struck their intended targets. Along with the Tomahawk that hit the Al Rashid hotel, one crashed into the ocean after it was launched, three fell into an orchard short of the target, and three more landed within the complex but missed any facilities. Of the seven buildings, four were destroyed, two severely damaged, and one moderately damaged.[14] UNSCOM inspectors visited the Zaafaraniyah complex soon after and "confirmed that only buildings with technical functions had been hit, and verified the destruction of many highly sensitive machine tools."[15] It is likely that the cruise missiles only struck those buildings with technical equipment because earlier UNSCOM inspections reports provided useful targeting information.[16]

Iraq, June 27, 1993
(Political success; Military success)

In April 1993, the Kuwaiti government uncovered an aborted assassination attempt on former President George H.W. Bush during his trip to Kuwait City that month. Kuwait alleged that an officer in the Iraqi Intelligence Service (the Mukhabarat) had recruited key suspects and provided the funding, explosives, and truck for the bombing plot.[17] After separate eight-week investigations by the CIA and Federal Bureau of Investigation (FBI), both agencies concluded in early June that the Mukhabarat, at its highest levels, was behind the assassination plot.[18]

During the investigations there were weeks of military planning, and a range of options were developed by the Joint Staff. President Bill Clinton chose the most limited military option presented by Chairman of the Joint Chiefs General Colin Powell, because Clinton wanted to avoid civilian casualties and believed that it was a proportionate response for the assassination attempt.[19] Though pressed by Clinton for a recommendation among the military options, the Joint Chiefs refused to provide one.[20] The cruise missile strikes, however, were supported by all NSC principals and Clinton's key political advisors.[21] Clinton later wrote, "I felt we would have been justified in hitting Iraq harder, but Powell made a persuasive case" for the more limited option.[22]

On June 27, at 12:22 A.M., the U.S. Navy destroyer *U.S.S. Peterson* in the Red Sea and cruiser *U.S.S. Chancellorsville* in the Persian Gulf fired twenty-three Tomahawk cruise missiles at the Mukhabarat headquarters in downtown Baghdad.[23] A twenty-fourth missile was supposed to have been fired, but its navigation system malfunctioned.[24] The number of Tomahawks was decided upon by a Navy analysis of what was necessary to destroy the complex.[25] Repeating an operational procedure used in the January 17 strikes, the Navy fired the Tomahawks from two different directions to confuse Iraqi air defense operators.[26] The cruise missiles landed shortly after 2:00 A.M., at a steep angle of descent to achieve maximum accuracy, to avoid killing non-essential staff.[27]

The political objective was to punish Iraq and deter it from attempting future attacks against the United States: it succeeded. According to Richard Clarke, counterterrorism czar to Presidents Clinton and George W. Bush, "Subsequent to that June 1993 retaliation, the U.S. intelligence and law enforcement communities never developed any evidence of further Iraqi support for terrorism directed against Americans."[28]

The military objective was to destroy one specific wing of the Mukhabarat headquarters compound in Baghdad: it succeeded. According to Admiral Michael Cramer, Joint Staff Director for Intelligence, "The strike damage assessment overall is that it was a successful strike. There was near complete destruction of the wing where the director and the leadership of the Iraqi Intelligence Service offices are located."[29] Sixteen of the twenty-three Tomahawks hit their aim-points, four landed elsewhere within the Mukhabarat compound, and three landed off-course by one hundred to six hundred meters, killing eight Iraqi civilians.[30] According to U.S. Navy officials, three of the Tomahawks "missed their aim points . . . because they were incorrectly programmed due to a mission planning software error. The missiles struck the aim points for which they were programmed."[31]

Bosnia and Herzegovina, February 28, 1994
(Political mixed success; Military success)

On October 9, 1992, the UN Security Council passed Resolution 781, which established "a ban on military flights in the airspace of Bosnia and Herzegovina."[32] With no enforcement mechanism, Bosnian Serb, Croatian, and Bosnian Muslim forces repeatedly violated the ban with medical, logistical, and military helicopter flights and fixed-wing airplane sorties. On March 31, 1993, the Security Council passed Resolution 816, which authorized UN member states to take all necessary measures to ensure compliance with the flight ban over Bosnia and Herzegovina.[33] The following month, NATO implemented Operation Deny Flight, a multi-national effort intended to enforce the NFZ, provide close air support to UN Protection Force (UNPROFOR) peacekeepers, and conduct airstrikes against targets that threatened UN-declared safe areas.[34]

On February 28, 1994, at 6:31 A.M., NATO E-3A Airborne Warning and Control System (AWACS) aircraft detected six Serb ground-attack planes, Jastrebs, flying above Bosnia and Herzegovina, in violation of the UN resolutions. Two U.S. Air Force F-16s enforcing the NFZ were deployed to engage the Jastrebs. The F-16s ordered the Serb pilots twice "to land or exit the airspace immediately or be engaged" on radio frequencies that the Serbs might not have been tuned into. The Serb pilots ignored NATO's warnings—or never heard them—and bombed a Bosnian munitions factory at Novi Travnik.[35] At 6:45 A.M., the lead F-16 fired an AIM-120 Advanced Medium-Range Air-to-Air Missile (AMRAAM), which destroyed a Jastreb. Within two minutes, the same F-16 fired two AIM-9 Sidewinder missiles, downing an additional two Serbian planes. The wing F-16 then fired a Sidewinder that missed and exploded on the ground. One minute later, two additional NATO F-16s arrived; the lead plane launched another Sidewinder, destroying a fourth Jastreb. The two remaining Serb planes exited the NFZs. The entire engagement—NATO's first military act in its forty-four-year history—took less than fifteen minutes.[36]

The political objective was to deter Bosnian Serb fixed-wing aircraft from flying over Bosnia and Herzegovina: it was a mixed success. The Bosnian Serbs reduced their violations of the UN no-fly zone for a short time, but did not end helicopter and fixed-wing flights within the prohibited airspace.[37]

The military objective was to shoot down Bosnian Serb Jastrebs that were violating the NFZs: it succeeded. According to NATO and civilians on the ground, all four Jastrebs were turned into fireballs, with no pilots observed bailing out.[38]

Bosnia and Herzegovina, April 10–11, 1994
(Political failure; Military success)

In early 1994, Bosnian Serb ground forces advanced on the UN-declared safe area of Gorazde, in central Bosnia and Herzegovina. By early April, the Serbs had blockaded roads surrounding Gorazde, penetrated the enclave with ground forces, and conducted sniper and artillery attacks on the 65,000 civilians trapped within the city.[39] On April 9, UN Secretary General Boutros Boutros-Ghali warned that "all available means"—meaning airstrikes—would be ordered if the Bosnian Serbs did not return "to the positions they held before the outbreak of the recent fighting [around Gorazde]."[40] The Secretary General's order was ignored.

On April 10, at 6:22 P.M., two U.S. Air Force F-16s on a routine patrol were requested by UNPROFOR peacekeepers near Gorazde to bomb a Serbian artillery command post four miles from the town center. The F-16s dropped three Mark 82 high-explosive bombs on the target, which was selected by a team of eight British Special Air Services officers disguised as UN military observers.[41] As the Bosnian Serb attacks on Gorazde continued, the following day, at 2:19 P.M., a force package of two U.S. Marine Corps F-18s dropped three more Mark 82 bombs and conducted a 20-millimeter strafing run on a tank and two armored personnel carriers.[42]

The political objective was to compel the Bosnian Serbs to return territory captured around the UN-declared safe area of Gorazde: it failed. The April 10 and 11 airstrikes did not protect Gorazde from attacks by the Bosnian Serbs, who advanced to the edge of the city center and shelled its inhabitants with tanks and artillery. By the end of April, however, a series of NATO and UN ultimatums eventually succeeded in compelling the Bosnian Serbs to disengage from Gorazde.[43]

The military objective was to destroy specific elements of the Bosnian Serb ground forces threatening Gorazde: it succeeded. Though the targeted Bosnian Serb forces were destroyed, bad weather, mountainous terrain, and poor communications between the British SAS officers and the NATO pilots limited the effectiveness of the airstrikes. On April 10, the F-16 pilots initially were directed to bomb Serb tanks attacking Gorazde but were unable to visibly acquire them while flying under cloud cover. The F-16s then proceeded to an alternative target, a Serbian hillside artillery command post, and after making eight passes overhead, dropped their ordnance on the post.[44]

Bosnia and Herzegovina, August 5, 1994
(Political mixed success; Military mixed success)

On February 9, 1994, Bosnian Serb leaders and a special representative to the UN secretary general reached an agreement that established a twelve-mile heavy weapons exclusion zone around Sarajevo, Bosnia and Herzegovina's capital. On August 5, Bosnian Serb forces raided the UN-controlled Ilidza Weapons Collection site, taking a T-55 tank, two armored personnel carriers, and a 30-millimeter anti-aircraft gun. Within hours, UN commanders requested a NATO airstrike against the offending Bosnian Serb units.[45]

On August 5, after 5:00 P.M., NATO dispatched four groups of four aircraft each consisting of a U.S. A-10 Warthog, a Dutch F-16, a French Mirage F-1, and a British Jaguar. At 6:32 P.M., two of the A-10s fired six hundred 30-millimeter gun rounds at a Bosnian Serb World War II–vintage anti-tank weapon.[46]

The political objective was to deter Bosnian Serb forces from future raids on UN-controlled munitions depots, and to compel them not to place heavy weapons within the twelve-mile exclusion zone: it was a mixed success. Although the Bosnian Serbs returned the four heavy weapons to the Ilidza Weapons Collection site hours after the strike, they continued the heavy artillery shelling of Sarajevo from within the exclusion zone.[47]

The military objective was to destroy one Bosnian Serb self-propelled anti-tank weapon: it was a mixed success. The anti-tank weapon was effectively destroyed, but it was only one of four targets originally selected for attack. The other three targets were not visible through the cloud-cover once the NATO pilots arrived.[48] No Bosnian Serbs were injured in the attack, because UN officials had warned them an hour in advance to move their soldiers. The British UNPROFOR commander for Bosnia, Lieutenant General Michael Rose, noted, "We do not think it is part of our business to kill anyone."[49]

Bosnia and Herzegovina, November 21, 1994
(Political failure; Military success)
Throughout the summer of 1994, Bosnian Serb forces and Bosnian and Herzegovinian government troops fought for control of the territory around the Bihac safe area in northwest Bosnia and Herzegovina. On November 9, as part of their offensive, Croatian Serbs—supporting their Bosnian kin—used the Ubdina air base in Serb-held Croatia for three air raids, which included dropping napalm and cluster bombs on civilian areas in Bihac.[50] On November 19, the UN Security Council passed Resolution 958, which authorized member states to use air power against targets in Croatia to enforce the no-fly zone over Bosnia and Herzegovina.[51] The following day, NATO formally decided to bomb Ubdina as soon as the weather allowed it.[52]

On November 21, starting at 1:00 P.M., U.S. F-18s, F-16s, F-15s, and F-111s, accompanied by British Jaguar bombers, French Jaguars and Mirages, and Dutch F-16s, began an air raid on the Croatian Serbs' Ubdina air base. The raid began with cluster-bomb strikes on SA-6 SAM sites and two anti-aircraft guns. Precision-guided munitions and gravity bombs were then dropped on the runway and taxiway. In total, during the forty-five minute air raid, thirty-nine NATO aircraft—two-thirds of which were American—dropped eighty bombs on the Ubdina air base.[53]

The political objective was to deter Bosnian Serbs from violating the NFZ and attacking the Bihac safe area: it failed. Bosnian Serbs violated the NFZ the following day, using helicopter gunships to attack Bosnian Muslims and firing SAMs at British combat aircraft patrolling the zone.[54] Furthermore, the Bosnian Serb ground forces continued tank and artillery attacks against Bihac, and escalated their threats and harassment against UN observers.[55] During the assault on Bihac, ten NATO planes were dispatched to bomb Bosnian Serb forces, but received no targets from British forward air controllers, as UNPROFOR Commander for Bosnia Lieutenant General Michael Rose—who opposed airstrikes—ordered the British scouts to not identify any targets.[56]

The military objective was to damage the runway, taxiway, anti-aircraft guns, and SAM sites at the Serbian-controlled Ubdina airfield: it succeeded. According to a senior Pentagon official, the air raid created five "major craters" at intersections between the runway and taxiway, one "direct hit" on the taxiway "with a couple of near misses," and hits on SAM sites and anti-aircraft guns.[57] While the airstrip and its support facilities were temporarily neutralized, General Bertrand de Lapresle, UNPROFOR commander for the former Yugoslavia, refused to allow NATO pilots to strike the air traffic control tower or the Serb light-attack aircraft sitting exposed on the ground.[58] Furthermore, within two weeks, the air field was repaired and working again. A spokesman for the Croatian Serb army described NATO's raid as "a little action . . . It gave us a little headache, nothing more."[59]

Bosnia and Herzegovina, May 25–26, 1995
(Political failure; Military success)

Between May 22 and 24, 1995, Bosnian Serb forces violated an earlier agreement when they seized five heavy weapons from a UN-controlled munitions storage depot near Sarajevo.[60] On May 24, Lieutenant General Rupert Smith, commander of UNPROFOR, warned the Muslim-led Bosnian and Herzegovinian government and the Bosnian Serb forces that they had until noon the following day to return any seized weapons and remove any heavy weapons from the exclusion zone around Sarajevo. Smith warned, "Failure to comply with either deadline will result in the offending party or parties being attacked from the air."[61] Bosnian Serb forces failed to comply with the deadline.[62]

On May 25, at 3:30 P.M., four U.S. F-16s and two U.S. F-18s, supported by many American logistics aircraft and Spanish, Dutch, and French fighters, dropped eleven bombs on two Bosnian Serb ammunition depots in the Jahorinski Potok military complex at Pale, the Serbs' political headquarters near Sarajevo.[63] Smith issued a second ultimatum, which was ignored by the Bosnian Serbs. The following day, at 10:30 A.M., twelve NATO aircraft bombed six more ammunition depots within the same complex.[64]

The political objective was to compel the Bosnian Serbs to return heavy weapons to

UN-monitored depots and to halt the shelling of Sarajevo: it failed. The Bosnian Serbs did not return the heavy weapons, and after a short pause resumed shelling Sarajevo.[65] Furthermore, Bosnian Serbs retaliated by raiding three additional UN-controlled heavy weapons depots, detaining more than three hundred UN peacekeepers, and handcuffing some of them onto other ammunition depots. The Bosnian Serbs' actions effectively deterred NATO from conducting additional airstrikes to protect Sarajevo.[66]

The military objective was to destroy eight ammunition depots in the Jahorinski Potok military complex: it succeeded. The first strike caused thick plumes of smoke, suggesting that it had ignited stored ammunition, and Admiral Leighton Smith, commander in chief of the Allied Forces Southern Region, said of the second strike, "we achieved hits on all six and either destroyed or damaged all six [depots]."[67]

Bosnia and Herzegovina, August 30–September 14, 1995
(Political success; Military success)

In the summer of 1995, following the fall of the Srebrenica and Zepa safe havens to the Bosnian Serbs, the Clinton administration decided to propose a settlement—behind the threat of NATO airpower—that would divide Bosnia and Herzegovina into two parts: a Bosnian-Croatian federation controlling 51 percent of the country, and the Serbs ruling over the other 49 percent.[68] The Bosnian Serbs were slow in complying with the agreement. On August 27, Ambassador Richard Holbrooke, the administration's negotiator for the Balkans, threatened that if the Serbs did not accept the concept of the proposed settlement, NATO would use force.[69] An unnamed State Department official clarified Holbrooke's threat, stating that "the reality is, if the Bosnian Serbs don't want to negotiate, then the game will basically be just to wait for the trigger for airstrikes."[70] The following day, that trigger arrived when a mortar shell fired by Bosnian Serb forces killed thirty-five and wounded eighty-eight civilians in a Sarajevo marketplace.

Starting on August 30, at 2:00 A.M., and ending September 14, at 10:00 A.M., NATO air forces flew 3,513 sorties against Bosnian Serb targets, dropping 1,026 high-explosive munitions on forty-eight Bosnian Serb target complexes, including 338 individual aim-points within those complexes. NATO airstrikes occurred on eleven of the seventeen days of the air campaign.[71] The United States flew two-thirds of the sorties, Great Britain 9 percent, France 8 percent, and other NATO member countries the remaining amount.[72] Starting on September 10, the U.S.S. Normandy fired thirteen Tomahawk cruise missiles at components of the Bosnian Serb integrated air-defense system near Banja Luka.[73] In conjunction with the bombing and cruise missile attacks, French and British ground forces belonging to NATO's Rapid Reaction Force shelled the Bosnian Serb's Lukavica barracks southwest of Sarajevo.

The political objective was to compel Bosnian Serb leaders to return to the negotiating table and agree to NATO's demands: it succeeded. Although all three warring parties resisted the U.S.-proposed settlement to various degrees, only the Bosnian

Serbs were targeted by NATO.[74] After several days of bombing, the Bosnian Serb leaders acceded to all of the key demands presented by Ambassador Holbrooke.[75]

The military objective was to degrade the Serbian Army's ability to conduct further offensive operations: it succeeded. Eased rules of engagement for NATO aircraft allowed for attacks of greater intensity and lethality. *Operation Deliberate Force*, combined with French and British artillery shelling and Croatian and Bosnian battlefield successes against the Serbs, reduced the territory controlled by the Serbian Army from 70 percent to 45 percent before the Dayton peace talks began.[76]

Iraq, September 3–4, 1996
(Political mixed success; Military mixed success)

In the summer of 1996, a cease-fire brokered by the State Department between the two main Kurdish political parties, the Kurdish Democratic Party (KDP) and the Patriotic Union of Kurdistan (PUK), unraveled over disagreements about dividing oil-smuggling revenues.[77] When the United States refused to decisively mediate this latest of many disputes, the two parties sought assistance from external powers: the PUK turned to Iran for weapons, logistics, and military advisors, while the KDP appealed directly to Saddam Hussein for Iraqi troops to intervene on their behalf.[78] On August 28 and 30, the United States warned Hussein not to intervene on the ground in northern Iraq, or else "it would be a serious mistake."[79] Ignoring the warnings, on August 31, two Iraqi Republican Guard divisions and three regular army divisions advanced on the Kurdish capital of Irbil.

In the days leading up to the Hussein regime's invasion of Kurdistan, senior NSC officials concluded that a military response was required, and considered a range of options.[80] For several reasons, it was decided not to directly attack the Iraqi Republican Guard and army divisions: the U.S. airwing at Incirlik, Turkey, consisted of planes not properly configured to identify and strike mobile ground forces; Saudi Arabia, Jordan, and Turkey would not permit their airspace to be used to bomb Iraq; and senior U.S. officials had no appetite for intervening in a Kurdish civil war.[81] In lieu of bombing Iraq's ground forces in Kurdistan, the White House made two choices: President Clinton opted for a military response that was "towards the middle" in severity among those presented to him; and the Pentagon announced that the northern edge of the southern NFZ would be expanded sixty-nine miles from Iraq's 32nd to the 33rd parallel.[82]

On September 3, at 7:00 A.M., the U.S. Navy destroyer *U.S.S. Laboon* and cruiser *U.S.S. Shiloh* launched fourteen Tomahawk cruise missiles, and two U.S. Air Force B-52Hs loitering in Kuwait fired thirteen Conventional Air-Launched Cruise Missiles (CALCMs) at components of the Iraqi integrated air-defense system that had been threatening planes enforcing the southern NFZ. Three more CALCMs from the B-52Hs malfunctioned and were not fired. The following day, seventeen more Tomahawk cruise missiles were launched from the U.S. Navy destroyers *Laboon* and *U.S.S.*

Hewitt and the submarine *U.S.S. Jefferson* against three targets that had been struck the day before, in addition to one new target.[83]

The political objectives were to compel Iraq to withdraw its armored divisions from Kurdistan and to deter Iraq from threatening pilots patrolling the no-fly zones: it was a mixed success. Having achieved its objectives, the Baathist regime quickly withdrew most of the armored divisions from Kurdistan, but Iraqi intelligence services remained. Iraq continued to threaten planes patrolling the expanded southern NFZ, and within a week began rebuilding its air defense systems damaged in the September 3–4 strikes.[84] Furthermore, America's reputation was harmed, as international opinion perceived the response to Baghdad's aggression as weak. As Director of Central Intelligence John Deutch summarized, "I believe that Saddam Hussein's position has been strengthened in the region recently," and "there is also perception of weakened determination of the coalition to meet Iraqi aggression."[85]

The military objective was to destroy eight SAM sites and seven command and control centers: it was a mixed success. Of the eight SAM sites targeted, five were destroyed or severely damaged, one damaged or abandoned, and two moved before the attacks. According to the Pentagon, of the seven command and control centers targeted, one was destroyed or severely damaged, four damaged, and two received minor or no damage.[86] According to a senior Pentagon official, the first strike was "about what the planners expected," but the second "wasn't worth a damn."[87] The problems were that Central Command planners lacked in-house expertise in cruise missiles, were rushed in the process of matching weapons with targets, and were instructed by the Pentagon to limit the number of missiles fired.[88]

Afghanistan and Sudan, August 20, 1998
(Political failure; Military failure)
See Chapter 4 for in-depth case study.

Iraq, December 16–19, 1998
(Political failure; Military mixed success)
By late summer 1997, Saddam Hussein, recognizing that the UN sanctions regime would persist while he remained in power, escalated Iraq's disruptive behavior toward the UN weapons inspectors. To compel Iraqi cooperation, the Clinton administration declared that it would use force. After a threatened U.S. bombing campaign was cancelled minutes before the first missiles were to be fired, on November 14, Iraqi diplomats pledged to "clearly and unconditionally" cooperate with the UN weapons inspection process and "allow the return of inspectors to resume all their activities on an immediate, unconditional and unrestricted basis."[89] On December 15, Richard Butler, the executive chairman of UNSCOM, reported that "Iraq's conduct ensured that no progress was able to be made in either the fields of disarmament or accounting for its prohibited

weapons programmes."[90] The following day, Clinton administration foreign policy officials unanimously supported extensive air and cruise missiles strikes against Iraq.[91]

Starting December 16, at 11:06 P.M., and ending December 19, at 10:00 P.M., U.S. and British forces in the Persian Gulf attacked one hundred regime targets throughout central and southern Iraq.[92] In total, 415 cruise missiles—325 U.S. Navy Tomahawks and ninety U.S. Air Force CALCMs—were fired, and 230 laser-guided bombs and about 250 Mark 82 "dumb-bombs" were dropped.[93] The target list consisted of twenty command and control sites, twelve WMD industry and production facilities, eighteen WMD security sites, nine Republican Guard barracks, six airfields, thirty-four air defense installations, and an oil refinery in Basra that the United States claimed was involved in oil smuggling outside of the UN sanctions regime.[94] *Operation Desert Fox* ended after four days, primarily because the Clinton administration did not want to bomb during Ramadan.[95]

The political objective was to compel Iraq to cooperate with the UNSCOM inspection process: it failed. The inspectors were barred from Iraq for four more years, until late 2002. As a consequence, the U.S. intelligence community lost its only direct access to Iraq's WMD programs, and provided estimates of Hussein's WMD arsenal that were outdated and proven to be false. As the U.S. Senate Select Committee on Intelligence noted in its report on pre-war intelligence of Iraq, "After the Gulf War, however, most of the intelligence community's knowledge of Iraqi WMD programs was obtained from, in conjunction with, and in support of the UNSCOM inspections. . . . When UN inspectors left Iraq in December 1998, the [Intelligence Community] was left with a limited unilateral collection capability against Iraq's WMD. . . . The CIA did not have any WMD sources in Iraq after 1998."[96]

The military objective was to degrade Iraq's ability to reconstitute its proscribed WMD and ballistic missile programs: it was a mixed success. The Pentagon's bomb damage assessment of the operation cited that of the one hundred targets, forty-three were severely damaged or destroyed, thirty moderately damaged, twelve lightly damaged, and thirteen untouched. According to Rear Admiral David Nichols, U.S. Central Command Deputy Director for Operations, U.S. and British forces successfully struck 211 out of 275 planned aim-points within the one hundred targets.[97] Iraq's ballistic missile production capabilities were set back by an estimated one to two years, and at least 1,400 of Hussein's elite military and security forces were killed or wounded.[98] Within fourteen months, U.S. satellite imagery and intelligence reports provided evidence that Iraq had rebuilt some of the suspected WMD and missile facilities damaged in the bombing.[99]

Iraq, February 16, 2001
(Political mixed success; Military mixed success)

Throughout 2000, Iraq enhanced its ability to track and target U.S. and British planes patrolling the southern NFZ through a system of radars networked by secure fiber-optic cables. Previously, Iraqi air-defense command and control centers had communicated via radio transmissions, which are susceptible to interception, jamming, or spoofing. The fiber-optic data links being supplied and installed by China allowed Iraqi air-defense operators to communicate in real-time. To degrade this threat, CENTCOM planners developed Response Option 4 to attack surveillance radars and fiber-optic nodes in central Iraq. On February 14, Chairman of the Joint Chiefs of Staff General Hugh Shelton presented Response Option 4 to the NSC; the following day President Bush approved it.[100]

On February 16, 2001, starting at 7:50 P.M. and ending at 9:40 P.M., eighteen U.S. combat planes—Air Force F-15Es and F-16s, and Navy F-18s—and six British Tornados bombed twenty-five targets at five separate air-defense sites in central Iraq: an early warning radar in Baghdad, command and control facilities at Al Taqaddum and Taji, and control stations at As Surwayrah and An Numiyah. Although the types and number of ordnance dropped was classified, anonymous Pentagon officials confirmed that they included twenty-eight AGM-130 precision-guided munitions, a few 2,000-lb. Paveway III laser-guided bombs, ten Standoff Land Attack Missiles, and twenty-eight of the recently-introduced AGM-154A Joint Stand-Off Weapons (JSOWs)—cluster bombs containing 145 anti-personnel bomblets. The raid was timed for the Muslim Sabbath, when work was halted, to reduce the likelihood of Chinese casualties.[101]

The political objective was to deter Iraq from continuing to threaten the pilots patrolling the southern NFZ: it was a mixed success. Although some of the crucial fiber-optic aim-points had been destroyed, reducing the air-defense threat, Iraq significantly increased the number of times that it tracked or fired on U.S. and British pilots patrolling the southern NFZ. Furthermore, by the summer of 2001, Baghdad had rebuilt much of the fiber-optic network that had been degraded in the February strike.[102]

The military objective was to destroy the Iraqi air-defense radars and command and control centers before they became interconnected through the fiber-optics network: it was a mixed success. Due to a human error in programming inaccurate guidance data, and high winds, all but two of the twenty-eight JSOWs impacted to the left of their aim-points by an average of more than a hundred yards. In addition, one or two of the AGM-130s also missed their targets. Consequently, by the Pentagon's own admission, within days at least two of the targeted air-defense radars were activated and working again.[103]

Yemen, November 3, 2002
(Political failure; Military success)

See Chapter 5 for in-depth case study.

Iraq, March 19, 2003
(Political failure; Military failure)

Two days before the Second Gulf War was scheduled to start, an Iraqi CIA source reported that Saddam Hussein and his sons would be at the Dora Farms complex near Baghdad on the morning of March 19, 2003.[104] Further human and imagery intelligence indicated an underground bunker at Dora, which meant that manned bombers would be required to drop 2,000-pound bombs to penetrate reinforced concrete. After receiving unanimous support from his senior civilian and military advisors, President Bush authorized a strike on the time-sensitive target.[105]

On March 19, from the Persian Gulf and the Red Sea, three U.S. Navy cruisers, a destroyer, and two submarines launched around twenty-four Tomahawk cruise missiles against Dora Farms and sixteen against Iraqi air-defense and command and control systems, to protect the manned bombers.[106] Some of the Tomahawks arrived late because of a delay in programming targeting data.[107] A strike package of two U.S. Marine EA-6B jamming aircraft, a KC-135 aerial refueling tanker, and two F-16CJs were assembled to accompany two F-117 stealth bombers.[108] Immediately after the two dozen cruise missiles made impact, and before the sun rose, the F-117s dropped four EGBU-27 2,000-pound bombs on the Dora Farms complex.[109]

The political objective was to decapitate the Iraqi political leadership to compel Iraq to surrender before the war started: it failed. Hussein and his sons survived, and a full-scale invasion was required to decapitate the regime.

The military objective was to kill Saddam Hussein: it failed. After the war, Hussein's personal secretary told U.S. interrogators that the Iraqi leader had not been to Dora Farms since 1995.[110] The complex was searched three times—once by the CIA and twice by the U.S. Army—and no underground bunkers or bodies were ever found.[111]

Pakistan, May 8, 2005
(Political mixed success; Military success)

Starting in early 2002, U.S. intelligence working alongside Pakistan counterterrorism forces began operating in northern Pakistan to capture or kill Osama Bin Laden, Ayman Al-Zawahiri, and second-tier Al Qaeda officials who were planning attacks against the United States.[112] Since early 2005 the CIA and American Special Operations forces had been tracking Haitham al-Yemeni—a senior Al Qaeda official and explosives expert—in northwest Pakistan in the hopes that he would lead them to Bin Laden. In early May, Pakistani security forces captured Abu Faraj al-Libbi, reportedly Al Qaeda's number three official. Concerned that al-Libbi's capture would compel al-Yemeni to go underground, U.S. officials decided to stop tracking him and attempt to kill him.[113]

On May 8, at approximately 2:00 A.M., a CIA-controlled Predator drone fired one Hellfire missile at a car driving near Toorikhel, a suburb of Mir Ali in the Pakistani province of North Waziristan. Tribal sources in the area said a rocket hit the car, while

the Pakistani government claimed that explosives being carried in the vehicle detonated accidentally. Though Pakistan's information minister both denied the event
took place and claimed having no knowledge that it might have happened near the
Afghanistan-Pakistan border, current and former U.S. officials confirmed that a CIA
Predator was responsible for the explosion.[114]

The political objective was to punish and deter Al Qaeda from using Pakistan
to plan and stage operations: it was a mixed success. Though Al Qaeda's objectives
might have been disrupted through killing or capturing second-tier officials such as
al-Yemeni, by late 2006 Al Qaeda remained entrenched in northern Pakistan, training
operatives and planning operations.[115]

The military objective was to kill Haitham al-Yemeni: it succeeded. Reportedly,
al-Yemeni and the passenger in his vehicle, named either Samiullah Khan or Imam
Din, were killed.[116]

Pakistan, November 5, 2005
(Political mixed success; Military failure)

In 2005, U.S. and Pakistani intelligence and military personnel were tracking Abu
Hamza Rabia, a senior Al Qaeda official who was involved in the 2003 assassination
plots against Pakistani President Pervez Musharraf. According to a Pakistani intelligence official, Rabia had for months been "playing hide-and-seek with the Americans,
who were on his tail."[117] Eventually, Rabia was tracked to the Mosaki village near Mi-
rali, in the North Waziristan province near the Afghan border.[118]

On November 5, a CIA-controlled Predator drone fired one or more Hellfire missiles at a house in Mosaki, reportedly killing Rabia's wife, daughter, and six others.[119]

The political objective was to punish and to deter Al Qaeda from using Pakistan
to plan and stage operations: it was a mixed success. Though Al Qaeda's objectives
might have been disrupted through the attempted killing of Rabia, by late 2006 Al
Qaeda remained entrenched in northern Pakistan, training operatives and planning
operations.[120]

The military objective was to kill Abu Hamza Rabia: it failed. Reportedly, Rabia
narrowly missed being killed in the attack, and suffered a slight leg wound.[121]

Pakistan, December 1, 2005
(Political mixed success; Military success)

After the failed attempt to kill Abu Hamza Rabia three weeks earlier, U.S. and Pakistani intelligence agents on the ground tracked him to an abandoned house in the
village of Haisori, in North Waziristan.[122]

On December 1, at 1:45 A.M., a CIA-controlled Predator drone fired one or more
Hellfire missiles at a mud-brick compound in Haisori, killing Rabia, a Syrian bodyguard,
and the seventeen-year-old son and eight-year-old nephew of the owner of the house.[123]

Villagers claimed to have heard at least two explosions, and reported seeing a white streak of light coming from a drone before the building was hit.[124] Villagers also uncovered pieces of shrapnel bearing the designation "AGM-114," the words "guided missile," and the initials "U.S."[125] To conceal American involvement, the Pakistani government created a cover story that Rabia blew himself up experimenting with explosives.[126]

The political objective was to punish and to deter Al Qaeda from using Pakistan to plan and stage operations: it was a mixed success. Though Al Qaeda's objectives might have been disrupted through the killing of Rabia, by late 2006 Al Qaeda remained entrenched in northern Pakistan, training operatives, and planning operations.[127]

The military objective was to kill Abu Hamza Rabia: it succeeded. According to Pakistani officials, Rabia's death was confirmed by tests of DNA evidence collected at the scene.[128] When Pervez Musharaff was asked to confirm Rabia's death, the Pakistani leader replied, "Yes indeed, two hundred percent confirmed."[129]

Pakistan, January 7, 2006
(Political mixed success; Military failure)

On January 7, 2006, at approximately 12:30 A.M., a CIA-controlled Predator drone fired one Hellfire missile at a residential compound in Saidgai, five miles inside the Afghan border. The compound, owned by religious leader Maulvi Noor Mohammad, had been searched by Pakistani security forces days earlier on suspicion that shelter was being provided to militants fighting in Afghanistan.[130]

The political objective was to punish and to deter Al Qaeda from using Pakistan to plan and stage operations: it was a mixed success. Al Qaeda remained entrenched in northern Pakistan, training operatives and planning operations.

The military objective was to kill an unidentified Al Qaeda official: it failed. Reportedly, eight local villagers inside the compound were killed: two women, two children, and four men. Injured villagers reported that U.S. soldiers had taken away a few tribesmen either just before or after the missile strike.[131]

Pakistan, January 13, 2006
(Political mixed success; Military failure)

Starting in late 2005, as part of their joint campaign to kill or capture high-value Al Qaeda or Taliban officials, U.S. and Pakistani intelligence tracked the movements of suspects in the Damadola region.[132] In conjunction, Pakistani intelligence officials developed information on Ayman al-Zawahiri's location from interrogations of Abu Faraj al-Libbi and from field agents.[133] The joint U.S.-Pakistani effort tracked Zawahiri to a compound of the religious leader Maulavi Liaqat, in the village of Damadola, four miles inside the Afghan border. Al-Zawahiri and three other senior Al Qaeda officials were reportedly meeting at the compound. Villagers reported seeing an unmanned drone circling the area for several days.[134]

On January 13, at 3:21 A.M. a few CIA-controlled Predator drones fired six to ten Hellfire missiles at the Liaqat compound. The strikes reportedly killed eighteen civilians, including women and children, and four suspected Al Qaeda militants.[135]

The political objective was to punish and to deter Al Qaeda from using Pakistan to plan and stage operations: it was a mixed success. Though four suspected Al Qaeda officials were killed, the terrorist group remained entrenched in northern Pakistan, training more operatives and planning operations. Furthermore, the civilian casualties led to mass protests throughout Pakistan, pressuring Pervez Musharraf to condemn the attack and to tell Under Secretary of State Nicholas Burns that it "must not be repeated."[136]

The military objective was to kill Ayman al-Zawahiri: it failed. Al-Zawahiri survived. According to Pakistani intelligence officials, al-Zawahiri ate dinner at the targeted compound of Maulavi Liaqat but left two hours before the missile strike.[137] Two weeks after the failed attack, al-Zawahiri appeared on an Al Jazeera videotape, in which he taunted the White House: "Bush, do you know where I am? I am among the Muslim masses."[138] In addition, Midhat Mursi al-Sayid Umar, who the CIA initially claimed was killed in the attack, survived, and continued his crucial role of overseeing Al Qaeda's efforts to develop or obtain WMD.[139] The other two senior Al Qaeda officials believed to be meeting al-Zawahiri and al-Sayid Umar at the compound both survived the strike.[140]

Somalia, January 7, 2007
(Political mixed success; Military failure)

In 2006, the United States began secret negotiations with Somali clans that were alleged to be harboring three highly wanted Al Qaeda operatives: Abu Talha al Sudani, Fazul Abdullah Mohamed, and Saleh Ali Saleh Nabhan.[141] The three were charged by the Bush administration for being involved in the 1998 African embassy bombings as well as the 2002 attacks against an Israeli airliner and a hotel in Mombasa, Kenya.[142] Efforts to obtain them by bargaining with the Somali clans failed. On December 24, 2006, with support in the form of detailed intelligence, military training, and Naval backing from the United States, the government of Ethiopia invaded Somalia with the goal of unseating the ruling Council of Islamic Courts (CIC).[143] As the Ethiopian offensive overwhelmed the CIC defenses, Somali militants and Al Qaeda affiliates fled south. Some of them were tracked visually with Predator drones, and through cell phone intercepts.[144]

On January 7, 2007, a U.S. Air Force Special Operations AC-130 gunship flying out of an airport in eastern Ethiopia fired on a convoy of escaping Islamic militants near the village of Ras Kamboni in southern Somalia near Kenya.[145]

The political objective was to punish and to deter Al Qaeda from using Somalia to plan and stage operations: it was a mixed success. The wanted Al Qaeda operatives survived, but were forced to take actions to protect themselves from the Ethiopian-backed government in Mogadishu and the U.S. military teams. Somali Islamic militants adopted some of Al Qaeda's tactics and provided shelter for sympathizers, some of whom supported terrorist attacks against the United States.[146]

The military objective was to kill any of the three senior Al Qaeda operatives: it failed. Although approximately ten suspected Somali militants died in the AC-130 raid, Ethiopian troops and U.S. Special Operations soldiers arriving after the attack confirmed that none of the three sought-after targets were killed.[147] Though Aden Hasi Ayro, a CIC military commander, was reportedly injured or killed, a U.S. official correctly warned at the time, "Frankly, I don't think we know who we killed."[148] Two months later, Ayro was named the head of Al Qaeda operations in Somalia, and he released an audiotape calling on the Islamic youth to fight the Ethiopians and other foreign forces in-country.[149]

Pakistan, January 16, 2007
(Political mixed success; Military unknown)

On January 16, 2007, at 6:55 A.M., one or more CIA-controlled Predator drones fired a few missiles into three compounds in the village of Zamzola, in South Waziristan. The Pakistani Army claimed to have struck the compounds itself with a helicopter assault, but CBS News reported that "the attack was carried out by the U.S., which allowed Pakistan to take credit." One journalist who arrived on the scene soon after the attack reported that there were two unexploded, half-buried missiles, one of which read, "AM York 0873."[150]

The political objective was to punish and to deter Al Qaeda from using Pakistan to plan and stage operations: it was a mixed success. Though some suspected Al Qaeda or Taliban operatives were killed, the terrorist group remained entrenched in northern Pakistan, training more operatives and planning operations.

The military objective was to kill an unknown number of unidentified Al Qaeda or Taliban operatives: result unknown. Between ten to thirty people were killed, described as woodcutters by local villagers and foreign terrorists by the Pakistani government.[151]

Somalia, January 22, 2007
(Political mixed success; Military failure)

On January 22, 2007, a U.S. Air Force Special Operations AC-130 gunship flying out of an airport in eastern Ethiopia fired on a senior Al Qaeda operative in southern Somalia.[152]

The political objective was to punish and to deter Al Qaeda from using Somalia to plan and stage operations: it was a mixed success. The three wanted Al Qaeda operatives survived again, and continued to take actions to protect themselves from U.S. military teams. Somali Islamic militants continued to adopt some of Al Qaeda's tactics and provide shelter for sympathizers.[153]

The military objective was to kill Sheik Ahmed Madobe, a senior leader of the

Islamic Council: it failed. Madobe survived the attack—as did any other senior Al Qaeda operatives who may have been present—but according to U.S. officials, Madobe was later captured by the Ethiopians.[154]

Pakistan, April 27, 2007
(Political mixed success; Military unknown)

On April 27, 2007, at 3:30 A.M., a CIA-controlled Predator drone fired one or two missiles at a compound owned by the religious leader Maulvi Noor Mohammad, in the village of Saidgai, in North Waziristan.

The political objective was to punish and to deter Al Qaeda from using Pakistan to plan and stage operations: it was a mixed success. Though some suspected Al Qaeda or Taliban operatives were killed, the terrorist group remained entrenched in northern Pakistan, training more operatives and planning operations.

The military objective was to kill an unknown number of unidentified Al Qaeda or Taliban operatives: result unknown. Reportedly, four local tribesmen staying at the house were killed and two others were injured.[155]

Somalia, June 1, 2007
(Political mixed success; Military failure)

On June 1, 2007, one or two fishing boats landed at the northern fishing port of Bargal with thirty-five well-armed Al Qaeda operatives that were attached to the deposed Islamist government. After the militants engaged in a running gun battle with local police forces, the regional government appealed to U.S. forces in Djibouti to conduct an attack.[156]

In response, a U.S. Navy destroyer in the Red Sea fired several cruise missiles against the suspected Al Qaeda operatives in Bargal.[157]

The political objective was to punish and to deter Al Qaeda from using Somalia to plan and stage operations: it was a mixed success. The three wanted Al Qaeda operatives survived again, and continued to take actions to protect themselves from U.S. military teams. Somalia Islamic militants continued to adopt some of Al Qaeda's tactics and provide shelter for sympathizers.[158] In a June 25, 2007, letter to a Security Council committee responsible for Somalia, the U.S. ambassador to the UN, Zalmay Khalilzad, wrote, "The United States has conducted several strikes in self-defense against al-Qaida terrorist targets in Somalia in response to on-going threats to the United States."[159]

The military objective, according to a U.S. official, was probably to kill Fazul Abdullah Mohammed, one of the three wanted Al Qaeda terrorists: it failed. Mohammed survived and remained at large. On the day after the cruise missile strikes, U.S. Special Operations soldiers and Somali security forces arrived at the scene to collect intelligence. Reportedly, they found the remains of eight militants, including some from Eritrea, Yemen, England, Sweden, and the United States.[160]

Pakistan, June 19, 2007
(Political mixed success; Military unknown)

On June 19, 2007, at around 10:30 A.M., one or more CIA-controlled Predator drones fired a few missiles into a religious compound in the border village of Mami Rogha, in North Waziristan. Local residents reported drones flying overhead moments before the strike. The Pakistani military claimed, again, that the explosions were caused when militants' bomb-making material accidentally detonated.

The political objective was to punish and to deter Al Qaeda from using Pakistan to plan and stage operations: it was a mixed success. Though some suspected Al Qaeda or Taliban operatives were killed, the terrorist group remained entrenched in northern Pakistan, training more operatives and planning operations.

The military objective was to kill an unknown number of unidentified Al Qaeda or Taliban operatives: result unknown. Reportedly, twenty to thirty people were killed, including some foreign militants and children.[161]

Pakistan, January 29, 2008
(Political mixed success; Military success)

In July 2002, Abu Laith al-Libi, a Libyan national and senior Al Qaeda lieutenant, emerged as a public figure when he announced that Osama Bin Laden and Taliban leader Mohammad Omar had survived the American-led invasion of Afghanistan.[162] Over the following five-and-a-half years, al-Libi was believed to have orchestrated the 2003 assassination attempts on President Pervez Musharraf; the 2005 prison breakout of al-Qaeda fighters from the U.S. military's prison at the Bagram Air Base; and the February 2007 bombing of the Bagram Air Base, during a visit by Vice President Dick Cheney, which killed twenty-three civilians.[163] An anonymous Western counterterrorism official labeled al-Libi the "senior paramilitary commander for Afghanistan."[164]

On June 17, 2007, U.S. Special Operations forces fired as many as five rockets from a High Mobility Artillery Rockets (HIMARS) system at a Taliban compound in the Paktika province of eastern Afghanistan, where al-Libi was believed to be living. Although seven children died, forensic tests by the U.S. military determined that al-Libi survived.[165]

After surviving the June attempt on his life in Afghanistan, al-Libi began operating freely in Pakistan, meeting foreign diplomats and visiting imprisoned Islamic militants.[166] In October 2007, U.S. officials offered a $200,000 bounty for information that could lead to his killing or capture. On January 9, 2008, Mike McConnell, Director of National Intelligence, and General Michael Hayden, director of the CIA, met with Musharraf to request greater latitude in conducting U.S. combat operations against Al Qaeda and the Taliban. While Musharraf reportedly refused an expanded American ground combat presence in Pakistan, he permitted enhanced intelligence sharing and an increase in the number and scope of patrols and strikes of the armed Predator sorties.[167]

During the time of McConnell and Hayden's visit, al-Libi resurfaced in North Waziristan and was reportedly planning a meeting with Baitullah Mehsud, a Pakistani Taliban commander.[168] Hours before the Predator strike, several local sources alerted the CIA to a convoy of vehicles believed to be carrying eight Al Qaeda operatives, including one senior official. Alerted to the convoy, the CIA watched the vehicles travel to a walled compound in the village of Khushali Torikel, located on the outskirts of Mir Ali, North Waziristan. A Predator was launched from a secret base located within Pakistan.[169]

On January 29, 2008, early in the morning, a CIA-controlled Predator drone fired two Hellfire missiles into a compound owned by Abdul Sattar—a local Taliban commander and associate of Mehsud. The compound was destroyed, and twelve or thirteen people were killed, most of them Arabs or Central Asians. Unlike with other Predator strikes in Pakistan, the CIA did not seek permission beforehand from Musharraf's government.[170]

The political objective was to punish and to deter Al Qaeda from using Pakistan to plan and stage operations: it was a mixed success. Though a senior Al Qaeda official was killed, Al Qaeda remained entrenched in northern Pakistan, training operatives and planning operations. A detailed *Washington Post* article about the al-Libi strike quoted a senior U.S. official describing its fortuitous but ephemeral impact: "Even a blind squirrel finds a nut now and then. But overall, we're in worse shape than we were 18 months ago."[171]

The military objective was to kill Abu Laith al-Libi: it succeeded. At least three unnamed U.S. officials and two Al Qaeda-affiliated websites confirmed al-Libi's death.[172] One month later, Al Qaeda also released a video eulogy showing al-Libi's corpse.[173]

Pakistan, February 28, 2008
(Political mixed success; Military unknown)

On February 28, 2008, at around 2:00 A.M., three missiles were fired into a house in the village of Kaloosha, South Waziristan, which was owned by Sher Mohammed Malikkheil, suspected of links to local and foreign militants. There were conflicting reports about whether the missiles were launched from a CIA-controlled Predator drone—which was seen circling above the area—or from a ground-based missile system located at a U.S. base in Machi Dat, Afghanistan.[174]

The political objective was to punish and to deter Al Qaeda from using Pakistan to plan and stage operations: it was a mixed success. Though some suspected Al Qaeda or Taliban operatives were killed, the terrorist group remained entrenched in northern Pakistan, training more operatives and planning operations.

The military objective was to kill an unknown number of unidentified Al Qaeda or Taliban operatives: result unknown. The missile strike reportedly killed between eight and thirteen people, including four Middle Eastern and two Central Asian men, and wounded five or six others. According to unnamed Pakistani security officials, the bodies of the dead were charred beyond recognition and removed soon after for burial by armed militants.[175]

Somalia, March 3, 2008
(Political mixed success; Military failure)

On March 3, 2008, at around 3:30 A.M., at least two Tomahawk cruise missiles were fired from a U.S. Navy submarine at a house owned by Mohammed Nuuriye Salaad in the town of Dobley, four miles from the Kenyan border.[176] Bryan Whitman, Pentagon spokesman, announced that "the United States conducted an attack against a known al Qaeda terrorist in southern Somalia."[177]

The political objective was to punish and to deter Al Qaeda from using Somalia to plan and stage operations: it was a mixed success. Highly sought-after Al Qaeda officials remained in Somalia. Furthermore, Somali Islamic militants adopted some of Al Qaeda's tactics and provided shelter for sympathizers, some of whom supported terrorist attacks against the United States.

The military objective was to kill Saleh Ali Saleh Nabhan, who was wanted by the FBI for questioning regarding his involvement in the 2002 attacks against an Israeli airliner and a hotel in Mombasa, Kenya: it failed.[178] The missile strikes reportedly killed up to six people and seriously wounded six to eight more, including a fifteen-year-old girl.[179] Nabhan was eventually killed by another U.S. DMO during a daylight helicopter raid on September 14, 2009.[180]

Pakistan, March 16, 2008
(Political mixed success; Military unknown)

On March 16, 2008, at around 3:30 P.M., between three and seven missiles were either dropped by U.S. drone aircraft or fired from across the Afghanistan border at a house owned by suspected Taliban sympathizer Noorullah Wazir in the village of Shahn-awaz Kot near the town of Wana in South Waziristan.[181] Major General Athar Abbas, spokesperson for the Pakistani Army, said that the Army had not carried out the attack and was not responsible for the deaths.[182]

The political objective was to punish and to deter Al Qaeda from using Pakistan to plan and stage operations: it was a mixed success. Though some suspected Al Qaeda or Taliban operatives were killed, the terrorist group remained entrenched in northern Pakistan, training more operatives and planning operations. In addition, the increase in U.S. missile strikes—and resultant civilian casualties—over the prior three months resulted in a worsening of relations between the United States and Pakistan. As a consequence, the incoming government of Prime Minister Yousaf Raza Gillani threatened to limit the scope of U.S. operations in Pakistan. As the leader of the second biggest party in Parliament, Nawaz Sharif, warned U.S. diplomats, "If America wants to see itself clean of terrorists, we also want that our villages and towns should not be bombed."[183]

The military objective was to kill an unknown number of unidentified Al Qaeda or Taliban operatives: result unknown. According to the *New York Times*, "The strike on Sunday did not appear to have killed a senior member of Al Qaeda or the Taliban, the [Pakistan security] official and residents said."[184] Between nine and twenty people were killed, including eight non-native militants, and Dr. Arshad Waheed, a kidney specialist who was convicted in Pakistan of providing material support to terrorists, only to have his conviction overturned by the Supreme Court.[185] Reportedly, no women or children were included among the dead.[186]

Somalia, May 1, 2008
(Political mixed success; Military success)

After surviving a U.S. AC-130 Special Forces attack in January 2007, Aden Hashi Ayro, CIC militant leader and senior operative in Al Qaeda's East Africa network, was the subject of intense and continuous U.S. intelligence collection efforts. In the spring of 2008, according to the *New York Times*, "American intelligence agents had been tracking Mr. Ayro for weeks through a combination of communications intercepts, satellite imagery and other intelligence."[187]

On May 1, 2008, at around 3:00 A.M., a U.S. Naval vessel in the Indian Ocean fired four or five Tomahawk cruise missiles into a small compound in the town of Dusa Marreb, in central Somalia. Major Sherri Reed, spokesperson for U.S. Central Command, confirmed that the United States had attacked "a known Al Qaeda target and militia leader in Somalia."[188]

The political objective was to punish and to deter Al Qaeda from using Somalia to plan and stage operations: it was a mixed success. Highly-sought-after Al Qaeda officials remained in Somalia. Furthermore, Somali Islamic militants adopted some of Al Qaeda's tactics and provided shelter for sympathizers, some of whom supported terrorist attacks against the United States. As an unnamed American official warned after the strike, "This will become a major recruiting tool."[189]

The military objective was to kill Aden Hashi Ayro: it succeeded. According to U.S. military and intelligence officials, and local Somalis, Ayro and several senior aides, as well as perhaps ten civilians, were killed in the missile strikes.[190] A spokesman for the militant group Shabab, which Ayro led, declared, "Infidel planes bombed Dusa Marreb. Two of our important people, including Ayro, were killed."[191]

Pakistan, May 14, 2008
(Political mixed success; Military success)

On May 14, 2008, late in the evening, one or two Hellfire missiles were fired by a Predator drone at a guesthouse belonging to former Afghan Taliban official Maulvi Obaidullah in the village of Damadola, just inside the Afghanistan border.[192] Major General Athar Abbas, spokesperson for the Pakistani Army, said that the Army had not carried out the attack and would protest it to the tripartite commission, which includes commanders from the U.S., Afghan, and Pakistani militaries.[193]

The political objective was to punish and to deter Al Qaeda from using Pakistan to plan and stage operations: it was a mixed success. Though suspected Al Qaeda or Taliban operatives were killed, the terrorist group remained entrenched in northern Pakistan, training more operatives and planning operations. In addition, the Predator strike led to massive protests in the local Banjur region, and Prime Minister Yousaf Raza Gillani told Pakistani television that if the United States conducted the attack, "we condemn it."[194]

The military objective was to kill a handful of Al Qaeda militants, including an Algerian-born, top-level financier of the group, Abu Suleiman al-Jaziery: it succeeded. According to Pakistani, U.S., and Western European officials, al-Jaziery and approximately fifteen others were killed, including a handful of Al Qaeda militants and civilians.[195] According to *Newsweek*, however, armed militants soon controlled the site, removing corpses for burial and keeping away local journalists and Pakistani security forces.[196]

Pakistan, September 3, 2008
(Political failure; Military mixed success)

After years of intense debate within the national security community, in July 2008, President Bush finally authorized U.S. Special Operations forces to conduct ground raids into Pakistan without the approval of the Pakistani government.[197]

On September 3, 2008, nearly two dozen Navy Seals hiked to the village of Angor Adda in South Waziristan, located one mile from the Afghan border. After a brief encounter, the Seals killed everyone within a targeted house. Nearby militants soon arrived and the Seals killed them too. With their cover blown, U.S. helicopters were dispatched from Afghanistan to quickly remove the Seals, none of whom were killed.[198]

The political objective was to punish and to deter Al Qaeda from using Pakistan to plan and stage operations: it failed. Though some suspected Al Qaeda or Taliban operatives were killed, as well as several civilians, the terrorist group remained entrenched in northern Pakistan, training more operatives and planning operations. Furthermore, the unprecedented deployment of U.S. troops across the Afghan border unleashed a backlash within Pakistan that led Army Chief General Ashfaq Kiyani to vow to defend Pakistani territory "at all cost." Twelve days after the raid, at 4:30 A.M., Pakistani border troops reportedly fired on U.S. forces that were poised to enter Pakistan. From then on, the United States was essentially deterred from deploying ground forces to Pakistan: to date, there have been no reported cross-border raids.

The military objective was to kill an unknown number of unidentified Al Qaeda or Taliban operatives: it was a mixed success. While some militants were killed, according to several anonymous U.S. officials, no high-value targets were captured or killed.[199]

Syria, October 27, 2008
(Political mixed success; Military success)

On October 27, 2008, around 5:00 P.M., in the village of Sukkariyah, six miles from the Iraqi border, around two dozen Special Operations Forces, transported in four Black Hawk helicopters, attacked a cell affiliated with Abu Ghadiyah, an Iraqi-born senior operative of Al Qaeda in Iraq (AQI). After a brief encounter, Ghadiyah, several of his bodyguards, and several civilians were killed.[200]

The political objective was to punish AQI and deter Syria from allowing its territory to be used to smuggle fighters and materials into Iraq to support the Sunni insurgency: it was a mixed success. While Ghadiyah was killed, according to an unnamed U.S. senior official, the message to Syria was, "You have to clean up the global threat that is in your back yard, and if you won't do that, we are left with no choice but to take these matters into our hands."[201] Syria did not take additional actions to prevent smuggling into Iraq as a result of the DMO, and the level of fighters and material flowing to Iraq remained steady.[202]

The military objective was to capture or kill Abu Ghadiyah: it succeeded. On February 28, 2008, the U.S. Department of the Treasury designated Ghadiyah as someone who assisted, sponsored, or provided material support to terrorism under Executive Order 13224 (2001), which froze any of his U.S.-based assets and prohibited U.S. citizens from having any business transactions with Ghadiyah.[203] The Treasury announcement claimed Ghadiyah "runs the AQI facilitation network, which controls the flow of money, weapons, terrorists, and other resources through Syria into Iraq."[204]

Indian Ocean, April 12, 2009
(Political mixed success; Military success)

On April 8, 2009, Richard Phillips, captain of an unarmed container ship, the *Maersk Alabama*, was taken hostage by four Somali pirates after a botched hijacking attempt several hundred miles off the coast of Somalia. The crew of the *Maersk Alabama* soon retook control of their ship, but the pirates fled with Captain Phillips on a lifeboat. U.S. Naval vessels and Navy Seals were deployed to the scene. In the course of negotiations, one pirate surrendered to the *U.S.S. Bainbridge*, which was towing the lifeboat in an effort to stabilize it. After being briefed seventeen times, President Barack Obama authorized the use of deadly force to free Phillips if the commander on the scene—Commander Frank Castellano—believed the hostage was in imminent danger. Central Command officials, meanwhile, developed the rules of engagement that governed the potential use of force.[205]

On April 12, 2009, at 7:19 P.M., one of the three pirates aimed an AK-47 assault rifle at Captain Phillips, who was tied up. Commander Castellano determined that Phillips's life was in imminent danger and ordered three Navy Seals positioned on the fantail of the boat to kill all three pirates with high-powered rifles, which they did.

The political objective was to punish the three Somalis and deter other prospective pirates from attempting to hijack ships in the Indian Ocean: it was a mixed success. The Somali pirates who threatened Captain Phillips were killed, but violent pirate hijackings against Western shipping in and around the Indian Ocean did not decrease.[206]

The military objective was to kill three Somali pirates threatening Captain Phillips: it succeeded. As one anonymous senior military official boasted, "Three pirates, three rounds, three dead bodies."[207]

APPENDIX II
NON-USES OF U.S. DISCRETE MILITARY OPERATIONS, 1991 TO JUNE 1, 2009

Summer 1992, Bosnia

The George H.W. Bush administration considered using military power, including ground troops, to ensure the delivery of humanitarian aid and deter Serbian aggression.[1] Public and private estimates by senior military officials of the number of U.S. troops required ranged from 60,000 to 200,000 to 400,000, depending on the intended objectives.[2] As a consequence of these large numbers, Bush—and later Bill Clinton—administration officials refused to deploy ground forces to end the fighting in the former Yugoslavia.[3]

August 1992, Iraq

After the government of Iraq repeatedly interfered with the work of UN weapons inspectors, the Bush administration decided to destroy valued regime targets if Baghdad interfered with an upcoming "challenge inspection." According to Richard Haass, then-Senior Director for Near East and South Asian Affairs, the administration learned that the *New York Times* was going to run a story that claimed the attack was, according to Washington bureau chief Howell Raines, intended to "help get the President re-elected." Haass unsuccessfully pled with Raines to kill the story because it was false and it would eliminate the element of surprise in an attack. The *Times* published the allegations, and Haass noted, "We couldn't and didn't attack after the story appeared."[4]

June 1994, North Korea

A range of airstrikes against key components of North Korea's nuclear facilities were developed and debated by the Clinton administration. The strikes were not conducted because a diplomatic agreement was reached at the last moment, and the South Korean president refused to participate in any intra-Korean war.[5]

July 1995, Bosnia

A range of military options were presented to the Principals Committee regarding Bosnia, but were rejected because troop requirements for the missions far exceeded what the White House believed Congress would support for deployment.

June 1996–1997, Iran

After the June 25, 1996, Khobar Towers bombing, a range of military options against Iran were presented to the NSC. Included was the "Eisenhower option"—a ground invasion of a half-million or more troops, cruise missile strikes against strategic assets on Iran's coast and WMD sites, and strikes against Iranian-sponsored terror camps in Lebanon. No military actions were taken. Instead, the CIA implemented a large-scale covert operation that "outed" Iranian agents around the world in order to deter Tehran from threatening U.S. intelligence agents and diplomatic institutions.[6]

May 1998–October 2000, Al Qaeda

Ten opportunities were developed by the CIA's Osama Bin Laden (OBL) Unit and were presented to the U.S. government, to kill or capture OBL using military means.[7] According to the *9/11 Commission Report*, "General Hugh Shelton developed as many as 13 strike options, and did not recommend any of them."[8] In his memoirs, President Clinton mentioned an October 2000 strike against Osama Bin Laden called off at the last minute by the CIA.[9] The attacks were not undertaken primarily because of a lack of actionable intelligence in finding Bin Laden.

Summer 1998–1999, Kosovo

A range of proposals to use ground forces in Kosovo were presented to the Principals Committee. None were employed because the diplomatic process was not concluded, there was congressional opposition to deploying any ground troops, and there was disagreement within NATO whether to go to war.[10]

August 20, 1998, Khartoum, Sudan

President Clinton decided not to strike a tannery reportedly linked to Osama Bin Laden in Khartoum, Sudan, because "it had no military value to al Qaeda and I wanted to minimize civilian casualties.[11] For further details, see Chapter 4.

November 15, 1998, Iraq

An attack on Iraqi military facilities and suspected WMD sites was called off by President Clinton fifteen to twenty minutes before it was scheduled to commence. Secretaries Cohen and Albright, and General Hugh Shelton, all supported going forward. The attack was not undertaken because Saddam Hussein agreed to allow UN weapons inspectors back into Iraq, there was concern for the United States' international reputation, and there was concern for civilian casualties—according to Clinton, the high-range estimate for innocent deaths was 2,000. The plans included a volley of three hundred cruise missile strikes, followed by bombing raids by B-52s, F-14s, and F-18s.[12]

Summer 2002, Khurmal, Iraq

See Chapter 6 for in-depth case study.

2005, Northern Pakistan

In early 2005, CIA and Special Operations teams in northern Pakistan reportedly developed intelligence giving them "80 percent confidence" about the future location of senior Al Qaeda lieutenants, including Ayman al-Zawahiri. (Some U.S. officials later argued that intelligence on al-Zawahiri's location was from a single source and unreliable.) Secretary of Defense Donald Rumsfeld called off a "snatch and grab" raid, which would have included more than one hundred U.S. Special Operations and CIA personnel, at the last moment because the size of the operation had grown too large.[13]

2006, Northern Pakistan

In 2006, U.S. intelligence was tracking Sheik Saiid al-Masri, an Egyptian who headed the Al Qaeda finance committee.[14] For months, military officials from the Joint Special Operations Command sought permission from Donald Rumsfeld to capture Al-Masri in northern Pakistan. Finally, in November 2006, Rumsfeld approved an operation using Special Operations teams to obtain Al-Masri. The operation, however, was shelved days later after Rumsfeld resigned on November 8.[15]

Summer 2007, Syria

In May 2007, Israeli intelligence officials provided evidence to the Bush administration that North Korea had supplied nuclear technology assistance to Syria. Specifically, it was demonstrated that a near carbon-copy version of North Korea's graphite-moderated plutonium reactor at Yongbyon was being built in the Euphrates River valley town of Al-Kibar. According to unnamed senior administration officials, the Pentagon drew up plans to attack Al-Kibar, but after several Oval Office debates President Bush decided he could not bomb another country that was only accused of possessing weapons of mass destruction. On the morning of September 6, 2007, Israeli aircraft conducted Operation Orchard, a raid that destroyed the Al-Kibar nuclear facility. The DMO resulted in no Israeli or Syrian casualties, and required only a small electronic and precision-guided attack against an air defense radar near the Turkish border.[16]

2005–2008, Darfur region of Sudan

Throughout his second term in office, President George W. Bush considered a range of unilateral military options against the Khartoum regime of Sudan to prevent its continued acts of genocide in Darfur. While the president and some senior civilian officials supported using force in Darfur, senior military advisors and Secretary of State Condoleezza Rice were opposed. As Rice reportedly said to Bush, "I don't think you can invade another Muslim country during this administration, even for the best of reasons." Two weeks before Bush's second term ended, National Security Advisor Stephen Hadley released a statement that declared, "more robust military options were considered by the President for Darfur," but humanitarian NGOs, U.S. Agency for International Development experts, Darfuri activists, and the African Union "reiterated that U.S. military action would only worsen the situation for the very people we are trying to save."[17]

NOTES

Chapter 1

1. Carl von Clausewitz, *On War*, trans. and ed. Michael Howard and Peter Paret (Princeton, NJ: Princeton University Press, 1984), p. 77.

2. PBS, *Newshour with Jim Lehrer*, January 9, 2001. See also Madeline Albright, with Bill Woodward, *Madame Secretary* (New York: Miramax Books, 2003), p. 182.

3. Michael Gordon, "Powell Delivers a Resounding No on Using Limited Force in Bosnia," *New York Times*, September 28, 1992, p. A1.

4. William Perry and Ashton Carter, "If Necessary, Strike and Destroy," *Washington Post*, June 22, 2006, p. A29; Phillip Zelikow, "Be Ready to Strike and Destroy North Korea's Missile Test," February 17, 2009 (www.foreignpolicy.com); Richard Cohen, "Predator for a Predator," *Washington Post*, December 9, 2008, p. A19; John Prendergast, "Time to Forcefully Oust Mugabe," *Christian Science Monitor*, January 16, 2009; "White House Would Welcome Hussein Assassination," *Washington Post*, October 1, 2002; and "Televangelist Urges Chavez Assassination," *Los Angeles Times*, August 23, 2006, p. A17.

5. Scott Sagan, "Rules of Engagement," *Security Studies*, Vol. 1, no. 1 (Autumn 1991), pp. 78–108.

6. The dataset compiled for this book includes all known U.S. unmanned drone attacks in Pakistan through June 1, 2008. It does not include unmanned drone attacks between June 2008 and June 2009. The reason is that in the June-July 2008 timeframe, President George W. Bush authorized a vast expansion in the scope and intensity of the use of the drones. As David Sanger reported, Bush lowered the threshold for an attack to what an anonymous U.S. official described as the "reasonable man" standard: "If it seemed reasonable, you could hit it." Consequently, while there were eleven known U.S. drone strikes in Pakistan between 2005 and June 2008, there have been over sixty from June 2008 to June 2009. This remarkable increase in covert operations has prevented journalists or researchers from consistently reporting on each individual strike. Thus, it is impossible to capture or evaluate whether the most recent drone attacks have met their intended political and military objectives. See Sanger, *The Inheritance: The World Obama Confronts and the Challenges to American Power* (New York: Harmony Books), p. 250.

7. This work relies on Clausewitz's insight that recent uses of military force are the most instructive for studying the phenomenon. As he noted, "The further back one goes, the less useful military history becomes, growing poorer and barer at the same time." *On War*, p. 173.

8. Department of Defense, "Fiscal Year 2011 Budget Request Overview" (Washington, DC: Office of the Under Secretary of Defense (Comptroller), February 2010); and Office of the Director of National Intelligence, "Media Conference Call with the Director of National Intelligence, Mr. Dennis Blair," September 15, 2009.

9. U.S. Army Field Manual 3.0, *Operations* (Washington, DC: Headquarters, Department of the Army, February 27, 2008), pp. 2-3–2-13.

10. While this book evaluates the direct political and military effects of DMOs on a specific adversary, the effects of DMOs on proximate and extended audiences is also an important topic in need of its own systematic research agenda and literature.

11. Despite its widespread use, this author cannot determine the origin of the term *theory of victory*. The earliest use uncovered was by Herman Kahn in "Issues of Thermonuclear War Termination," *Annals of the American Academy of Political and Social Science*, Vol. 392, no. 1 (November 1970), p. 164. Barry Posen defines a theory of victory as "a notion of the combination of human and material resources and tactics that [a military organization] believes is most likely to produce success on the battlefield." Posen, "Measuring the European Conventional Balance: Coping with Complexity in Threat Assessments," *International Security*, Vol. 9, no. 3 (Winter 1984–1985), p. 51. See also William Martel, *Victory in War: Foundations of Modern Military Policy* (Cambridge, UK: Cambridge University Press, 2007); and J. Boone Bartholomees, "Theory of Victory," *Parameters* (Summer 2008), pp. 25– 36.

12. "Text of President's Speech on National Drug Control Strategy," *New York Times*, September 6, 1989, p. B6. President Nixon earlier declared a "war on drugs" in 1971.

13. Jonathan M. House, *Combined Arms Warfare in the Twentieth Century* (Lawrence, KS: University Press of Kansas, 2001), pp. 189–230; Michael Carver, "Conventional Warfare in the Nuclear Age," in Peter Paret (ed.), *Makers of Modern Strategy: From Machiavelli to the Modern Age* (Princeton, NJ: Princeton University Press, 1986), pp. 783–789; and Morton Halperin, "Nuclear Weapons and Limited War," *Journal of Conflict Resolution*, Vol. 5, no. 2 (June 1961), pp. 146–166.

14. Robert Osgood, *Limited War: The Challenge to American Strategy* (Chicago: University of Chicago Press, 1957), pp. 1–2. Like NATO's military planners during the Cold War, Osgood believed that "limited war" could include the use of tactical nuclear weapons with the destructive power of up to 15 kilotons. See pp. 251–259. The concept of DMOs used in this book will not include nuclear weapons.

15. A. Hamish Ion and E. J. Errington (eds.), *Great Powers and Little Wars: The Limits of Power* (Westport, CT: Praeger, 1993); and Max Boot, *The Savage Wars of Peace: Small Wars and the Rise of American Power* (New York: Basic Books, 2002).

16. Examples include Northern Iraq (1991), Somalia (December 1992–1994), and the Asian tsunami (2004–2005). For an overview of non-DMO limited uses of force, see Daniel Byman, *Keeping the Peace: Lasting Solutions to Ethnic Conflicts* (Baltimore: Johns Hopkins University, 2002), pp. 177–212.

17. Examples include Kosovo (June 1999–present), Iraq (May 2003–present), and Afghanistan (December 2001–present).

18. Alan Vick, David T. Orletsky, Abram N. Shulsky, and John Stillion, *Preparing the U.S. Air Force for Military Operations Other Than War* (Santa Monica, CA: RAND, 1997), Appendix A, "USAF MOOTW Operations, 1916–1996."

19. U.S. Department of Justice, *Report to the Deputy Attorney General on the Events at Waco, Texas: February 28 to April 19, 1993* (Washington, DC: Department of Justice, October 8, 1993).

20. Ann Scott Tyson and Robin Wright, "U.S. Helps Turkey Hit Rebel Kurds in Iraq," *Washington Post*, December 18, 2007, p. A1; and Yochi Dreazen, "Turkey Told U.S. About Strike Plan," *Wall Street Journal*, February 27, 2008, p. A10.

21. Scott Johnson, "Hard Target: The Hunt for Africa's Last Warlord," *Newsweek*, May 25, 2009, p. 61.

22. Interview with Gen. David Petraeus, February 10, 2010; Dana Priest, "U.S. Playing Key Role in Yemen Attacks," *Washington Post*, January 27, 2010, p. A1; and Eric Schmitt and Robert Worth, "U.S. Widens Terror War to Yemen, a Qaeda Bastion," *New York Times*, December 28, 2009, p. A1.

23. William C. Wohlforth, "The Stability of a Unipolar World," *International Security*, Vol. 24, no. 1 (Summer 1999), pp. 5–41; and Daniel Nexon and Thomas Wright, "What's at Stake in the American Empire Debate," *American Political Science Review*, Vol. 101, no. 2 (May 2007), pp. 253–271.

24. Stephen Biddle, *American Grand Strategy After 9/11: An Assessment* (Carlisle, PA: Strategic Studies Institute, U.S. Army War College, April 2005), pp. 3–5.

25. Micah Zenko, "Speeding Up: The Global Trend Toward Rapidly-Deployable Forces," International Studies Association Conference, March 2003.

26. William Arkin, "War Games," Early Warning blog, *Washington Post*, November 4, 2005, http://washingtonpost.com; and Arkin, "War Plans Meaner, Not Leaner," *Los Angeles Times*, March 21, 2004, p. M1. According to Arkin, the United States has seventy war plans.

27. Sarah McLaughlin Mitchell and Will Moore, "Presidential Uses of Force During the Cold War: Aggregation, Truncation, and Temporal Dynamics," *American Journal of Political Science*, Vol. 46, no. 2 (April 2002), pp. 438–452.

28. Ward Thomas, *The Ethics of Destruction: Norms and Force in International Relations* (Ithaca, NY: Cornell University Press, 2001). Although DMOs are perceived as a more usable option, this does not mean they are the preferred option, especially among senior military officials.

29. Richard Eichenberg, "Victory Has Many Friends: U.S. Public Opinion and the Use of Military Force, 1981–2005," *International Security*, Vol. 30, no. 1 (Summer 2005).

30. One Clinton administration NSC staffer recalled the large ground combat proposals presented by the military as "the usual two-division, $2 billion option." Daniel Benjamin and Steven Simon, *The Age of Sacred Terror* (New York: Random House, 2002), p. 294. See also testimony of Lt. Gen. Barry McCaffrey before the Senate Armed Services Committee, "Situation in Bosnia and Appropriate Western Responses," August 11, 1992; David Halberstam, *War in a Time of Peace: Bush, Clinton, and the Generals* (New York: Scribner, 2001), p. 45; Richard Clarke, *Against All Enemies: Inside America's War on Terrorism* (New York: Free Press, 2004), pp. 143–144; and Richard H. Shultz Jr., "Showstoppers: Nine Reasons Why We Never Sent Our Special Operations Forces After Al Qaeda Before 9/11," *Weekly Standard*, January 26, 2004. In fall 1998, when the Pentagon presented a range of options to the White House for stopping Serbian ethnic cleansing in Kosovo, the largest included deploying as many as 200,000 NATO troops. As a senior administration official stated, "The numbers came in high. No one said yes, no one said no; it was taken off the table. . . . It was a complete eye-roller." John F. Harris, "Advice Didn't Sway Clinton on Airstrikes," *Washington Post*, April 1, 1999, p. A1.

31. Howard Fineman, "A President Finds His True Voice," *Newsweek*, September 24, 2001, p. 50.

32. National Commission on Terrorist Attacks Upon the United States, *9/11 Commission Report* (New York: W.W. Norton, 2004), p. 189; and Benjamin and Simon, *The Age of Sacred Terror*, p. 318. For Clinton's interest in using limited force, see William J. Clinton, *My Life* (New York: Knopf, 2004), p. 804; George Stephanopoulos, *All Too Human* (Boston: Little, Brown, 1999), pp. 217–218; and Halberstam, *War in a Time of Peace*, p. 317.

33. Anonymous (later revealed as Michael Scheur), "Note to the Members of the Senate Select Committee on Intelligence," date September or October 2004, as printed in "How *Not* to Catch a Terrorist," *Atlantic Monthly*, December 2004, p. 52; and National Commission on Terrorist Attacks, *9/11 Commission Report*, pp. 119–143.

34. Russell Weigley, *The American War of War: A History of U.S. Military Strategy and Policy* (New York: Macmillan, 1973); F. G. Hoffman, *Decisive Force: The New American Way of War* (Westport, CT: Praeger, 1996), pp. 8–12; Ralph Peters, "In Praise of Attrition," *Parameters*, Summer 2004, pp. 24–32; and Shultz Jr., "Showstoppers."

35. Andrew Krepinevich, *The Army and Vietnam* (Baltimore: Johns Hopkins University Press, 1984); Deborah Avant, *Political Institutions and Military Change: Lessons from Peripheral Wars* (Ithaca, NY: Cornell University Press, 1994); and David Johnson, *Preparing Potential Senior Army Leaders for the Future: An Assessment of Leader Development Efforts in the Post–Cold War Era* (Santa Monica, CA: RAND, 2002).

36. As General Colin Powell wrote in a *New York Times* op-ed during a national

debate about using DMOs in Bosnia: "Decisive means and results are always to be pre-ferred, even if they are not always possible. So you bet I get nervous when so-called experts suggest that all we need is a little surgical bombing or a limited attack. When the desired result isn't obtained, a new set of experts then comes forward with talk of a little escalation." Powell, "Why Generals Get Nervous," *New York Times,* October 8, 1992, p. A35.

37. From interviews and Halberstam, *War in a Time of Peace;* Tommy Franks, with Malcolm McConnell, *American Soldier* (New York: HarperCollins, 2004), pp. 250–251; Bob Woodward, *The Commanders* (New York: Pocket Star Books, 1991), pp. 214, 220; Shultz Jr., "Showstoppers"; and National Commission on Terrorist Attacks, *9/11 Commission Report,* p. 351.

38. Richard Betts, *Soldiers, Statesmen, and Cold War Crises,* 2nd ed. (New York: Columbia University Press, 1991), p. 170.

39. J. F. Guilmartin Jr., *A Very Short War: The Mayaguez and the Battle of Koh Tang* (College Station, TX: Texas A&M Press, 1995).

40. Department of Defense, Adm. J. L. Holloway III, chair, *Rescue Mission Report* (Washington, DC: Government Printing Office, August 23, 1980). *Desert One* was a hostage-rescue operation deep into an adversary's territory that was expected to include extensive casualties and destruction. Therefore, it would be considered a DMO.

41. David C. Wills, *The First War on Terrorism: Counter-Terrorism Policy During the Reagan Administration* (Lanham, MD: Rowman and Littlefield, 2003), pp. 76–77.

42. William Arkin, "America Cluster Bombs Iraq," Early Warning blog, *Washington Post,* February 26, 2001 (http://washingtonpost.com).

43. Under the War Powers Resolution of 1973, the president is required to notify Congress of the "introduction of United States Armed Forces into hostilities, or into situations where imminent involvement in hostilities is clearly indicated by the circum-stances, and to the continued use of such forces in hostilities or in such situations." Most DMOs are accompanied by a presidential notification to Congress "consistent with the War Powers Resolution" only after the attack is under way. Some DMOs, such as the December 1998 attacks on suspected Iraqi WMD facilities and regime military targets, are never reported to Congress. Other times, senior congressional members are never told (February 16, 2001, bombing of Iraq), or are told at the last minute (1986 attack on Libya). Other DMOs, under George W. Bush, have fallen under the blanket notification to Congress of being "in support of the global war on terrorism." See Richard F. Grim-mett, *The War Powers Resolution: After Thirty Years,* Congressional Research Service (CRS), Report RL32267, March 11, 2004; Grimmett, *War Powers Resolution: Presidential Compliance,* CRS, Report IB81050, May 24, 2005; James Dao and Steven Lee Myers, "U.S. and British Jets Strike Air-Defense Centers in Iraq," *New York Times,* February 17, 2001, p. A1; and Barry Blechman, *The Politics of National Security: Congress and U.S. Defense Policy* (Oxford, UK: Oxford University Press, 1992).

44. Peter Feaver and Christopher Gelpi, *Choosing Your Battles: American Civil-Military Relations and the Use of Force* (Princeton, NJ: Princeton University Press, 2004), p. 53.

45. Colin Powell, with Joseph E. Persico, *My American Journey* (New York: Ballantine Books, 1995); Wesley Clark, *Waging Modern War: Bosnia, Kosovo, and the Future of Combat* (New York: Public Affairs, 2001); Jacob Van Staaveren, *Gradual Failure: The Air War Over North Vietnam, 1965–1966* (Washington, DC: United States Air Force, 2002); and Mark Clodfelter, *The Limits of Air Power: The American Bombing of North Vietnam* (New York: Free Press, 1989).

46. Jonathan Mercer, *Reputation and International Politics* (Ithaca, NY: Cornell University Press, 1996); and Daryl Press, "Does Backing Down Damage Credibility? Evidence from the 'Appeasement Crises,'" *International Security*, Vol. 29, no. 3 (Winter 2004-2005), pp. 136–169.

47. The phrase "all or nothing" as a description of the U.S. military's preference for using force is traced to Les Aspin, while he was chairman of the House Armed Services Committee. Aspin, "Role of U.S. Military in Post–Cold War World," address before the Jewish Institute for National Security Affairs, September 21, 1992.

48. Eliot Cohen, "The Mystique of U.S. Air Power," *Foreign Affairs*, January-February 1994, p. 109.

49. The day-to-day enforcement of the northern and southern Iraqi no-fly zones is counted as one DMO. Each attack against the territory of Iraq—located between the southern and northern no-fly zones—is counted as another DMO. The distinction is justified because the strikes against central Iraq were in pursuit of a different set of political and military goals, were larger and more lethal, and each required specific presidential authorization.

50. See Chapter 3.

51. See Chapter 4.

52. See Chapter 5.

53. See Chapter 6.

54. Van Evera, *Guide to Methods for Students of Political Science*, (Ithaca, NY: Cornell University Press, 1997), pp. 77–88.

55. For rules to selecting negative cases, see Gary Goertz, *Social Science Concepts: A User's Guide* (Princeton, NJ: Princeton University Press, 2006), pp. 177–210.

56. Kenneth Pollack, *The Persian Puzzle: The Conflict Between Iran and America* (New York: Random House, 2004), pp. 284–285, 291; and Clarke, *Against All Enemies*, pp. 118–121.

57. Robert Gates, *From the Shadows: The Ultimate Insider's Story of Five Presidents and How They Won the Cold War* (New York: Simon and Schuster, 1996), pp. 497–498.

58. Evan Thomas, "Into Thin Air," *Newsweek*, September 3, 2007, p. 24; and Mark Mazzetti, "U.S. Aborted Raid Against Al Qaeda in Pakistan in '05," *New York Times*, July 8, 2007, pp. 1, 6.

Chapter 2

1. Kenneth Waltz, *Theory of International Politics* (Boston: McGraw-Hill, 1979), p. 113.

2. Thucydides, *History of the Peloponnesian War*, trans. Rex Warner (London, UK: Penguin Group, 1954), p. 84.

3. Robert Gates, *From the Shadows: The Ultimate Insider's Story of Five Presidents and How They Won the Cold War* (New York: Simon and Schuster, 1996), p. 275.

4. Carl von Clausewitz, *On War*, trans. and ed. Michael Howard and Peter Paret (Princeton, NJ: Princeton University Press, 1984), p. 69.

5. Rupert Smith, *The Utility of Force: The Art of War in the Modern World* (New York: Alfred Knopf, 2007), p. 13.

6. Thomas Schelling, "Bargaining, Communication, and Limited War," *Conflict Resolution*, Vol. 1, no. 1 (March 1957), p. 19.

7. Thomas Schelling, *Arms and Influence* (New Haven, CT: Yale University Press, 1966), p. 10.

8. Ibid, pp. 1–34.

9. For other early contributors to these typologies see Morton Kaplan, *The Strategy of Limited Retaliation* (Princeton, NJ: Center of International Studies, Woodrow Wilson School of Public and International Affairs, 1959); Robert Osgood, *Limited War: The Challenge to American Strategy* (Chicago: University of Chicago Press, 1957); Henry Kissinger, *The Necessity for Choice* (New York: Harper and Row, 1961); and Daniel Ellsberg, "The Theory and Practice of Blackmail," lecture at the Lowell Institute, Boston, March 10, 1959; reprinted by the RAND Corporation in July 1968. These are by no means the only types of political uses of military force. Robert Art, for example, has presented the diffuse category of *swaggering*: peaceful use of force with the goal of "displaying one's military might" or to "enhance the national pride of a people or to satisfy the personal ambitions of its ruler." See Art, "To What Ends Military Power?" *International Security*, Vol. 4, no. 4 (Spring 1980), p. 10.

10. Alexander George and Richard Smoke, *Deterrence in American Foreign Policy: Theory and Practice* (New York: Columbia University Press, 1974), p. 11.

11. White House, "President Bush's Statement on North Korea Nuclear Test," Washington, DC, Office of the Press Secretary, October 9, 2006.

12. Barton Gellman, "The Path to Crisis: How the United States and Its Allies Went to War," *Washington Post*, April 18, 1999, p. A30.

13. Ivo Daalder and Michael O'Hanlon, *Winning Ugly: NATO's War to Save Kosovo* (Washington, DC: Brookings Institution Press, 2000), pp. 27–28.

14. Patrick Morgan, *Deterrence: A Conceptual Analysis*, 2nd ed. (Beverly Hills, CA: Sage, 1983); and Paul Huth and Bruce Russett, "General Deterrence Between Enduring Rivals: Testing Three Competing Models," *American Political Science Review*, Vol. 87, no. 1 (March 1993), pp. 61–73.

15. White House, "Address to a Joint Session of Congress and the American People," Washington, DC, Office of the Press Secretary, September 20, 2001.

16. See Appendix I for descriptions of both of these DMOs.

17. There are many ways to define *coercive diplomacy*. This section uses the term interchangeably with *compellence* following scholars such as Paul Gordon Lauren, Gordon A. Craig, and Alexander George, *Force and Statecraft: Diplomatic Challenges of Our Time*, 2nd ed., (New York: Oxford University Press, 1990), p. 197; Barry Posen, "Military Responses to Refugee Disasters," *International Security*, Vol. 21, no. 1 (1996), p. 85; and Forest Morgan, *Compellence and the Strategic Culture of Imperial Japan: Implications for Coercive-Diplomacy in the Twenty-First Century* (Boulder, CO: Praeger, 2003).

18. Ivo Daalder, *Getting to Dayton: The Making of America's Bosnia Policy* (Washington, DC: Brookings Institution Press, 2000); Daalder and O'Hanlon, *Winning Ugly*; Micah Zenko, "Coercive Diplomacy Before the War in Kosovo: America's Approach in 1998," Pew Case Studies in International Affairs, Case 252, (Washington, DC: Institute For the Study of Diplomacy, Georgetown University, 2001). James A. Baker III, Secretary of State in the George H.W. Bush administration, wrote in his memoirs of the U.S. mission in the Persian Gulf in August 1990 as "undoing of Iraq's invasion of Kuwait by the pursuit of a policy of coercive diplomacy against Saddam Hussein." Baker III, with Thomas M. DeFrank, *The Politics of Diplomacy: Revolution, War and Peace, 1989–1992* (New York: G.P. Putnam's Sons, 1995), p. 277. William Perry, Secretary of Defense, explained the U.S. approach to North Korea in 1994: "We felt if we could ratchet up on diplomatic pressure, we could probably stop [Pyongyang's nuclear weapons program]. So we set off on a course of what could fairly be called 'coercive diplomacy.' It was diplomacy, but it was diplomacy that was backed with a very credible threat of military force." See PBS, *Frontline*, "Kim's Nuclear Gamble," April 10, 2003.

19. CNN, Presidential Debate hosted by Wolf Blitzer, February 21, 2008. See also Jill Lawrence, "Treatment of Troops 'Outrageous'," *USA Today*, April 12, 2007, p. A6; Jonathan Darman, "'A Much Fuller Understanding'," interview with Hillary Clinton, *Newsweek*, September 17, 2007, p. 33; and CNN, Presidential Debate hosted by Wolf Blitzer, Scott Spradling, and Jennifer Vaughn, June 3, 2007.

20. Peter Baker, Dafna Lizner, and Thomas Ricks, "U.S. Is Studying Military Strike Options on Iran," *Washington Post*, April 9, 2006, p. A1; and Mark Mazzetti, Steven Lee Myers, and Thom Shanker, "Questions Linger Over Scope of Iran's Role in Iraq Fighting," *New York Times*, April 26, 2008, p. A1.

21. Adapted from Alexander George, "The Development of Doctrine and Strategy," in George, David Hall, and William Simons (eds.), *The Limits of Coercive Diplomacy: Laos, Cuba, Vietnam* (Boston: Little, Brown, 1971), pp. 1–35; Alexander George, *Forceful Persuasion: Coercive Diplomacy as an Alternative to War* (Washington, DC: United States Institute of Peace Press, 1991), pp. xii–xiii; and Lauren, Craig, and George, *Force and Statecraft*, pp. 198–219.

22. Robert Art, "Introduction," in Art and Patrick Cronin (eds.), *The United States and Coercive Diplomacy* (Washington, DC: United States Institute of Peace Press, 2003), p. 10.

23. Barry M. Blechman and Stephen S. Kaplan, *Force Without War: U.S. Armed Forces as a Political Instrument* (Washington, DC: Brookings Institution Press, 1978).

24. Philip Zelikow, "The United States and the Use of Force: A Historical Summary," in George Osborn and Asa Clark (eds.), *Democracy, Strategy, and Vietnam: Implications for American Policymaking* (Lexington, MA: D.C. Heath, 1987), pp. 31–81. See also Zelikow, "Force Without War, 1975–82," *Journal of Strategic Studies*, Vol. 7, no. 1 (March 1984), pp. 29–54. For another scholar who utilized Blechman and Kaplan's typology of non-kinetic political uses of force, see James David Meernik, *The Political Use of Military Force in U.S. Foreign Policy* (Burlington, VT: Ashgate, 2004).

25. George, *Forceful Persuasion*; and Art and Cronin (eds.), *The United States and Coercive Diplomacy*.

26. Daniel Byman and Matthew Waxman, *The Dynamics of Coercion: American Foreign Policy and the Limits of Military Might* (Cambridge, UK: Cambridge University Press, 2002), p. 58.

27. Peter Feaver, "Civil-Military Relations," *Annual Review of Political Science*, Vol. 2, no. 1 (1999), pp. 211–241.

28. Richard Betts, *Soldiers, Statesmen, and Cold War Crises*, 2nd ed. (New York: Columbia University Press, 1991), p. 4.

29. The "senior" designation used throughout the book refers to officials that participate in debates over military options within the Joint Chiefs of Staff, geographic Combatant Commands, Joint Staff, Office of the Secretary of Defense—and affiliated civilian offices, or at the Deputies or Principals Committee level of the National Security Council. See "Appendix: Civilian and Military Elites," in Thomas Szayna, et al., *The Civil-Military Gap in the United States: Does It Exist, Why, and Does It Matter?* (Santa Monica, CA: RAND, 2007), pp. 161–169.

30. Harry Summers, *On Strategy: A Critical Analysis of the Vietnam War* (Novato, CA: Presidio Press, 1982); Andrew Krepinevich Jr., *The Army and Vietnam* (Baltimore: Johns Hopkins University Press, 1986); and David Petraeus, *The American Military and the Lessons of Vietnam: A Study of Military Influence and the Use of Force in the Post-Vietnam Era*, Princeton University, unpublished dissertation, 1987, pp. 256–265.

31. For one expression of this frustration from a retired senior military official, see Richard Myers, with Malcolm McConnell, *Eyes on the Horizon: Serving on the Front Lines of National Security* (New York: Threshold Editions, 2009), pp. 59–60.

32. Peter Feaver, *Armed Servants: Agency, Oversight, and Civil-Military Relations* (Cambridge, MA: Harvard University Press, 2003), p. 59. See also Peter H. Wilson, "Defining Military Culture," *Journal of Military History*, Vol. 72, no. 1 (January 2008), pp. 11–41.

33. Interview with Professor Robert Baumann, U.S. Army Command and General Staff College, February 6, 2007.

34. Joint Publication 1-02, "DOD Dictionary of Military and Associated Terms." As amended through March 4, 2008.

35. Cheryl Marcum et al., *Department of Defense Political Appointments: Positions and Process* (Santa Monica, CA: RAND, 2001), pp. 15–16.

36. Colin S. Gray, *Modern Strategy* (Oxford, UK: Oxford University Press, 1999), p. 61.

37. These differ from the "All or Nothing" and "Limited War" schools utilized by Christopher Gacek, who described the beliefs of military and civilian officials for all uses of force. See Gacek, *The Logic of Force: The Dilemma of Limited War in American Foreign Policy* (New York: Columbia University Press, 1994).

38. *Webster's Third New International Dictionary, Unabridged,* Merriam-Webster online, 2002.

39. Interview with Gen. Jack Keane, September 27, 2006. As Gen. Colin Powell would repeat in Principals Committee debates, in 1993, over U.S. military options for Bosnia-Herzegovina: "Tell me what the objective is, and I'll tell you what it will take and what the consequences are." Elizabeth Drew, *On the Edge: The Clinton Presidency* (New York: Simon and Schuster), p. 149.

40. For an example of one senior military officer opposed to the Powell Doctrine, see Tom Clancy, with Tony Zinni and Tony Koltz, *Battle Ready* (New York: G.P. Putnam's Sons, 2004), p. 424.

41. Betts, *Soldiers, Statesmen, and Cold War Crises,* 2nd ed., p. 214.

42. David C. Wills, *The First War on Terrorism: Counter-Terrorism Policy During the Reagan Administration* (Lanham, MD: Rowman and Littlefield, 2003), p. 173

43. Peter Feaver and Christopher Gelpi, *Choosing Your Battles: American Civil-Military Relations and the Use of Force* (Princeton, NJ: Princeton University Press, 2004), pp. 5 and 53; Ole Holsti, "Of Chasms and Convergences: Attitudes and Beliefs of Civilian and Military Elites at the Start of a New Millennium," in Feaver and R. H. Kohn (eds.), *Soldiers and Civilians: The Civil-Military Gap and American National Security* (Cambridge, MA: MIT Press, 2001), p. 39; Szayna et al., *The Civil-Military Gap in the United States,* pp. 141–145; Alice E. Hunt, *Civil-Military Relations and Humanitarian Intervention: A Re-examination of the Politics of Military Advice and the Use of Force,* unpublished master's thesis, American University, 2006; Feaver, *Armed Servants,* p. 52; Todd Sechser, "Are Soldiers Less War-Prone Than Statesmen?," *Journal of Conflict Resolution,* Vol. 48, no. 5 (October 2004), pp. 746–774; Michael Desch, *Civilian Control of the Military: The Changing Security Environment* (Baltimore: Johns Hopkins University Press, 1999), pp. 22–38; Charles Fairbanks, "War-Limiting," in Klaus Knorr (ed.), *Historical Dimensions of National Security Problems* (Lawrence, KS: University Press of Kansas, 1976), p. 175; and Gacek, *The Logic of Force.*

44. For a good account of this bargaining process, in the case of the April 1986 raid on Tripoli, Libya, see William Crowe Jr., with David Chanoff, *The Line of Fire: From Washington to the Gulf, the Politics and Battles of the New Military* (New York: Simon and Schuster, 1993), pp. 132–145.

45. Baker III, with DeFrank, *The Politics of Diplomacy*, pp. 648–651; and Daalder, *Getting to Dayton*, pp. 6–7.

46. Interview with Gen. Barry McCaffrey, February 13, 2007.

47. Hearing before the Senate Armed Services Committee, "Situation in Bosnia and Appropriate U.S. and Western Responses," August 11, 1992. After his Senate testimony, McCaffrey was asked by Powell, "Where the fuck did you get those numbers?" McCaffrey replied, "I made them up, based on my understanding of the parties and the situation. I know more about Bosnia than anyone I know." Interview with McCaffrey, February 13, 2007.

48. Remarkably, Halberstam goes on to note that "One reason [Powell] had always put the number of troops needed to do the job so high—over two hundred thousand—was *not necessarily that he felt it would take that many*. It was a test for civilians. How much do you really want this, how high a price are you willing to pay? Are you willing to cover worst-case scenario possibilities?" (emphasis added). See Halberstam, *War in a Time of Peace: Bush, Clinton, and the Generals* (New York: Scribner, 2001), pp. 36 and 42.

49. Confirmed in interviews with George H.W. Bush, Clinton, and George W. Bush administration officials. See also George H.W. Bush and Brent Scowcroft, *A World Transformed* (New York: Alfred A. Knopf, 1998), pp. 431–432; Wesley Clark, *Waging Modern War: Bosnia, Kosovo, and the Future of Combat* (New York: Public Affairs, 2001), p. 440; Hunt, *Civil-Military Relations and Humanitarian Intervention*, p. 113; Tim Wiener, "U.S. Cancels Plans for Raid on Bosnia to Capture 2 Serbs," *New York Times*, July 26, 1998, p. 1; John Harris, "Advice Didn't Sway Clinton on Airstrikes," *Washington Post*, April 1, 1999, p. A1; Richard H. Shultz Jr., "Showstoppers: Nine Reasons Why We Never Sent Our Special Operations Forces After Al Qaeda Before 9/11," *Weekly Standard*, January 26, 2004; Daniel Benjamin and Steven Simon, *The Age of Sacred Terror* (New York: Random House, 2002), pp. 294–296 and 318–320; Mark Mazzetti, "U.S. Aborted Raid Against Al Qaeda in Pakistan in '05," *New York Times*, July 8, 2007, p. 1; and CBS News, reported by Chip Reid, "McChrystal Wanted 50,000 Troops," October 7, 2009.

50. Bush and Scowcroft, *A World Transformed*, p. 431.

51. Feaver, *Armed Servants*, pp. 58–75.

52. As Rupert Smith has warned, "Politicians quite rightly expect the military to respond to their requirements, but too often do so without any comprehension of the practical considerations of the matter, let alone conceptual ones. If force is to continue to be used, and to have utility, this situation must change." Smith, *The Utility of Force*, p. xiv. For someone who defends the right of civilians to choose to use force in a way that

seems "unmilitary" to senior officers, see Martin Cook, "The Proper Role of Military Advice in Contemporary Uses of Force," *Parameters* (Winter 2002–2003), pp. 21–33.

53. State Department Memorandum to the President, June 28, 1961, *Foreign Relations of the United States, Berlin Crisis 1961–1962*.

54. The military was so opposed to the NSC effort that, according to Wills, "The Pentagon did as it was asked but in a way that was sure to be rejected; planners designed an invasion that required at least three divisions be pulled from Europe." Wills, *The First War on Terrorism*, p. 173. In Bob Woodward's reporting of the incident, "The Pentagon argued that an American military operation might eventually require six divisions, 90,000 men. Pentagon planners were asking, for practical purposes, 'Do we want a war with Libya?'" Woodward, *Veil: The Secret Wars of the CIA, 1981–1987* (New York: Simon and Schuster, 1987), p. 420.

55. National Commission on Terrorist Attacks Upon the United States, *9/11 Commission Report* (New York: W.W. Norton, 2004), p. 189; and Benjamin and Simon, *The Age of Sacred Terror*, p. 318.

56. Interview with Clinton administration Pentagon official, June 4, 2009.

57. Gates, *From the Shadows*, p. 559. Or, as Gates noted more colorfully in 1996, "I have seen a lot of civilians make a lot of proposals for a lot of silly military actions that eventually did not take place." PBS, *Frontline*, "The Gulf War," January 9, 1996.

58. Interview with Gen. Richard Myers, October 8, 2007. It can be added that many people wearing military uniforms do not understand how to provide politically aware military advice. E-mail communication with Col. Kevin Benson, July 10, 2008.

Chapter 3

1. Methodological note: While the American enforcement of the northern and southern Iraqi NFZs is counted as one DMO, the six attacks against the Iraq territory located in-between the NFZs are each counted as separate DMOs—three in 1993 and one each in 1996, 1998, and 2001. This distinction between these six DMOs and the NFZs is justified because each strike against central Iraq was in pursuit of a distinct set of political and military goals, they were larger and more lethal in nature, and they required specific presidential authorization. Furthermore, while the Iraqi NFZs are considered one DMO, the NFZ enforced by NATO over Bosnia between October 1992 and December 1995 is not. This distinction arises because, unlike in Iraq, NATO's rules of engagement (ROE) for the Bosnian NFZ were so severely proscribed that pilots were not permitted to shoot down Serbian, Bosnian Muslim, or Croatian planes that flew in violation. With one exception, the Bosnian NFZ went unenforced. NATO did, however, bomb Serb ground and air forces, airfields, and command and control bunkers. Since these raids were only conducted by U.S. pilots, each is counted as a separate DMO in this work's dataset. See Ronald Reed, "Chariots of Fire: Rules of Engagement in Operation Deliberate Force," in Roger Owen (ed.), *Deliberate Force: A Case Study for Effective Air Campaigning* (Maxwell,

AL: Air University Press, 2000), pp. 394–406; NATO, Air Force South Fact Sheet, updated: July 18, 2003; and Roberto Corsini, "The Balkan War: What Role for Airpower?" *Airpower Journal*, Winter 1995. As Madeline Albright, U.S. Ambassador to the UN at the time, admitted in her autobiography, "We voted to enforce no-fly zones, but the Serbs violated them hundreds of times without paying a significant price." See Albright, with Bill Woodward, *Madame Secretary* (New York: Miramax Books, 2003), p. 181.

2. President George H.W. Bush, "Remarks to the American Association for the Advancement of Science," and "Remarks to Raytheon Missile Systems Plant Employees in Andover, Massachusetts," February 15, 1991.

3. Andrew Cockburn and Patrick Cockburn, *Out of the Ashes: The Resurrection of Saddam Hussein* (New York: HarperCollins, 1999), p. 13; and Michael Gordon and Bernard Trainor, *The Generals' War: The Inside of the Conflict in the Gulf* (Boston: Little, Brown, 1994), pp. 434–435.

4. Ofra Bengio, "Baghdad Between Shi'a and Kurds," *Policy Focus* no. 18, Washington Institute for Near East Policy, February 1992, p. 26, fn 44.

5. Jonathan Randal, "Kurdish Uprising Aided by Clandestine Army Contacts," *Washington Post*, March 23, 1991, p. A1; and Human Rights Watch, "Iraq and Occupied Kuwait," *World Report 1992*.

6. Human Rights Watch, "Iraq and Occupied Kuwait," *World Report 1992*.

7. Jonathan Randal, "Kurdish Troops Reported Set to Join Rebellion," *Washington Post*, March 7, 1991, p. A31.

8. Cockburn and Cockburn, *Out of the Ashes*, p. 20; and Jonathan Randal and Valerie Strauss, "Rebels Said to Control Much of Northern Iraq," *Washington Post*, March 15, 1991, p. A37.

9. H. Norman Schwarzkopf, with Peter Petre, *The Autobiography: It Doesn't Take a Hero* (New York: Bantam Books, 1992), p. 489; PBS, Schwarzkopf interview with David Frost, March 27, 1991; and Ann Devroy and Molly Moore, "Winning the War and Struggling with Peace," *Washington Post*, April 14, 1991, p. A1.

10. George H.W. Bush and Brent Scowcroft, *A World Transformed* (New York: Alfred A. Knopf, 1998), p. 490.

11. Eric Schmitt, "Allies Tell Iraq Not to Fly Planes," *New York Times*, March 18, 1991, p. 1.

12. Barton Gellman, "U.S. Downs Iraqi Jet as Insurgency Continues," *Washington Post*, March 21, 1991, p. A1.

13. The Iraqi regime also did not violate an American-imposed condition of the Safwan Accords that they refrain from using chemical weapons against the Kurds or the Shias.

14. Gordon and Trainor, *The Generals' War*, p. 455.

15. Kenneth Pollack, *The Threatening Storm: The Case for Invading Iraq* (New York: Random House, 2002), p. 51.

16. James A. Baker III, with Thomas M. DeFrank, *The Politics of Diplomacy:*

Revolution, War and Peace, 1989–1992 (New York: G.P. Putnam's Sons, 1995), pp. 438–439; Bush and Scowcroft, *A World Transformed*, pp. 488–492; and Elizabeth Drew, "Letter from Washington," *New Yorker*, May 6, 1991. In fact, the United States actively restrained the uprisings by destroying captured Iraqi weapons and munitions stockpiles, returning them to the Iraqis, or transferring them to the mujahideen in Afghanistan. See Steve Coll, *Ghost Wars: The Secret History of the CIA, Afghanistan, and Bin Laden, from the Soviet Invasion to September 10, 2001* (New York: Penguin Press, 2004), p. 226; and Ronald Brown, *Humanitarian Operations in Northern Iraq, 1991: With Marines in Operation Provide Comfort* (Washington, DC: Headquarters, U.S. Marine Corps, 1995), p. 72.

17. Jonathan Randal, *After Such Knowledge, What Forgiveness?: My Encounters with Kurdistan* (New York: Farrar, Straus and Giroux, 1997), p. 52.

18. Human Rights Watch/Middle East, *Iraq's Crime of Genocide: The Anfal Campaign Against the Kurds* (New Haven, CT: Yale University Press, 1995), pp. 262–265.

19. PBS, "Saddam's Road to Hell," *Frontline* broadcast, January 24, 2006.

20. UN, Security Council Resolution 688, April 5, 1991.

21. Blaine Harden, "Turkey to Move Iraqi Refugees," *Washington Post*, April 16, 1991, p. A1. Though there were three times more Kurdish refugees in Iran than in Turkey, the U.S.-led coalition did not assist them. The U.S. spokesman for Operation Provide Comfort, Cmdr. John Woodhouse, stated: "We are not in the business of trying to supply aid along the Iranian border." See Blaine Harden, "U.S., Iraqi Officers to Meet on Aid Plan," *Washington Post*, April 19, 1991, p. A1.

22. Elaine Sciolino, "U.S. Warns Against Attack by Iraq on Kurdish Refugees," *New York Times*, April 11, 1991, p. 10.

23. Brown, *Humanitarian Operations in Northern Iraq, 1991*, p. 6.

24. Devroy and Moore, "Winning the War and Struggling with Peace," p. A1; and Baker III, with DeFrank, *The Politics of Diplomacy*, pp. 430–435.

25. Brown, *Humanitarian Operations in Northern Iraq, 1991*, pp. 4–5.

26. Interview with Maj. Gen. Scott Gration, April 13, 2006; and Randal, *After Such Knowledge, What Forgiveness?*, p. 67.

27. Barton Gellman, "Last Coalition Units Are Leaving Iraq," *Washington Post*, July 13, 1991, p. A1; and Clyde Haberman, "Allied Strike Force Aimed at Iraq Forms in Turkey," *New York Times*, July 25, 1991, p. 3.

28. Operation Provide Comfort was initially re-dubbed "Operation Poised Hammer," but that name was rejected by Turkey because it was too bellicose. See Haberman, "Allied Strike Force Aimed at Iraq Forms in Turkey," p. 3.

29. UN Security Council Resolution 687, April 3, 1991.

30. UN Security Council Resolution 707, August 15, 1991; and UN Security Council Resolution 715, October 11, 1991. The quote is from Resolution 715.

31. Michael Knights, *Cradle of Conflict: Iraq and the Birth of Modern U.S. Military Power* (Annapolis, MD: Naval Institute Press, 2005), pp. 126–127.

32. The term was first used by White House Press Secretary Marlin Fitzwater on September 26, 1991.

33. Knights, *Cradle of Conflict*, pp. 127–128.

34. Knights, *Cradle of Conflict*, p. 128; and CIA, "The Destruction of Iraq's Southern Marshes," September 1, 1994, declassified April 21, 2001.

35. Eric Schmitt, "Iran Strafes Rebels in Iraq," *New York Times*, April 6, 1992, p. 3; and Knights, *Cradle of Conflict*, p. 128.

36. Robin Wright and William Tuohy, "U.S. Allies to Enforce 'No Fly' Zone," *Los Angeles Times*, August 19, 1992, p. 1.

37. David Fulghum, "Pentagon Halts Planned Attack on Iraqi Sites," *Aviation Week and Space Technology*, August 10, 1992, p. 23; Youssef Ibrahim, "Among the Arabs, Little Enthusiasm," *New York Times*, August 17, 1992, p. 6; and Barton Gellman and Caryle Murphy, "U.N. Pushes Inspections in Iraq," *Washington Post*, August 17, 1992, p. A1.

38. William Beecher, "U.S. Considers New Curbs on Iraq Air Operations," *Minneapolis Star-Tribune*, July 7, 1992, p. A11; and Michael Gordon, "U.S. Thinks Iraq Prepares for Big Push on the Shiites," *New York Times*, August 18, 1992, p. 6.

39. John Lancaster, "'No-Fly Zone' in Iraq Is Set, Scowcroft Says," *Washington Post*, August 20, 1992, p. A24.

40. President George H.W. Bush, "Remarks on Hurricane Andrew and the Situation in Iraq and an Exchange with Reporters," August 26, 1992.

41. Michael Gordon, "Most Iraqi Planes Leave South, but Mirages Arrive," *New York Times*, August 26, 1992, p. 10.

42. "No-Fly in Iraq. Why?," *New York Times*, August 28, 1992, p. 24; "'No Fly' Zone Doesn't Fly," *Boston Globe*, August 21, 1992, p. 18; and Douglas Jehl and John Broder, "'No-Fly' Zone in Iraq Starts Today, Bush Says," *Los Angeles Times*, August 27, 1992, p. 1.

43. Jehl and Broder, "'No-Fly' Zone in Iraq Starts Today, Bush Says," p. 1.

44. Gellman and Murphy, "U.N. Pushes Inspections in Iraq," *Washington Post*, August 17, 1992, p. A1.

45. Anthony Lake, "From Containment to Engagement," Johns Hopkins University, School of Advanced International Studies, September 21, 1993.

46. Anthony Cordesman and Ahmed Hashim, *Iraq: Sanctions and Beyond* (Boulder, CO: Westview Press, 1997) p. 187; and Michael Gordon, "U.S. Sees Signs of Iraqi Retreat but Continues Buildup," *New York Times*, October 12, 1994, p. A1.

47. Joseph Treaster, "U.S. Jets Fly Dry Runs on Iraq Targets to Show 'We're Here,'" *New York Times*, October 18, 1994, p. A17.

48. National Intelligence Council Memorandum, "Iraq: Refurbished Equipment South of 32 Degrees," November 30, 1995, declassified November 2005.

49. Thomas Lippman and Bradley Graham, "Iraqi Troops Move Near Kuwaiti Border," *Washington Post*, October 8, 1994, p. A1. In this same vein, Clinton administration officials would often express thoughts such as "Thank god we have Saddam Hussein as

an adversary, or else we would have to get real allies." See interview with Clinton administration official, September 2006.

50. UN Security Council Resolution 949, October 15, 1994.

51. Daniel Williams, "U.S., in Easing Pressure on Iraq, Feared Coalition Breakup and Shiite State," *Washington Post*, October 14, 1994, p. A34.

52. John Darnton, "Almost a Nation: The Kurds in Iraq," *New York Times*, January 21, 1994, p. 1.

53. Interview with Maj. Gen. Scott Gration, April 13, 2006.

54. Interview with Maj. Gen. Larry New, August 29, 2006.

55. Interview with Maj. Gen. Scott Gration, April 13, 2006; interview with Maj. Gen. Larry New, August 29, 2006; interview with Michael Knights, September 7, 2006; and Thomas Ricks, "Containing Iraq: A Forgotten Mission," *Washington Post*, October 25, 2000, p. A1.

56. Interview with Vice Adm. Scott Fry, February 16, 2009.

57. Department of Defense Dictionary of Military and Associated Terms, s.v. "Rules of Engagement," http://www.dtic.mil/doctrine/jel/doddict/ (accessed October 20, 2009).

58. Scott Sagan, "Rules of Engagement," *Security Studies*, Vol. 1, no. 1 (Autumn 1991), pp. 78–108.

59. The Turks even placed either a colonel or a lieutenant colonel on board the U.S. Air Force AWACS plane monitoring the northern NFZ. Interview with Maj. Gen. Scott Gration, April 13, 2006; interview with Maj. Gen. Larry New, August 29, 2006; and John Robinson, "Years After the War, Air Force Sharpens Operations Over Iraq," *Defense Daily*, June 14, 1996.

60. Interview with Amb. Marc Grossman, December 8, 2006. According to Grossman, brokering the ROE between the U.S. commanders and Ankara "was a constant and main focus of our attention," which took up "hours, and hours, and hours, and hours."

61. Interview with Maj. Gen. Scott Gration, April 13, 2006; and Ricks, "Containing Iraq," p. A1.

62. Knights, *Cradle of Conflict*, p. 243.

63. Cockburn and Cockburn, *Out of the Ashes*, p. 232.

64. Pollack, *The Threatening Storm*, p. 81

65. Amatzia Baram, *Building Toward Crisis: Saddam Husayn's Strategy for Survival*, Policy Paper no. 47, Washington Institute for Near East Policy, 1998, p. 51.

66. Testimony of Bruce Riedel, Deputy Assistant Secretary of Defense for Near East and South Asian Affairs, before the House Committee on National Security, September 26, 1996; and Pollack, *The Threatening Storm*, p. 82.

67. Knights, *Cradle of Conflict*, p. 155.

68. Interview with Bruce Riedel, January 23, 2007; Tara Soneshine and John Barry, "Putting Iraq on Notice," *Newsweek*, September 9, 1996, p. 48; and Riedel, testimony before the House Committee on National Security.

69. Cockburn and Cockburn, *Out of the Ashes*, p. 242.

70. Interview with Bruce Riedel, January 23, 2007.

71. Pollack, *The Threatening Storm*, p. 83.

72. Knights, *Cradle of Conflict*, p. 154.

73. David Fulghum, "Hard Lessons in Iraq Lead to New Attack Plan as Saddam Rebuilds," *Aviation Week and Space Technology*, September 16, 1996, p. 24.

74. Interview with Clinton administration official, September 27, 2006.

75. E-mail communication with Gen. Wesley Clark, February 28, 2010.

76. Interview with Clinton administration official, September 27, 2006; and Knights, *Cradle of Conflict*, pp. 158–160.

77. David Fulghum and Paul Mann, "No Clear Winners Emerge from U.S.-Iraq Clash," *Aviation Week and Space Technology*, September 9, 1996, p. 35.

78. Baram, *Building Toward Crisis*, p. 51; Cordesman and Hashim, *Iraq: Sanctions and Beyond*, pp. 89–95; Paul K. White, *Crises After the Storm: An Appraisal of U.S. Air Operations in Iraq since the Persian Gulf War*, Washington Institute for Near East Policy, Military Research Paper, no. 2, 1999, p. 48; and Daniel Byman and Matthew Waxman, *Confronting Iraq: U.S. Policy and the Use of Force Since the Gulf War* (Santa Monica, CA: RAND, 2000), pp. 62–63.

79. Andrew Phillips et al., "Why Saddam Won," *Maclean's*, September 16, 1996, p. 16.

80. "Saddam Thumbs His Nose, Barzani Strolls to Power," *Economist*, September 14, 1996, p. 42.

81. "Saddamned," *Economist*, September 7, 1996, p. 17.

82. Testimony of John Deutch before the Senate Select Committee on Intelligence, September 19, 1996.

83. Bruce Clark, "Distractions Get in the Way of Diplomacy," *Financial Times*, April 11, 1997, p. 4; Clark and Roula Khalaf, "U.S. Retreats from Iraq Showdown," *Financial Times*, April 23, 1997, p. 4; Jim Hoagland, "Diplomacy in Denial," *Washington Post*, May 22, 1997, p. A25; and Pollack, *The Threatening Storm*, pp. 86–87.

84. Thomas Ricks, *Fiasco: The American Military Adventure in Iraq* (New York: Penguin Press, 2006), p. 13.

85. Interview with Maj. Gen. Scott Gration, April 13, 2006.

86. Interview with Maj. Gen. Scott Gration, April 13, 2006.

87. Charles Duelfer, *Hide and Seek: The Search for Truth in Iraq* (New York: Public Affairs, 2009), p. 132.

88. Charles Wilson, *Strategic and Tactical Aerial Reconnaissance in the Near East* (Washington, DC: Washington Institute for Near East Policy, 1999), p. 84.

89. Knights, *Cradle of Conflict*, pp. 176–177.

90. Knights, *Cradle of Conflict*, pp. 176–177.

91. Knights, *Cradle of Conflict*, p. 181.

92. John Lancaster and John Harris, "U.S. at Crossroads on Iraq—and Its Choices Appear Bleak," *Washington Post*, November 22, 1997, p. A1.

93. Knights, *Cradle of Conflict*, pp. 183–184.

94. William Arkin, "The Difference Was in the Details," *Washington Post*, January 17, 1999, p. B1.

95. U.S. Senate Armed Services Committee, "Hearing on Military Readiness," statement of Gen. Hugh Shelton, January 5, 1999; and Tom Clancy, with Tony Zinni and Tony Koltz, *Battle Ready* (New York: G.P. Putnam's Sons, 2004), pp. 16–19.

96. Interview with Clinton administration Pentagon official, June 4, 2009.

97. The aspiration to remove Saddam Hussein from power was formalized in the *Iraq Liberation Act of 1998*, public law 105–338, October 31, 1998.

98. Suzanne Chapman, "The War Before the War," *Air Force Magazine*, February 2004. Anonymous parties also reportedly threatened U.S. pilots and their families stationed in the United States. See Terry Boyd, "Northern Watch Keeps a Tight Reign on Iraq," *European Stars and Stripes*, May 8, 2000, p. 3.

99. Robert Wall, "Iraq SAM Firings Trigger U.S. Attacks," *Aviation Week and Space Technology*, January 4, 1999, p. 24; and Wall and David Fulghum, "Aggressive Iraq Violates No-Fly Zones with Aircraft Missiles," *Aviation Week and Space Technology*, January 11, 1999, p. 42.

100. White, *Crises After the Storm*, pp. 62–63.

101. Knights, *Cradle of Conflict*, p. 213.

102. Interview with Vice Adm. Scott Fry, February 16, 2009; and Department of Defense News Briefing, "Subject: Defense Reform Initiative," March 1, 1999.

103. Knights, *Cradle of Conflict*, pp. 217–225.

104. Ron Suskind, *The Price of Loyalty: George W. Bush, the White House, and the Education of Paul O'Neil* (New York: Simon and Schuster, 2004), pp. 70–75.

105. Jim Hoagland, "A Risky No-Fly Zone Over Iraq," *Washington Post*, February 11, 2001, p. B7.

106. Warren Strobel, "Bush Didn't Realize International Weight of Iraq Bomb Raid," *Knight Ridder Tribune*, April 26, 2001; and Knights, *Cradle of Conflict*, pp. 235–237.

107. David Fulghum and Robert Wall, "Strikes Hit Old Targets, Reveal New Problems," *Aviation Week and Space Technology*, February 26, 2001, p. 24; Thomas Ricks, "Bombs in Iraq Raid Fell Wide Of Targets," *Washington Post*, February 22, 2001, p. A1; and William Arkin, "America Cluster Bombs Iraq," *Washington Post*, February 26, 2001. The operation infuriated both Condoleezza Rice and Donald Rumsfeld. Rice was not told that several IADS targets were close enough to Baghdad that they would be seen on CNN broadcasts. President Bush, meanwhile, had his first international visit, with President Vicente Fox of Mexico, upstaged by a military strike against Iraq that was larger than he had thought. Rumsfeld was particularly furious that as Secretary of Defense he was not fully informed of the extent of the mission, and that it took six to ten hours for

him to learn of the results. According to Vice Adm. Scott Fry, the bombing "was a mess, and set the tone for much of the bad blood between Rumsfeld and the military." One senior administration official referred to the result as "a rookie mistake" since "none of us were sufficiently educated to know if this would cause air-raid alarms to go off in Baghdad." Interview with senior Bush administration official, March 2007; interview with Vice Adm. Scott Fry, February 16, 2009; interview with Bush administration official, September 2006; Knights, *Cradle of Conflict*, pp. 236–238; and Bob Woodward, *State of Denial* (New York: Simon and Schuster, 2006), p. 22.

108. Interview with Vice Adm. Scott Fry, February 16, 2009.

109. Bob Woodward, *Plan of Attack* (New York: Simon and Schuster, 2004), p. 14.

110. Woodward, *Plan of Attack*, pp. 11, 64–65.

111. Michael Gordon and Bernard Trainor, *Cobra II: The Inside Story of the Invasion and Occupation of Iraq* (New York: Pantheon Books, 2006), pp. 48–49. According to General Tommy Franks, "Blue would call for air operations followed by ground operations, to establish an enclave inside Iraq that would be expanded by rapidly deploying follow-on forces." See Tommy Franks, with Malcolm McConnell, *American Soldier* (New York: HarperCollins, 2004), p. 363.

112. Secretary of Defense Donald Rumsfeld interview with Bob Woodward, October 23, 2003; as released by the Department of Defense (DoD), April 19, 2004.

113. Russell Watson and Roy Gutman, "Bush vs. Iraq: The Rematch," *Newsweek*, February 26, 2001, p. 38.

114. Michael O'Hanlon, *Defense Policy Choices for the Bush Administration, 2001–05* (Washington, DC: Brookings Institution Press, 2001), pp. 55–57; and Ricks, *Fiasco*, pp. 43–45.

115. Interview with former George W. Bush administration official, July 13, 2006. Former Director of Central Intelligence Stansfield Turner claims, "We did not detect India's preparations for reopening its testing of nuclear weapons, something that should have been discernible from satellite photography. The reason was that the photographic satellites were all focused on Iraq. There, well before our invasion in March 2003, our military had imposed no-fly zones. It was important to the military to keep close track of Iraq's anti-air defenses, which might attack our aircraft on patrol in the no-fly zones." See Turner, *Burn Before Reading: Presidents, CIA Directors, and Secret Intelligence* (New York: Hyperion, 2005), p. 164.

116. John Diamond, "U.S. Rethinks Patrols of Iraq No-Fly Zones," *Chicago Tribune*, March 10, 2001, p. 1; and Diamond, "U.S. Reviews Its Missions in Iraq Zones," *Chicago Tribune*, March 29, 2001, p. 4.

117. Interview with Lt. Gen. Gregory Newbold, August 29, 2006.

118. Thomas Ricks and Alan Sipress, "Cuts Urged in Patrols Over Iraq," *Washington Post*, May 9, 2001, p. A1.

119. Interview with Douglas Feith, August 9, 2006.

120. Department of Defense, "Media Availability with Secretary Rumsfeld," August 3, 2001.

121. Thomas Ricks, "U.S., British Jets Attack Three Iraqi Air Defense Sites," *Washington Post*, August 11, 2001, p. A18; and "Iraqi Missile Nearly Hits U.S. Spy Plane," *Washington Post*, July 26, 2001, p. A4.

122. Interview with Lt. Gen. Gregory Newbold, August 29, 2006.

123. Woodward, *Plan of Attack*, p. 121.

124. Woodward, *Plan of Attack*, p. 25.

125. Franks, with McConnell, *American Soldier*, pp. 346–352.

126. Interviews with Bush administration officials; Susan Page et al., "Iraq Course Set from Tight White House Circle," *USA Today*, September 11, 2002, p. A1; and Ivo Daalder and James Lindsay, *America Unbound: The Bush Revolution in Foreign Policy* (Washington, DC: Brookings Institution Press, 2003), pp. 131–132. On April 4, Bush told British journalists, "I made up my mind that Saddam needs to go." See "Interview of the President by Sir Trevor McDonald of Britain's ITV Television Network," April 4, 2002.

127. Woodward, *Plan of Attack*, pp. 108–109.

128. Warren Strobel and John Walcott, "Bush Aims to Topple Iraq's Hussein," *San Diego Union Tribune*, February 13, 2002, p. A1.

129. Knights, *Cradle of Conflict*, p. 257.

130. Knights, *Cradle of Conflict*, p. 257.

131. Interview with senior Bush administration official, March 2007.

132. *Washington Post* staff writer, "Leaflets Warn Iraq Not to Target Allied Jets," *Washington Post*, October 4, 2002, p. A22; Scott Simmie, "Truths, Half-Truths and Untruths," *Toronto Star*, March 16, 2003, p. F3; and Department of Defense, Press Briefing with Assistant Secretary of Defense (Public Affairs) Rear Admiral David Gove, October 4, 2002.

133. Elaine Grossman, "Decision to Hasten Ground Attack into Iraq Presented New Risks," *Inside the Pentagon*, March 18, 2004; and Knights, *Cradle of Conflict*, pp. 258–260.

134. Michael Gordon, "U.S. Attacked Iraqi Air Defenses in 2002," *New York Times*, July 20, 2003.

135. Douglas Feith, *War and Decision: Inside the Pentagon at the Dawn of the War on Terrorism* (New York: Harper Paperbacks, 2008), p. 211.

136. Albright, with Wooodward, *Madame Secretary*, p. 275; and interviews with Clinton administration officials.

137. Knights, *Cradle of Conflict*, pp. 213–217; Department of Defense News Briefing, "Subject: Defense Reform Initiative," March 1, 1999; and Albright, with Wooodward, *Madame Secretary*, p. 287.

138. Scott Snook, *Friendly Fire: The Accidental Shootdown of U.S. Black Hawks Over Northern Iraq* (Princeton, NJ: Princeton University Press, 2000); Edward Cody, "Under

Iraqi Skies, a Canvas of Death," *Washington Post*, June 16, 2000, p. A1; Matthew Hay Brown, "Stray Missiles, Shattered Lives," *Hartford Courant*, October 24, 2000; and Hugh Pope, "U.S.-Iraq Tensions Mount in No-Fly Zones," *Wall Street Journal*, November 20, 2002, p. A2.

139. Department of Defense, *Conduct of the Persian Gulf War: Final Report to Congress* (Washington, DC: DoD, April 1992), p. 182.

140. Craig Hoyle, "Grounded: Why Iraq's Air Force Won't Fight," *Jane's Defence Weekly*, April 9, 2003.

141. George W. Bush, "President Bush Participates in Roundtable with Travel Pool," Heiligendamm, Germany, June 6, 2007; Guy Dinmore, "Blair Backs Plan for No-Fly Zone Over Darfur," *Financial Times*, December 13, 2006, p. 1; John McCain and Bob Dole, "Rescue Darfur Now," *Washington Post*, September 10, 2006, p. B7; and Save Darfur, "The Genocide in Darfur—Briefing Paper," June 2007.

Chapter 4

1. CBS, *60 Minutes*, "Bin Laden's Bodyguard," April 2, 2006.

2. John Barry and Russell Watson, "'Our Target Was Terror'," *Newsweek*, August 31, 1998, p. 24.

3. Donald Petterson, *Inside Sudan: Political Islam, Conflict, and Catastrophe* (Boulder, CO: Westview Press, 1999), pp. 84–85. Petterson was the U.S. Ambassador to Sudan from 1992 to 1995.

4. Jonathan Randal, "Sudan's Urbane Islamic Leader Sends Shivers from Behind the Scenes," *Washington Post*, May 9, 1995, p. A14.

5. Peter Woodward, *U.S. Foreign Policy and the Horn of Africa* (Aldershot, UK: Ashgate, 2006), pp. 47–49.

6. Jonathan Randal, *Osama: The Making of a Terrorist* (New York: Alfred A. Knopf, 2004), pp. 117–120.

7. Judith Miller, "Faces of Fundamentalism," *Foreign Affairs*, November-December 1994, p. 134.

8. Joseph Fried, "Sheikh and 9 Followers Guilty of a Conspiracy of Terrorism," *New York Times*, October 2, 1995, p. A1.

9. Petterson, *Inside Sudan*, p. 69.

10. Meghan L. O'Sullivan, *Shrewd Sanctions: Economic Statecraft in an Age of Global Terrorism* (Washington, DC: Brookings Institution Press, 2003), pp. 238–240.

11. Anonymous, *Through Our Enemies' Eyes: Osama Bin Laden, Radical Islam, and the Future of America* (Washington, DC: Brassey's, 2002), pp. 122–124; and Steve Coll, *Ghost Wars: The Secret History of the CIA, Afghanistan, and Bin Laden, From the Soviet Invasion to September 10, 2001* (New York: Penguin Press, 2004), p. 268.

12. National Commission on Terrorist Attacks Upon the United States, *9/11 Commission Report* (New York: W.W. Norton, 2004), pp. 57–58.

13. National Commission on Terrorist Attacks Upon the United States, *9/11 Commission Report*, pp. 57–61; and Moises Naim, *Illicit: How Smugglers, Traffickers, and Copycats Are Hijacking the Global Economy* (New York: Doubleday, 2005), pp. 145–146.

14. Daniel Benjamin and Steven Simon, *The Age of Sacred Terror* (New York: Random House, 2002), p. 113.

15. John Goshko, "Security Council Approves Limited Penalty for Sudan," *Washington Post*, April 27, 1996, p. A20; and National Commission on Terrorist Attacks Upon the United States, *9/11 Commission Report*, p. 62.

16. O'Sullivan, *Shrewd Sanctions*, pp. 240–241.

17. National Commission on Terrorist Attacks Upon the United States, *9/11 Commission Report*, pp 62–63.

18. National Commission on Terrorist Attacks Upon the United States, *9/11 Commission Report*, pp. 479–480 (fn) 7.

19. National Commission on Terrorist Attacks Upon the United States, Eighth Public Hearing, March 23, 2004; and Coll, *Ghost Wars*, p. 323.

20. Barton Gellman, "U.S. Was Foiled Multiple Times in Efforts to Capture Bin Laden or Have Him Killed," *Washington Post*, October 3, 2001, p. A1.

21. Coll, *Ghost Wars*, pp. 325–326.

22. Testimony of George E. Moose, Assistant Secretary for African Affairs, "Terrorism and Sudan," before Senate Foreign Relations Committee, Subcommittee on Africa, May 15, 1997.

23. Gellman, "U.S. Was Foiled Multiple Times in Efforts to Capture Bin Laden or Have Him Killed," p. A1; Coll, *Ghost Wars*, p. 271; and Anthony Lake, *6 Nightmares: Real Threats in a Dangerous World and How America Can Meet Them* (Boston: Little, Brown, 2000), p. 64. Within weeks of the decision to withdraw U.S. diplomats and spies from Khartoum, the CIA formally withdrew over a hundred intelligence reports regarding Sudan because they were based on an unreliable foreign intelligence source. Many of those CIA reports covered threats to Americans in Sudan. See Tim Weiner and James Risen, "Decision to Strike Factory in Sudan Based on Surmise Inferred from Evidence," *New York Times*, September 21, 1998, p. A1.

24. National Commission on Terrorist Attacks Upon the United States, *9/11 Commission Report*, pp. 479–480 (fn) 7; and Timothy Carney and Mansoor Ijaz, "Intelligence Failure? Let's Go Back to Sudan," *Washington Post*, June 30, 2002, p. B4.

25. Coll, *Ghost Wars*, pp. 190–221.

26. Larry P. Goodson, *Afghanistan's Endless War: State Failure, Regional Politics, and the Rise of the Taliban* (Seattle, WA: University of Washington Press, 2001), p. 73.

27. Coll, *Ghost Wars*, p. 228.

28. Goodson, *Afghanistan's Endless War*, 73–76; and Peter Mardsen, *The Taliban: War, Religion and the New Order in Afghanistan* (London: Zed Books, 1998), pp. 37–42.

29. Goodson, *Afghanistan's Endless War*, p. 77.

30. Benjamin and Simon, *The Age of Sacred Terror*, p. 145, and Coll, *Ghost Wars*, p. 299. See also Richard Mackenzie, "The United States and the Taliban," in William Maley (ed.), *Fundamentalism Reborn? Afghanistan and the Taliban* (New York: New York University Press, 1998), pp. 90–103.

31. John F. Burns, "With Kabul Largely in Ruins, Afghans Get Respite from War," *New York Times*, February 20, 1995, p. A1; and John Lee Anderson, "Afghans Say City Is Calmer Under Militants," *Washington Post*, March 2, 1995, p. A23.

32. Coll, *Ghost Wars*, pp. 334–335.

33. National Commission on Terrorist Attacks Upon the United States, *9/11 Commission Report*, pp. 63–67.

34. Benjamin and Simon, *The Age of Sacred Terror*, pp. 138–139; and National Commission on Terrorist Attacks Upon the United States, "Overview of the Enemy," Staff Statement no. 15, p. 11.

35. National Commission on Terrorist Attacks Upon the United States, *9/11 Commission Report*, pp. 110–111.

36. Coll, *Ghost Wars*, pp. 395–396; National Commission on Terrorist Attacks Upon the United States, *9/11 Commission Report*, pp. 111–115; and James Risen: *The Secret History of the CIA and the Bush Administration* (New York: Free Press, 2006), p. 184.

37. Interview with Bruce Riedel, January 23, 2007. Riedel is Senior Director for Near East Affairs on the NSC. He accompanied Ambassador Richardson on his trip to Afghanistan.

38. Lawrence Wright, *The Looming Tower: Al-Qaeda and the Road to 9/11* (New York: Alfred A. Knopf, 2006), pp. 267–268, 288–289; and Alan Cullison and Andrew Higgins, "U.S. Attack on Afghanistan Reunited al Qaeda, Taliban," *Wall Street Journal*, August 2, 2002, p. A1.

39. Benjamin and Simon, *The Age of Sacred Terror*, p. 118.

40. Lisa Anderson, "Witness Details Bin Laden," *Chicago Tribune*, February 7, 2001, p. 3.

41. National Commission on Terrorist Attacks Upon the United States, Staff Statement no. 15, "Overview of the Enemy," p. 4.

42. Mark Bowden, *Black Hawk Down: A Story of Modern War* (New York: Penguin, 1999), p. 110; and Paul Watson and Sidhartha Barua, "Somalian Link Seen to Sudan," *Los Angeles Times*, February 25, 2002, p. A1.

43. Benjamin and Simon, *The Age of Sacred Terror*, p. 130.

44. Benjamin and Simon, *The Age of Sacred Terror*, p. 130.

45. Peter Bergen, *Holy War Inc.: Inside the Secret World of Osama Bin Laden* (New York: Touchstone, updated version, 2002), p. 108.

46. Mark S. Hamm, *Crimes Committed by Terrorist Groups: Theory, Research and Prevention*, research report submitted to the Department of Justice, June 1, 2005, p. 77.

47. Henry Chu and Zulfiqar Ali, "Al Qaeda Operative Is Targeted," *Los Angeles Times*, April 14, 2006, p. A26.

48. Adm. William J. Crowe Jr., chairman, *Report of the Accountability Review Board*, January 1999; Southern District of New York, Count One, "Conspiracy to Kill United States Nationals," December 20, 2000; and David E. Kaplan and Stefan Lovgren, "On Terrorism's Trail," *U.S. News and World Reports*, November 23, 1998, p. 30.

49. Coll, *Ghost Wars*, p. 404; and Michael Elliot, "Terror Times Two," *Newsweek*, August 17, 1998, p. 23.

50. Richard Clarke, *Against All Enemies: Inside America's War on Terrorism* (New York: Free Press, 2004), p. 183.

51. The known members of the Small Group included President Clinton, Madeline Albright, Samuel Berger, William Cohen, Janet Reno, George Tenet, Gen. Hugh Shelton, Gen. Joseph Ralston, James Steinberg, Lt. Gen. Donald Kerrick, Richard Clarke, Mary McCarthy, and Bruce Riedel.

52. Madeline Albright, with Bill Woodward, *Madame Secretary* (New York: Miramax Books, 2003), p. 364.

53. National Commission on Terrorist Attacks Upon the United States, *9/11 Commission Report*, p. 116; Barry and Watson, "'Our Target Was Terror,'" p. 24; and Coll, *Ghost Wars*, p. 410.

54. Bob Woodward, "CIA Had Afghans Tracking Bin Laden for Four Years," *Washington Post*, December 23, 2001, p. A9; George Tenet, with Bill Harlow, *At the Center of the Storm: My Years at the CIA* (New York: HarperCollins, 2007), p. 115; and Clarke, *Against All Enemies*, p. 184.

55. Coll, *Ghost Wars*, p. 410; and interview with Bruce Riedel, January 23, 2007.

56. Interview with Bruce Riedel, January 23, 2007.

57. James Risen, "To Bomb Sudan Plant, or Not: A Year Later, Debates Rankle," *New York Times*, October 27, 1999, p. A1; and James Risen, *State of War: The Secret History of the CIA and the Bush Administration* (New York: Free Press, 2006), p. 153.

58. Clarke, *Against All Enemies*, p. 184.

59. Coll, *Ghost Wars*, p. 407; and Albright, with Wooodward, *Madame Secretary*, p. 364.

60. William J. Clinton, *My Life* (New York: Knopf, 2004), pp. 803–805; and interview with Lt. Gen. Donald Kerrick, November 2, 2006.

61. Coll, *Ghost Wars*, pp. 407–408.

62. National Commission on Terrorist Attacks Upon the United States, *9/11 Commission Report*, p. 116. Berger later noted that "Cruise missiles are not generally conceived of as a law enforcement technique. We were trying to kill Bin Laden and his lieutenants." See Berger testimony before the House and Senate Select Committees on Intelligence, "Hearing on Iraq," September 18, 2002.

63. Risen, "To Bomb Sudan Plant, or Not," p. A1; and Seymour Hersh, "The Missiles

of August," *New Yorker*, October 12, 1998. FBI Director Louis Freeh was asked for his opinion about the strength of evidence implicating Al Qaeda for the embassy bombings, but was not asked for his recommendation about whether or not to attack. See Freeh testimony before the Senate Judiciary Committee, Subject: U.S. Counterterrorism Policy, September 3, 1998.

64. Interview with James Steinberg, February 27, 2007.

65. Interview with Gen. Anthony Zinni, February 13, 2008.

66. Risen, "To Bomb Sudan Plant, or Not," p. A1; Scott Macleod, "The Paladin of Jihad," *Time*, May 6, 1996, p. 51; and Robert Block, "In War on Terrorism, Sudan Struck a Blow by Fleecing Bin Laden," *Wall Street Journal*, December 3, 2001, p. A1.

67. Benjamin and Simon, *The Age of Sacred Terror*, p. 259.

68. Risen, "To Bomb Sudan Plant, or Not," p. A1; and Coll, *Ghost Wars*, p. 411.

69. Risen, "To Bomb Sudan Plant, or Not," p. A1.

70. Vernon Loeb, "U.S. Wasn't Sure Plant Had Nerve Gas Role," *Washington Post*, August 21, 1999, p. A1. Six weeks after the Small Group debates, Clinton told historian Taylor Branch that among the intelligence justifying the El-Shifa strike was "soil samples, connecting an element in nerve gas found there and in Afghanistan at similarly high concentrations." See Taylor Branch, *The Clinton Tapes: Wrestling History with the President* (New York: Simon and Schuster, 2009), p. 512.

71. Weiner and Risen, "Decision to Strike Factory in Sudan Based on Surmise Inferred from Evidence," p. A1.

72. Interview with Lt. Gen. Donald Kerrick, November 2, 2006.

73. Risen, "To Bomb Sudan Plant, or Not," p. A1.

74. See National Commission on Terrorist Attacks Upon the United States, *9/11 Commission Report*, p. 117; and David S. Cloud, "Colleagues Say C.I.A. Analyst Played by Rules," *New York Times*, April 23, 2006, p. 1.

75. Interview with Clinton administration intelligence official, July 2006.

76. Interview with Paul Pillar, September 28, 2006. Writing seven years after the fact, Louis Freeh recalled that he "wasn't much convinced by the evidence" presented by Berger and Tenet for attacking El-Shifa beforehand. See Freeh, with Howard Means, *My FBI: Bringing Down the Mafia, Investigating Bill Clinton, and Fighting the War on Terror* (New York: St. Martin's Press, 2005), p. 223. Zinni, who reviewed the El-Shifa intelligence as a CIA contract employee after he retired from the military, noted that "you could see right away there were big problems with it." Interview with Gen. Anthony Zinni, February 13, 2008.

77. Risen, "To Bomb Sudan Plant, or Not," p. A1.

78. Risen, "To Bomb Sudan Plant, or Not," p. A1.

79. Interview with senior military official, October 2006.

80. Interview with Bruce Riedel, January 23, 2007; and interview with James Steinberg, February 27, 2007.

81. Risen, "To Bomb Sudan Plant, or Not," p. A1. The worry about being blamed for a future chemical attack on the United States is consistent with the comments of an anonymous senior CIA official, who recalled, "[Tenet] was quite clear with policy-maker saying 'we don't know everything about [El-Shifa].' The policy guys decided to accept the risk [of being wrong] given the possibility that Al Qaeda could carry out some kind of chemical-based attack. They didn't want to take that kind of risk." Ted Gup, *Nation of Secrets: The Threat to Democracy and the American Way of Life* (New York: Doubleday, 2007), pp. 74–75.

82. Coll, *Ghost Wars*, p. 412; and National Commission on Terrorist Attacks Upon the United States, *9/11 Commission Report*, p. 116.

83. Risen, "To Bomb Sudan Plant, or Not," p. A1; interview with Gen. Anthony Zinni, February 13, 2008; and Hersh, "The Missiles of August." According to a news report, "As the president was deciding whether to attack the facilities in Sudan and Afghanistan, there was no classified briefing in the Pentagon 'tank' with the heads of the four military services and the chairman and vice chairman of the Joint Chiefs of Staff." See Brian Duffy, "The Price of Payback," *U.S. News and World Report*, September 7, 1998, p. 22. Furthermore, State Department officials in the regional bureau that included Afghanistan believed that they knew that the high-level Al Qaeda meeting would have ended before the cruise missiles made impact. According to Deputy Assistant Secretary of State for South Asian Affairs Edward Lanpher, however, these regional experts were never consulted before the bombing. Interview with Edward Gibson Lanpher, Association for Diplomatic Studies and Training Foreign Affairs Oral History Project, June 25, 2002.

84. Clinton, *My Life*, p. 803.

85. William Clinton, "Remarks on the 35th Anniversary of the March on Washington," Oak Bluffs, Massachusetts, August 28, 1998.

86. Barry and Watson, "'Our Target Was Terror,'" p. 24.

87. Interview with Lt. Gen. Donald Kerrick, November 2, 2006.

88. Richard Newman et al., "America Fights Back," *U.S. News and World Reports*, August 31, 1998, p. 38. Interview with Gen. Anthony Zinni, February 13, 2008. See also Michael Knights, *Cradle of Conflict: Iraq and the Birth of Modern U.S. Military Power* (Annapolis, MD: Naval Institute Press, 2005), p. 187; and Tom Clancy, with Tony Zinni and Tony Koltz, *Battle Ready* (New York: G.P. Putnam's Sons, 2004), p. 340.

89. Newman et al., "America Fights Back," p. 38; and Eugene Robinson and Dana Priest, "Reports of U.S. Strikes' Destruction Vary," *Washington Post*, August 22, 1998, p. A1.

90. Barry and Watson, "'Our Target Was Terror,'" p. 24.

91. Loeb, "U.S. Wasn't Sure Plant Had Nerve Gas Role," p. A1; "A Bit of Collateral Damage," *Economist*, August 26, 2000; and James Astill, "Strike One," *The Guardian*, October 2, 2001, p. 2.

92. Department of Defense News Briefing, William Cohen and Gen. Hugh Shelton, August 20, 1998.

93. Interview with Gen. Anthony Zinni, February 13, 2008.

94. Interview with Gen. Joseph Ralston, October 25, 2006.

95. Interview with Gen. Joseph Ralston, October 25, 2006.

96. Clarke, *Against All Enemies*, pp. 186–190; and interview with Lt. Gen. Donald Kerrick, November 2, 2006.

97. Interviews with James Steinberg, February 27, 2007; Bruce Riedel, January 23, 2007; and Gen. Anthony Zinni, February 13, 2008.

98. Tenet, with Harlow, *At the Center of the Storm*, p. 117.

99. David A. Fulghum, "Secrecy About Raids Hints More to Come," *Aviation Week and Space Technology*, August 31, 1998, p. 30.

100. Robinson and Priest, "Reports of U.S. Strikes' Destruction Vary," p. A1; and Human Rights Watch, *Ticking Time Bombs: NATO's Use of Cluster Munitions in Yugoslavia*, "Appendix A: Descriptions of Cluster Bomb Types," June 1999.

101. Peter Finn, "Secret Tape Suggests China-Bin Laden Link," *Washington Post*, October 20, 2001, p. A17; and Lawrence Wright, "The Man Behind Bin Laden," *New Yorker*, September 16, 2002.

102. Bob Woodward and Thomas Ricks, "CIA Trained Pakistanis to Nab Terrorist," *Washington Post*, October 3, 2001, p. A1; Benjamin and Simon, *The Age of Sacred Terror*, p. 260; and Clarke, *Against All Enemies*, p. 189.

103. William Cohen, "We Are Ready to Act Again," *Washington Post*, August 23, 1998, p. C1.

104. Barton Gellman and Dana Priest, "U.S. Strikes Terrorist-Linked Sites in Afghanistan, Factory in Sudan," *Washington Post*, August 21, 1998, p. A1.

105. National Commission on Terrorist Attacks Upon the United States, *9/11 Commission Report*, p. 134.

106. National Commission on Terrorist Attacks Upon the United States, *9/11 Commission Report*, pp. 134–143, and 194; National Commission on Terrorist Attacks Upon the United States, "The Military," Staff Statement, no. 6; and Coll, *Ghost Wars*, pp. 421–422. To support this final effort, the CIA's Special Activities Division deployed to Afghanistan in 1999 to prepare an airstrip to evacuate Bin Laden if the tribesmen captured him. Barton Gellman, "Broad Effort Launched After '98 Attacks," *Washington Post*, December 19, 2001, p. A1.

107. Richard H. Shultz Jr., "Showstoppers: Nine Reasons Why We Never Sent Our Special Operations Forces After Al Qaeda Before 9/11," *Weekly Standard*, January 26, 2004; Benjamin and Simon, *The Age of Sacred Terror*, p. 264; and Albright, with Woodward, *Madame Secretary*, pp. 374–375. On the concerns of civilian casualties, Gen. Zinni recalled, "They wanted me to shoot Kandahar when bin Laden might or might not be there and there would be 1,500 casualties. I refused. I told [Secretary of Defense] Cohen, if you order me to do it, I'll have to resign." Derek Chollet and James Goldgeier, *America Between the Wars: From 11/9 to 9/11* (New York: Public Affairs, 2008), pp. 268–269. No officials interviewed for this book could recall this incident.

108. Benjamin and Simon, *The Age of Sacred Terror*, p. 295.

109. Interview with James Steinberg, February 27, 2007.

110. Interview with Lt. Gen. Donald Kerrick, November 2, 2006.

111. Interview with Lt. Gen. Donald Kerrick, November 2, 2006.

112. Interview with Gen. David Petraeus, February 2010.

113. Interview with Vice Adm. Scott Fry, February 16, 2009.

114. Michael Elliot, "They Had a Plan," *Time*, August 12, 2002, p. 28; and National Commission on Terrorist Attacks Upon the United States, *9/11 Commission Report*, p. 187.

115. Interview with Lt. Gen. Gregory Newbold, August 29, 2006.

116. Interview with senior military official, October 2006.

117. National Commission on Terrorist Attacks Upon the United States, "Counter-terrorism Policy," eighth public hearing, March 23–24, 2004.

118. Interview with James Steinberg, February 27, 2007.

119. White House, "Press Briefing on U.S. Strikes in Sudan and Afghanistan," by Madeline Albright and Sandy Berger, August 20, 1998; and PBS, *Newshour,* interview with Samuel Berger, August 21, 1998.

120. Interview with Gen. Jack Keane, September 27, 2006.

121. Branch, *The Clinton Tapes*, pp. 136, 512, and 552; John Broder, "From Baptism of Fire to Kosovo," *New York Times*, April 8, 1999, p. A1; and George Stephanopoulos, *All Too Human* (Boston: Little, Brown, 1999), p. 160.

122. William Clinton, Oval Office address, Washington, DC, August 20, 1998.

123. Albright, with Woodward, *Madame Secretary*, p. 368; and Risen, "To Bomb Sudan Plant, or Not," p. A1.

124. Interview with Gen. Anthony Zinni, February 13, 2008.

125. Coll, *Ghost Wars*, p. 421; and Benjamin and Simon, *The Age of Sacred Terror*, p. 294.

126. Tenet, with Harlow, *At the Center of the Storm*, p. 111.

127. Gellman, "Broad Effort Launched After '98 Attacks," p. A1.

128. Barry and Watson, "'Our Target Was Terror'," p. 24.

129. Press Briefing with Madeline Albright and Sandy Berger, White House, August 20, 1998.

130. Statement of George J. Tenet as Prepared for Delivery Before the Senate Armed Services Committee Hearing on Current and Projected National Security Threat, February 2, 1999.

131. National Commission on Terrorist Attacks Upon the United States, *9/11 Commission Report*, p. 121.

132. These suspects, Pakistani nationals, were offered by the Sudanese to the United States one week after the embassy bombings. Some members of the Small Group were unaware of the offer, while others thought it was too close to the date of the planned cruise missile strikes. See Randal, *Osama*, p. 132–139. See also Benjamin and Simon, *The*

Age of Sacred Terror, p. 505; and James Risen, "Sudan, Angry at U.S. Attack, Freed Bomb Suspects, Officials Say," *New York Times*, July 30, 1999, p. A4.

133. Paul Pillar, *Terrorism and U.S. Foreign Policy* (Washington DC: Brookings Institution Press, 2001), p. 109.

134. Daniel Byman, *Deadly Connections: States That Sponsor Terrorism* (Cambridge, UK: Cambridge University press, 2005), pp. 202–203; and Cullison and Higgins, "U.S. Attack on Afghanistan Reunited al Qaeda, Taliban," p. A1.

135. Tim Wiener, "Missile Strikes Against Bin Laden Won Him Esteem in Muslim Lands, U.S. Officials Say," *New York Times*, February 8, 1999, p. A13.

136. Interview with James Steinberg, February 27, 2007. For this concern, see also Albright, with Wooodward, *Madame Secretary*, pp. 374–375.

137. National Commission on Terrorist Attacks Upon the United States, "Ninth Public Hearing," testimony of Dr. Condoleezza Rice, April 8, 2004.

138. National Commission on Terrorist Attacks Upon the United States, *9/11 Commission Report*, p. 213.

Chapter 5

1. Stephen Gaghan, writer and director, *Syriana* (Burbank, CA: Warner Brothers, 2005).

2. Kenneth Pollack, *The Threatening Storm: The Case for Invading Iraq* (New York: Random House, 2002), p. 15.

3. Department of Energy, "Persian Gulf Oil and Gas Exports Fact Sheet," September 2004.

4. Department of Energy, World Oil Transit Chokepoints, "Bab-el-Mandeb," November 2005. Furthermore, American war material shipped through the Mediterranean Sea during both Persian Gulf Wars traveled through the Bab-el-Mandeb.

5. Ahmed Noman and Kassim Almadhagi, *Yemen and the United States: A Study of a Small Power and Super-State Relationship, 1962–1994* (London: I.B. Tauris, 1996); pp. 105–186.

6. Ronald Reagan, "President's News Conference," October 1, 1981; and Steve A. Yetiv, *Crude Awakenings: Global Oil Security and American Foreign Policy,* (Ithaca, NY: Cornell University Press, 2004), p. 66.

7. Joseph Kostiner, *Yemen: The Tortuous Quest for Unity, 1990–1994* (London: Royal Institute for International Affairs, 1996), pp. 93–105; Nora Boustany, "Yemen's North-South Struggle Spreads," *Washington Post*, May 7, 1994, p. A13; Boustany, "Civil War in Yemen Heightens Worries of Wider Instability," *Washington Post*, June 18, 1994, p. A19; and Elaine Sciolino and Eric Schmitt, "Saudi Arabia, Its Purse Thinner, Learns How to Say 'No' to U.S.," *New York Times*, November 4, 1994, p. A1.

8. Carlyle Murphy, "Yemen Tries to Liberalize, Sell Oil—But Faces Saudi Anger," *Washington Post*, July 12, 1992, p. A20.

9. Eric Watkins, "Success of Yemeni Elections Prompts Worries for Saudis," *Financial Times*, May 14, 1993, p. 4; and Sheila Carapico, "Elections and Mass Politics in Yemen," *Middle East Report* (November-December 1993), pp. 2–6.

10. "Total Group Has Hefty Oil Find in South Yemen," *Oil & Gas Journal*, August 21, 1995, p. 29; "Yemen's Oil Production Climbing, Potential Great," *Oil & Gas Journal*, March 5, 2001, p. 82; and CIA, *The World Factbook*, "Rank Order-Oil-Exports," various years.

11. Department of Energy, Country Analysis Brief, Yemen, "Natural Gas," October 2005.

12. Andrew Higgins and Allan Cullison, "Friend or Foe: The Story of a Traitor to al Qaeda," *Wall Street Journal*, December 20, 2002, p. A1; and Patrick Tyler, "Yemen, an Uneasy Ally, Proves Adept at Playing Off Old Rivals," *New York Times*, December 19, 2002, p. 1.

13. Shefagh Weir, "A Clash of Fundamentalisms: Wahhabism in Yemen," *Middle East Report* (July-September 1997), pp. 22–26.

14. Lawrence Wright, *The Looming Tower: Al-Qaeda and the Road to 9/11* (New York: Alfred A. Knopf, 2006), pp. 153–154; and Jonathan Randal, *Osama: The Making of a Terrorist* (New York: Alfred A. Knopf, 2004), pp. 99–103.

15. Anonymous, *Through Our Enemies' Eyes: Osama Bin Laden, Radical Islam, and the Future of America* (Washington, DC: Brassey's, 2002), p. 112. See also Randal, *Osama*, p. 200.

16. Sue Lackey, "Yemen: Unlikely Key to Western Security," *Jane's Intelligence Review*, October 12, 2000.

17. Robert Kaplan, *Imperial Grunts: The American Military on the Ground* (New York: Random House, 2005), p. 31; Chris Hedges, "Yemenis Battle for the Control of a Major City," *New York Times*, May 10, 1994, p. A1; and Nora Boustany, "Going Great Guns in Yemen," *Washington Post*, May 3, 1993, p. A13.

18. Kostiner, *Yemen: The Tortuous Quest for Unity, 1990–1994*, p. 86.

19. Peter Bergen, *Holy War Inc.: Inside the Secret World of Osama Bin Laden* (New York: Touchstone, updated version, 2002), p. 178.

20. This quote appeared in the "Yemen" section of the *Patterns* report throughout the 1990s.

21. Rohan Gunaratna, *Inside Al Qaeda: Global Network of Terror* (New York: Columbia University Press, 2002), p. 12. For a summary of Al Qaeda communications between Afghanistan and Yemen, see Allan Cullinson, "Inside Al-Qaeda's Hard Drive," *Atlantic Monthly*, September 2004, pp. 50–70.

22. Eric Watkins, "Terror Main Weapon in Yemen War of Political Wills," *Financial Times*, January 7, 1994, p. 4; Richard Clarke, *Against All Enemies: Inside America's War on Terrorism* (New York: Free Press, 2004), p. 233; and Lackey, "Yemen: Unlikely Key to Western Security."

23. National Commission on Terrorist Attacks Upon the United States, *9/11 Commission Report* (New York: W.W. Norton, 2004), p. 148; Andrew Higgins and Christo-

pher Cooper, "Cloak and Dagger: A CIA-Backed Team Used Brutal Means to Crack Terror Cell," *Wall Street Journal*, November 20, 2001, p. A1; and Higgins and Alan Cullison, "Terrorist's Odyssey: Saga of Dr. Zawahiri Illuminates Roots of al Qaeda Terror," *Wall Street Journal*, July 2, 2002, p. A1.

24. Lawrence Wright, "The Man Behind Bin Laden," *New Yorker*, September 16, 2002, pp. 56–85.

25. In early 1997, Bin Laden sent emissaries to Yemen to determine if tribal sheikhs would host him in the mountainous northwest region. Bin Laden remained in Afghanistan. See Bergen, *Holy War Inc.*, p. 181.

26. Bergen, *Holy War Inc.*, p. 179.

27. National Commission on Terrorist Attacks Upon the United States, *9/11 Commission Report*, p. 232; and Jonathan Mahler, "The Bush Administration vs. Salim Hamdan," *New York Times Magazine*, January 8, 2006, p. 44.

28. Tim Weiner, "Man with Mission Takes On the U.S. at Far-Flung Sites," *New York Times*, August 21, 1998, p. A1.

29. Shaul Shay, *The Red Seat Terror Triangle: Sudan, Somalia, Yemen, and Islamic Terror*, trans. Rachel Liberman (New Brunswick, NJ: Transaction, 2005), pp. 121–122; and Clarke, *Against All Enemies*, p. 88.

30. Stephen Barr, "U.S. Stops Using Yemen Support Base," *Washington Post*, January 3, 1993, p. A18.

31. Anonymous, *Through Our Enemies' Eyes*, p. 135.

32. National Commission on Terrorist Attacks Upon the United States, *9/11 Commission Report*, pp. 152–153; and 491 (31).

33. National Commission on Terrorist Attacks Upon the United States, *9/11 Commission Report*, pp. 190–191.

34. Kim Cragin and Scott Gerwehr, *Dissuading Terror: Strategic Influence and the Struggle Against Terrorism* (Santa Monica, CA: RAND, 2005), p. 42.

35. Clarke, *Against All Enemies*, p. 213.

36. Tom Clancy, with Tony Zinni and Tony Koltz, *Battle Ready* (New York: G.P. Putnam's Sons, 2004), pp. 337–338, and 350–352.

37. John Burns, "How a Mighty Power Was Humbled by a Little Skiff," *New York Times*, October 28, 2000, p. A6; Daniel Benjamin and Steven Simon, *The Age of Sacred Terror* (New York: Random House, 2002), p. 323; and Benjamin and Simon, *The Next Attack: The Failure of the War on Terror and a Strategy for Getting It Right* (New York: Henry Holt, 2005), p. 46.

38. Shay, *The Red Seat Terror Triangle*, p. 127.

39. Steve Coll, *Ghost Wars: The Secret History of the CIA, Afghanistan, and Bin Laden, from the Soviet Invasion to September 10, 2001* (New York: Penguin Press, 2004), p. 532.

40. James Dao and Eric Schmitt, "U.S. Sees Battles in Lawless Areas After Afghan War," *New York Times*, January 8, 2002, p. A1.

41. Department of Defense, "Secretary Rumsfeld News Briefing in Brussels," December 18, 2001.

42. Robert McFadden, "An Inauguration, an Attack on a Convoy, Questions for the Captured," *New York Times*, December 22, 2001, p. B1.

43. Roula Khalaf, "Yemen Develops Its Own Type of Anti-Terrorist Campaign," *Financial Times*, February 18, 2002, p. 18.

44. Interview with Clinton administration official, September 2006.

45. Nora Boustany, "Yemeni Proclaims His Nation's Solidarity with U.S. in Fight Against Terrorism," *Washington Post*, November 27, 2002, p. A13.

46. Robert Worth, "For Yemen's Leader, a Balancing Act Gets Harder," *New York Times*, June 21, 2008, p. A8.

47. Interview with Bush administration NSC official, July 2006.

48. Jeffrey Gettleman, "Yemen, Once a Magnet, Now Expels Terrorists," *Los Angeles Times*, October 10, 2001, p. A11; Yaroslav Trofimov, "Yemen Is Eager to Remain a U.S. Ally," *Wall Street Journal*, October 31, 2001, p. A16; Trofimov, "Nations Supporting Jihads of Yesteryear Now Close," *Wall Street Journal*, November 16, 2001, p. A1; and Raymond Bonner, "Long at Odds with the U.S., Yemen Is Now Cooperating to Fight Terror," *New York Times*, November 25, 2001, p. 1.

49. John Burns, "FBI's Inquiry in Cole Attack Is Nearing Halt," *New York Times*, August 21, 2001, p. A1.

50. Saleh noted of the U.S. investigators in an *Al Jazeera* interview, "We denied them access to Yemen with forces, planes and ships. We put them under direct monitoring by our security forces. They respected our position and surrendered to what we did." Walter Pincus, "Yemen Hears Benefits of Joining U.S. Fight," *Washington Post*, November 28, 2001, p. A8. See also James Risen and Raymond Bonner, "Officials Say Bomber of the Cole Was in Yemeni Custody Earlier," *New York Times*, December 7, 2001, p. 1.

51. Department of State, "Middle East Overview," *Patterns of Global Terrorism: 2001*, May 21, 2002.

52. Boustany, "Yemeni Proclaims His Nation's Solidarity with U.S. in Fight Against Terrorism," p. A13.

53. Interview with Barbara Bodine, April 6, 2006; John Donnelly, "CIA Paying Millions in Qaeda Hunt," *Boston Globe*, November 24, 2002, p. A1; and James Bamford, "Big Brother Is Listening," *Atlantic Monthly*, April 2006, p. 67.

54. Brookings Institution, Policy Briefing with Abd Al-Kareem Al-Iryani, Special Advisor to the President of Yemen, November 26, 2002.

55. Bonner, "Long at Odds With the U.S., Yemen Is Now Cooperating to Fight Terror," p. 1

56. "No Holds Barred—Yemen and the War on Terrorism," *Economist*, November 9, 2002, p. 49.

57. Tyler, "Yemen, an Uneasy Ally, Proves Adept at Playing Off Old Rivals," p. 1.

58. Greg Jaffe and David Cloud, "U.S. Prepares to Send Troops to Yemen," *Wall Street Journal*, March 1, 2002, p. A3.

59. Clancy, with Zinni and Koltz, *Battle Ready*, p. 337. After the *U.S.S. Cole* bombing, U.S. counterterrorism training with Yemen was frozen. See Dana Priest, *The Mission: Waging War and Keeping Peace with America's Military* (New York: W.W. Norton, 2003), p. 109.

60. Carla Anne Robbins, Jay Solomon, and Yaroslav Trofimov, "U.S. Finds Extending the War on Terrorism Raises New Problems," *Wall Street Journal*, March 11, 2002, p. A1; and Michael Gordon, "Cheney Asks Yemen to Join the Pursuit of Al Qaeda's Remnants," *New York Times*, March 15, 2002, p. 10.

61. Internal Revenue Service, "Combat Zones," http://www.irs.gov/newsroom/article/0,,id=108331,00.html (accessed October 20, 2009).

62. Thom Shanker and Eric Schmitt, "U.S. Moves Commandos to Base in East Africa," *New York Times*, September 18, 2002, p. A20.

63. Dana Priest, "Foreign Network at Front of CIA's Terror Fight," *Washington Post*, November 18, 2005, p. A1.

64. Thomas Ricks, "U.S. Arms Unmanned Aircraft," *Washington Post*, October 18, 2001, p. A1; David Fulghum, "Predator B to Increase Lethality of UAV Fleet," *Aviation Week and Space Technology*, November 11, 2002, p. 34.

65. Walter Pincus, "U.S. Strike Kills Six in Al Qaeda," *Washington Post*, November 5, 2002, p. A1; and Pincus, "CIA Fails in Bid to Kill Afghan Rebels with a Missile," *Washington Post*, May 10, 2002, p. A24.

66. Bob Woodward, *Bush at War* (New York: Simon and Schuster, 2002), p. 327.

67. Tyler, "Yemen, an Uneasy Ally, Proves Adept at Playing Off Old Rivals," p. 1; and Dana Priest, "Help from France Key in Covert Operations," *Washington Post*, July 3, 2005, p. A1.

68. U.S. Senate Select Committee to Study Governmental Operations with respect to Intelligence Activities, *Alleged Assassination Plots Involving Foreign Leaders*, an interim report, November 20, 1975, p. 1; and Rhodri Jeffreys-Jones, *Cloak and Dollar: A History of American Secret Intelligence* (New Haven, CT: Yale University Press, 2002), pp. 205–231.

69. *Weekly Compilation of Presidential Documents*, Vol. 12, No. 8, February 23, 1976.

70. Ward Thomas, *The Ethics of Destruction: Norms and Force in International Relations* (Ithaca, NY: Cornell University Press, 2001), p. 49.

71. Bob Woodward, "Antiterrorist Plan Rescinded After Unauthorized Bombing," *Washington Post*, May 12, 1985, p. A1; David C. Wills, *The First War on Terrorism: Counter-Terrorism Policy During the Reagan Administration* (Lanham, MD: Rowman and Littlefield, 2003), pp. 209–210; Stephen Engelberg, "Reagan Agreed to Prevent Noriega Death," *New York Times*, October 17, 1989, p. A10; Engelberg and Susan Rasky, "White House, Noriega and Battle in Congress," *New York Times*, October 25, 1989, p. A10; and

Yossi Melman, "Why the Plot to Kill Hussein Failed," *Los Angeles Times*, July 21, 1991, pp. M1–2. On one occasion, a senior U.S. official supported an assassination attempt. Director of Central Intelligence George Casey, working through Saudi Arabia, approved an assassination plot against Sheikh Mohammed Hussein Fadlallah, the leader of Hezbollah. Casey's involvement, however, was done outside of Congressional oversight and without the knowledge of the rest of the CIA, or even President Reagan, who claimed, "Never would I sign anything that would authorize an assassination. I never have, and I never will, and I didn't." On March 8, 1985, a car bomb exploded outside of Fadlallah's residence in Beirut. Eighty people were killed, and two hundred wounded. Fadlallah was uninjured. See Bob Woodward, *Veil: The Secret Wars of the CIA, 1981–1987* (New York: Simon and Schuster, 1987), pp. 396–397; and Reagan, "Remarks on Federal Loan Asset Sales," Washington, DC, September 30, 1987.

72. Wills, *The First War on Terrorism*, pp. 209–210; and Steven Erlanger, "NATO Strikes Serb State TV; Casualties Seen," *New York Times*, April 23, 1999, p. A1.

73. Paul Pillar, *Terrorism and U.S. Foreign Policy* (Washington DC: Brookings Institution Press, 2001), pp. 120–123; Philip Heymann and Juliette Kayyem, *Protecting Liberty in an Age of Terror* (Cambridge, MA: MIT Press, 2005), pp. 59–68; Daniel Byman, "Do Targeted Killings Work?" *Foreign Affairs*, March-April 2006, pp. 95–111; Thomas, *The Ethics of Destruction*, pp. 47–85; and Tim Wiener, "Rethinking the Ban on Political Assassinations," *New York Times*, August 30, 1998, p. 3.

74. National Commission on Terrorist Attacks Upon the United States, *9/11 Commission Report*, pp. 131–133; Coll, *Ghost Wars*, pp. 423–428; Clarke, *Against All Enemies*, pp. 203–204; William J. Clinton, *My Life* (New York: Knopf, 2004), p. 804; and Barton Gellman, "Broad Effort Launched After '98 Attacks," *Washington Post*, December 19, 2001, p. A1. One particular Memorandum of Notification, dated December 24, 1998, included a starkly written, one-page "kill" authorization for Bin Laden. Although the memorandum was written at Tenet's request, when the CIA director was questioned by the 9/11 Commission in 2004, he claimed to have never heard of it. Philip Shenon, *The Commission: The Uncensored History of the 9/11 Investigation* (New York: Twelve, 2008), pp. 357–360.

75. George Tenet, with Bill Harlow, *At the Center of the Storm: My Years at the CIA* (New York: HarperCollins, 2007), p. 110.

76. National Commission on Terrorist Attacks Upon the United States, *9/11 Commission Report*, pp. 211–212.

77. Barton Gellman, "CIA Weighs 'Targeted Killing' Missions," *Washington Post*, October 28, 2001, p. A1.

78. Woodward, *Bush at War*, p. 101; James Risen and David Johnston, "Bush Has Widened Authority of C.I.A. to Kill Terrorists," *New York Times*, December 15, 2002, p. 1; and John Lumpkin, "Bush War Rules Let U.S. Kill Its Own," *Houston Chronicle*, December 4, 2002, p. 1.

79. Gellman, "CIA Weighs 'Targeted Killing' Missions," p. A1.

80. Dana Priest, "Covert CIA Program Withstands New Furor," *Washington Post*, December 30, 2005, p. A1; and Douglas Waller, "The CIA's Secret Army," *Time*, February 3, 2003, p. 22.

81. Bob Woodward, "CIA Told to Do 'Whatever Necessary' to Kill Bin Laden," *Washington Post*, October 21, 2001, p. A1. As Cofer Black, head of the CIA's Counterter- rorist Center, described the transition, "This is a highly classified area, but I have to say that all you need to know: There was a before 9/11, and there was an after 9/11. After 9/11 the gloves came off." Testimony before the Joint House and Senate Intelligence Committee, September 26, 2002.

82. Risen and Johnston, "Bush Has Widened Authority of C.I.A. to Kill Terrorists," p. 1; Jaffe and Cloud, "U.S. Prepares to Send Troops to Yemen," p. A3; and ABC News, *Nightline*, "Hot Spot: Are They with Us or Against the U.S.? Yemen's Seeming Support of U.S. Mission to Eliminate Terrorism," January 17, 2002.

83. Jaffe and Cloud, "U.S. Prepares to Send Troops to Yemen," p. A3; and ABC News, *Nightline*, "Hot Spot: Are They with Us or Against U.S.?" Al-Harithi and others were sought by the United States before 9/11, but the Yemeni government consistently claimed that they could not be located. See interview with Barbara Bodine, April 6, 2006.

84. "What Went Wrong?," *Yemen Times*, December 24–30, 2001; "Manhunt for Al Qaeda Suspects Continues," *Yemen Times*, January 14–21, 2002; and "Tribes Do Not Harbor Al-Harethi: Sheikh al-Okaimi," *Yemen Times*, January 14–21, 2002.

85. ABC News, *Nightline*, "Hot Spot: Are They With Us or Against U.S.?"

86. "What Went Wrong?," *Yemen Times*, December 24–30, 2001; and "No Holds Barred," p. 49.

87. Karl Vick, "Yemen Pursuing Terror Its Own Way," *Washington Post*, October 17, 2002, p. A14; and Evan Thomas and Mark Hosenball, "The Opening Shot," *Newsweek*, November 18, 2002, p. 48.

88. Neil MacFarquhar, "Unmanned U.S. Planes Comb Arabian Desert for Suspects," *New York Times*, October 23, 2002, p. A14.

89. PBS, *Frontline*, "In Search of Al Qaeda," November 21, 2002, interview with Abu Bakr Al-Qirbi, Foreign Minister of Yemen; Michael DeLong, with Noah Lukeman, *Inside CENTCOM: The Unvarnished Truth About the Wars in Afghanistan and Iraq* (Washing- ton, DC: Regnery, 2004), p. 70; and Rowan Scarborough, *Rumsfeld's War: The Untold Story of America's Anti-Terrorist Commander* (Washington: Regnery, 2004), pp. 24–25.

90. Philip Smucker, "The Intrigue Behind the Drone Strike," *Christian Science Mon- itor*, November 12, 2002, p. 1; and Bruce Finley, "Anti-Terror Tactics Costing U.S. Allies," *Denver Post*, September 9, 2002, p. A1.

91. Rod Nordland, Sami Yousafzai, and Babak Dehghanpisheh, "How Al Qaeda Slipped Away," *Newsweek*, August 19, 2002, p. 34; "Confessions of Detainees Helped Ar- rest Top Al-Qa'idh Man," *Al Hayat*, November 25, 2002 (translated by BBC Monitoring

Middle East); Don Van Natta, "Questioning Terror Suspects in a Dark and Surreal World," *New York Times*, March 9, 2003, p. 1; Christopher Dickey, "Shadowland: Evil Genius," *Newsweek*, February 20, 2003, http://www.newsweek.com/id/62699 (accessed October 20, 2009); and David Kaplan, "Playing Offense," *U.S. News and World Report*, June 2, 2003, p. 18. According to CIA director Michael Hayden, al-Nashiri was one of three Al Qaeda detainees waterboarded. See testimony before the Senate Select Committee on Intelligence, February 5, 2008. U.S. officials claimed that al-Nashiri had been captured at an undisclosed Persian Gulf country in early November 2002. Within a month, however, a UAE spokesman acknowledged that al-Nashiri had been captured in *late October* and handed over to the United States. See Alaa Shahine, "UAE Says al-Qaida Member Planned Attack," *Associated Press*, December 24, 2002; and "UAE Admits It Handed Over to CIA Top Al-Qaeda Operations Manager," *Al-Babwa*, December 24, 2002.

92. Seymour Hersh, "Manhunt," *New Yorker*, December 23, 2002.

93. Policy Briefing with Abd Al-Kareem Al-Iryani, November 26, 2002.

94. Bamford, "Big Brother Is Listening," p. 67.

95. Abdul-Aziz Oudah, "Marib Operation Joint Yemeni-American Action," *Yemen Observer*, November 16, 2002; "Military Units Deployed in Mareb, Jowf, & Shabwa," *Yemen Times*, August 19–25, 2002; Policy Briefing with Abd Al-Kareem Al-Iryani; and Seymour Hersh, *Chain of Command: The Road from 9/11 to Abu Gharib* (New York: HarperCollins, 2004), p. 265.

96. DeLong, with Lukeman, *Inside CENTCOM*, p. 70.

97. Doyle McManus, "A U.S. License to Kill," *Los Angeles Times*, January 11, 2003, p. A1.

98. Bamford, "Big Brother Is Listening," p. 67.

99. Ron Suskind, *The One Percent Doctrine: Deep Inside America's Pursuit of Its Enemies Since 9/11* (New York: Simon and Schuster, 2006), p. 181; and DeLong, with Lukeman, *Inside CENTCOM*, pp. 70–71. Gen. Tommy Franks, CENTCOM commander, was in Qatar during the Predator strike.

100. Priest, "Covert CIA Program Withstands New Furor," p. A1; and Suskind, *The One Percent Doctrine*, p. 181.

101. Dana Priest, "CIA Killed U.S. Citizen in Yemen Missile Strike," *Washington Post*, November 8, 2002, p. A1; and DeLong, with Lukeman, *Inside CENTCOM*, p. 71. CIA officials claimed that they did not know Hijazi was in the SUV. See James Risen and Marc Santora, "Man Believed Slain in Yemen Tied by U.S. to Buffalo Cell," *New York Times*, November 10, 2002, p. 17.

102. John Barry and Evan Thomas, "Up in the Sky, an Unblinking Eye," *Newsweek*, June 9, 2008, p. 42.

103. Interview with Richard Armitage, February 15, 2007.

104. DeLong, with Lukeman, *Inside CENTCOM*, pp. 70–71.

105. Thomas and Hosenball, "The Opening Shot," p. 48; "Leading al Qaeda Suspect

Killed in Yemen Car Blast," Reuters, November 4, 2002; "Yemeni Security Investigates Car Explosion," *Saba*, November 4, 2002 (translated by BBC Monitoring Middle East); and Karl Mueller et al., *Striking First: Preemptive Preventive Attack in U.S. National Security Policy* (Santa Monica, CA: RAND, 2006), pp. 241–256.

106. John Lumpkin, "U.S. Kills Senior Al-Qaeda Operative in Yemen with Missile Strike," *Associated Press*, November 4, 2002; and NBC, *Nightly News*, "CIA Bombs Car Allegedly Carrying Al-Qaeda Operative Abu Ali al-Harithi," Jim Miklaszewski reporting, November 4, 2002.

107. DeLong, with Lukeman, *Inside CENTCOM*, pp. 71–72; and CNN, *Live Today*, interview with Paul Wolfowitz, November 5, 2002.

108. Thomas and Hosenball, "The Opening Shot," p. 48.

109. Smucker, "The Intrigue Behind the Drone Strike," p. 1.

110. Thomas and Hosenball, "The Opening Shot," p. 48.

111. For a list, and narrative description, of all known U.S. Predator attacks in Pakistan from May 2005 through June 1, 2008, see Appendix I.

112. Joby Warrick and Robin Wright, "Unilateral Strike Called a Model for U.S. Operations in Pakistan," *Washington Post*, February 19, 2008, p. A1.

113. Karen DeYoung and Joby Warrick, "For Obama Administration, Fatal Blows Take Precedence," *Washington Post*, February 14, 2010, p. A1.

114. Or succeed without creating substantial collateral damage. See Stephen Hosmer, *Operations Against Enemy Leaders* (Santa Monica, CA: RAND, 2001), pp. 40–45.

115. Greg Miller, "Despite Apparent Success in Yemen, Risks Remain," *Los Angeles Times*, November 6, 2002, p. A8.

116. David Johnston and David Sanger, "Fatal Strike in Yemen Was Based on Rules Set Out by Bush," *New York Times*, November 6, 2002, p. A12.

117. Hersh, *Chain of Command*, p. 262.

118. Interview with Richard Armitage, February 15, 2007.

119. Suskind, *The One Percent Doctrine*, p. 182.

120. For a partial list, see Bruce Jenkins, *Unconquerable Nation: Knowing Our Enemy, Strengthening Ourselves* (Santa Monica, CA: RAND, 2006), pp. 179–184.

121. Jim Landers, "Despite the Odds, Yemen Not al-Qaeda's Playground," *Dallas Morning News*, May 2, 2004, p. A1.

122. Kevin Whitelaw, "On a Dagger's Edge," *U.S. News and World Report*, March 13, 2006, pp. 38–45.

123. Interview with Gen. David Petraeus, February 10, 2010; and Dana Priest, "U.S. Playing Key Role in Yemen Attacks," *Washington Post*, January 27, 2010, p. A1.

124. Interview with a senior U.S. Central Command official, February 2006.

125. Tyler, "Yemen, an Uneasy Ally, Proves Adept at Playing Off Old Rivals," p. 1.

126. Robert Worth, "Yemen's Deals with Jihadists Unsettle U.S.," *New York Times*, January 28, 2008, p. 1; Craig Whitlock, "Probe of USS Cole Bombing Unravels,"

Washington Post, May 4, 2008, p. A1; and Ali Soufan, "Coddling Terrorists in Yemen," *Washington Post*, May 17, 2008, p. A17.

127. Transcript of Daniel Benjamin, U.S. Department of State Coordinator for Counterterrorism, briefing with the Defense Writers Group, Washington, D.C., January 20, 2010.

128. Suskind, *The One Percent Doctrine*, p. 182.

129. Deborah West, *Combating Terrorism in the Horn of Africa and Yemen*, World Peace Foundation Report, no. 40, 2005; and Robert Burrowes, "Yemen: Political Economy and the Effort Against Terrorism," in Robert Rotberg (ed.), *Battling Terrorism in the Horn of Africa* (Washington, DC: Brookings Institution Press, 2005), pp. 141–172.

130. Interview with Gen. David Petraeus, February 10, 2010; and "General David Petraeus: Full Transcript of Interview with *The Times*," *The Times (London)*, January 25, 2010.

131. For an endorsement of this position, see Office of the Director of National Intelligence, "Summary of the High Value Terrorist Detainee Program," September 6, 2006.

Chapter 6

1. President George W. Bush, "Address to a Joint Session of Congress and the American People," September 20, 2001.

2. Sebastian Rotella, "Terrorism's Reach: A Road to Ansar Began in Italy," *Los Angeles Times*, April 28, 2003, p. A1.

3. Interview with Gen. Richard Myers, October 8, 2007.

4. Interview with Gen. Jack Keane, September 27, 2006.

5. John Darnton, "Almost a Nation: The Kurds in Iraq," *New York Times*, January 21, 1994, p. 1.

6. Andrew Cockburn and Patrick Cockburn, *Out of the Ashes: The Resurrection of Saddam Hussein* (New York: HarperCollins, 1999), p. 232.

7. International Crisis Group (ICG), "Radical Islam in Iraqi Kurdistan: The Mouse That Roared?," ICG Middle East Briefing, February 7, 2003, p. 3; and Michael Rubin, "The Islamist Threat in Iraqi Kurdistan," Middle East Intelligence Bulletin, jointly published by the United States Committee for a Free Lebanon and the Middle East Forum, December 2001.

8. Michael Howard, "Under Fire from Militants," *The Guardian*, February 5, 2003, p. 1.

9. Karl Vick, "In Remote Corner of Iraq, an Odd Alliance," *Washington Post*, March 12, 2003, p. A1. According the U.S. Department of the Treasury "Bin Laden provided [Ansar] with an estimated $300,000 to $600,000 in seed money." See Office of Public Affairs, "Treasury Department Statement Regarding the Designation of Ansar al-Islam," February 20, 2003.

10. Human Rights Watch, "Ansar al-Islam in Iraqi Kurdistan," *HRW Backgrounder*, February 5, 2003; and ICG, "Radical Islam in Iraqi Kurdistan," p. 5.

11. Jason Burke, *Al-Qaeda: Casting a Shadow of Terror* (London: I.B. Tauris, 2003), pp. 202–204, 242–244; and C. J. Chivers, "Kurds Face a Second Enemy," *New York Times*, January 13, 2003, p. 1.

12. Ed Blache, "Northern Iraq Seething as War Looms," *Jane's Islamic Affairs*, December 20, 2002; Scott Peterson, "The Rise and Fall of Ansar al-Islam," *Christian Science Monitor*, October 16, 2003, p. 1; and Catherine Taylor, "Taliban-Style Group Grows in Iraq," *Christian Science Monitor*, March 15, 2002, p. 1.

13. ICG, "Radical Islam in Iraqi Kurdistan," p. 4.

14. Taylor, "Taliban-Style Group Grows in Iraq," p. 1.

15. Mary Anne Weaver, "Inventing Al-Zarqawi," *Atlantic Monthly* (July-August 2006), pp. 87–100; and Mark Hosenball, "Terrorism: Following Zarqawi's Footsteps in Iran," *Newsweek*, October 25, 2004, p. 6.

16. C. J. Chivers, "Instruction and Methods from Al Qaeda Took Root in North Iraq with Islamic Fighters," *New York Times*, April 27, 2003, p. 26.

17. Jonathan Schanzer, "Ansar al-Islam: Back in Iraq," *Middle East Quarterly* (Winter 2004), pp. 41–50.

18. Ron Suskind, *The Price of Loyalty: George W. Bush, the White House, and the Education of Paul O'Neil* (New York: Simon and Schuster, 2004), pp. 70–75.

19. Karen DeYoung, *Soldier: The Life of Colin Powell* (New York: Alfred A. Knopf, 2006), pp. 398–399; George Tenet, with Bill Harlow, *At the Center of the Storm: My Years at the CIA* (New York: HarperCollins, 2007), pp. 307–309; and interview with Douglas Feith, August 9, 2006.

20. Interview with Douglas Feith, August 9, 2006; interview with Amb. Richard Armitage, February 15, 2007; and James Mann, *Rise of the Vulcans: The History of Bush's War Cabinet* (New York: Viking, 2004), pp. 332.

21. Mann, *Rise of the Vulcans*, pp. 332–334.

22. Interview with Amb. Richard Armitage, February 15, 2007.

23. DeYoung, *Soldier*, p. 399.

24. Human Rights Watch/Middle East, *Iraq's Crime of Genocide: The Anfal Campaign Against the Kurds* (New Haven, CT: Yale University Press, 1995), pp. 262–265.

25. Jeffrey Goldberg, "The Great Terror," *New Yorker*, March 25, 2002, pp. 52–75. British journalist and long-time Al Qaeda watcher Jason Burke interviewed Shahab a year after Goldberg and concluded flatly: "Shahab is a liar." See Burke, "The Missing Link?" *Observer*, February 9, 2003.

26. Goldberg, "The Great Terror."

27. CNN, *Late Edition*, March 24, 2002.

28. NPR, *All Things Considered*, March 18, 2002; and CNBC, *Hardball with Chris Matthews*, March 18, 2002.

29. Goldberg, "The Great Terror," p. 52.

30. John Mintz, "Iraq, Al Qaeda Run Extremist Group in Kurdish Territory," *Washington Post*, March 18, 2002, p. A12.

31. Interview with Douglas Feith, August 9, 2006. See also Douglas Feith, *War and Decision: Inside the Pentagon at the Dawn of the War on Terrorism* (New York: Harper Paperbacks, 2008), pp. 261–262.

32. Interview with Douglas Feith, August 9, 2006; and interview with senior administration official, March 2007.

33. Bob Woodward, *Plan of Attack* (New York: Simon and Schuster, 2004), pp. 140–142; Tenet, with Harlow, *At the Center of the Storm*, pp. 389–391; and Tim Judah, "Kurdish Guerillas Poised to Fire First Shots Against Iraq," *The Observer*, August 11, 2002, p. 2.

34. Peter Roman and David Tarr, "The Joint Chiefs of Staff: From Service Parochialism to Jointness," *Political Science Quarterly* (Spring 1998), p. 105.

35. Interview with Gen. Jack Keane, September 27, 2006; and e-mail communication with Lt. Gen. Gregory Newbold, August 29, 2006.

36. Interview with Lt. Gen. Gregory Newbold, August 29, 2006.

37. Ibid.

38. Interview with Gen. Jack Keane, September 27, 2006.

39. Ibid.

40. Interview with Amb. Marc Grossman, December 8, 2006.

41. Interview with Amb. Marc Grossman, December 8, 2006.

42. DeYoung, *Soldier*, p. 427.

43. According to Amb. Richard Armitage, "There were also some concerns within the administration that [Khurmal] was very close to the Iranian border, and we didn't want to get into a fight with Iran." Interview with Armitage, February 15, 2007.

44. Michael Knights, *Cradle of Conflict: Iraq and the Birth of Modern U.S. Military Power* (Annapolis, MD: Naval Institute Press, 2005).

45. Interview with Gen. Jack Keane, September 27, 2006; interview with Gen. Richard Myers, October 8, 2007; and Myers, with McConnell, *Eyes on the Horizon*, p. 219.

46. Interview with Gen. Jack Keane, September 27, 2006; and interview with Douglas Feith, August 9, 2006.

47. Interview with U.S. Air Force colonel, February 2007; and Richard Myers, with Malcolm McConnell, *Eyes on the Horizon: Serving on the Front Lines of National Security* (New York: Threshold Editions, 2009), p. 219. See also Linda Robinson, *Masters of Chaos: The Secret History of the Special Forces* (New York: Public Affairs, 2004), p. 298.

48. Interview with U.S. Air Force colonel, February 2007.

49. Ibid.

50. Interview with Gen. Jack Keane, September 27, 2006.

51. Scot Paltrow, "Questions Mount Over Failure to Hit Zarqawi's Camp," *Wall Street Journal*, October 25, 2004, p. A3.

52. Interview with Gen. Richard Myers, October 8, 2007; and interview with Gen. Jack Keane, September 27, 2006.

53. Thomas Ricks, "Military Bids to Postpone Iraq Invasion," *Washington Post*, May 24, 2002, p. A1. See also David Moniz and Jonathan Weisman, "Military Question Iraq Plan," *USA Today*, May 23, 2002, p. A1; and Thom Shanker and Eric Schmitt, "Military Would Be Stressed By a New War, Study Finds," *New York Times*, May 24, 2002, p. A8.

54. Interview with Amb. Richard Armitage, February 15, 2007; interview with Amb. Marc Grossman, December 8, 2006; and interview with senior administration official, March 2007.

55. Interview with Gen. Richard Myers, October 8, 2007.

56. ABC, *World News Tonight*, reported by John McWethy, August 19, 2002; and David Cloud, "Kurdish Militants May Have Run Chemical-Weapons Tests in Iraq," *Wall Street Journal*, August 20, 2002, p. A4.

57. Tenet, with Harlow, *At the Center of the Storm*, pp. 277, 350–351.

58. Tenet, with Harlow, *At the Center of the Storm*, pp. 350–351.

59. Secretary Colin Powell, "Remarks to the United Nations Security Council," New York City, February 5, 2003. The allegations of al-Zarqawi's connections to Baghdad would turn out to be false. According to the Senate Select Committee on Intelligence report into the use of intelligence in the period preceding the Iraq war, "Saddam viewed al-Zarqawi as an outlaw and attempted, unsuccessfully, to locate and capture him. Similarly, Saddam Hussein viewed the al-Qa'ida affiliate group Ansar al-Islam operating in Kurdish-controlled northeastern Iraq as a threat to his regime. A May 2002 intelligence document indicates that the Iraqi regime was concerned that the United States would use the presence of Ansar al-Islam, operating in an area that Baghdad had not controlled since 1991, to support claims of links between the regime and al-Qa'ida." See U.S. Senate Select Committee on Intelligence, *The Use by the Intelligence Community of Information Provided by the Iraqi National Congress*, September 8, 2006, pp. 181–182.

60. U.S. Department of State, "Designation of Ansar al-Islam," February 20, 2003.

61. Tenet, with Harlow, *At the Center of the Storm*, p. 350.

62. Paltrow, "Questions Mount Over Failure to Hit Zarqawi's Camp," p. A3.

63. Michael Scheuer, *Marching Toward Hell: America and Islam After Iraq* (New York: Free Press, 2008), p. 126.

64. Paltrow, "Questions Mount Over Failure to Hit Zarqawi's Camp," p. A3. Emphasis added.

65. Evan Thomas and Rod Nordland, "Death of a Terrorist," *Newsweek*, June 19, 2006, p. 22.

66. Robinson, *Masters of Chaos*, p. 322.

67. Interview with Lt. Gen. Gregory Newbold, August 29, 2006.

68. An exhaustive search of Turkish-language media, as translated by the U.S.

Department of Commerce, National Technical Information Service's World News Connection, could not find this article. Several administration officials, however, have referred to this article. It is doubtful that this one article would have definitely alerted Ansar al-Islam members to flee Khurmal, as a close reading of all translated Turkish media articles published between June 1 and August 31 demonstrates that there were persistent rumors of an imminent U.S. or Turkish military invasion of Iraq.

69. Woodward, *Plan of Attack*, p. 142.

70. ABC, *World News Tonight*, August 19, 2002.

71. CNN, *Live at Daybreak*, reported by Barbara Starr, August 20, 2002.

72. Walter Pincus, "U.S. Effort to Link Terrorists to Iraq Focuses on Jordanian," *Washington Post*, February 5, 2003, p. A17.)

73. Interview with Douglas Feith, August 9, 2006.

74. Interview with U.S. Air Force colonel, February 2007.

75. According to a February 2003 news report, "Lawmakers who have attended classified briefings on the camp say that they have been stymied for months in their efforts to get an explanation for why the United States has not launched a military strike on the compound near the village of Khurmal." See Greg Miller, "Ongoing Iraqi Camp Questioned," *Los Angeles Times*, February 7, 2003, p. A1. On the day after his Security Council presentation, Powell was asked by Sen. Joseph Biden at a Senate Foreign Relations Committee hearing, "Why hadn't we taken direct military action [at Khurmal]?" Powell replied, "I would rather not in this setting go into what contingency plans we had looked at or what we might or might not have done. But I can assure you that it is a place that has been very much in our minds and something we have been studying very carefully." See Senate Foreign Relations Committee, "Hearing on U.S. Foreign Policy," February 6, 2003.

76. Interview with Douglas Feith, April 5, 2007.

77. Paltrow, "Questions Mount Over Failure to Hit Zarqawi's Camp," p. A3.

78. Interview with Douglas Feith, August 9, 2006; and interview with Marc Grossman, December 8, 2005.

79. Interview with Douglas Feith, August 9, 2006.

80. American Enterprise Institute, *America After 9/11: Public Opinion on the War on Terrorism, the War with Iraq, and America's Place in the World*, updated December 26, 2003, pp. 94–95.

81. ABC News/*Washington Post* poll, February 22–25, 2007; and Roper Center, "Job Performance Ratings for President Bush," http://www.ropercenter.uconn.edu/ (accessed March 1, 2007).

82. Ann Scott Tyson, "Invading Iraq: Would the Public Go Along?" *Christian Science Monitor*, July 17, 2002, p. 2; and Richard Morin and Claudia Deane, "Poll: Americans Cautiously Favor War in Iraq," *Washington Post*, August 13, 2002, p. A10. The concerted Bush administration effort to highlight the threat of Saddam Hussein did not begin

in earnest until early September, because, in the words of White House Chief of Staff Andy Card, "From a marketing point of view, you don't introduce new products in August." See Elisabeth Bushmiller, "Bush Aides Set Strategy to Sell Policy on Iraq," *New York Times,* September 7, 2002, p. A1.

83. The formal decision for regime change might have been reached even earlier. A February 2002 news report quoted an anonymous senior administration official: "This is not an argument about whether to get rid of Saddam Hussein. That debate is over. This is . . . how you do it." See Warren Strobel and John Walcott, "Bush Has Decided to Overthrow Hussein," *Knight-Ridder,* February 13, 2002.

84. White House, "Interview of the President by Sir Trevor McDonald of Britain's ITV Television Network," April 4, 2002.

85. Nicholas Lemann, "How It Came to War," *New Yorker,* March 31, 2006, p. 36.

86. Lemann, "How It Came to War," p. 36. Haass was not the only member of the diplomatic corps cut out of the loop on Iraq. State Department employees later recounted that by mid-June staffers from the vice president's office and the Pentagon were "too cocky" and acting "like they know something we don't." See DeYoung, *Soldier,* p. 399.

87. As reprinted in "The Secret Downing Street Memo," *The Sunday Times,* May 1, 2005, p. 1. According to George Tenet, Dearlove told him after the Memo was leaked "that upon returning to London in July 2002, he expressed the view, based on his conversations, that the war in Iraq was going to happen." See Tenet, with Harlow, *At the Center of the Storm,* p. 310. For more on the July 2002 meetings that informed Dearlove's assessment, see James Risen, *State of War: The Secret History of the CIA and the Bush Administration* (New York: Free Press, 2006), pp. 112–114.

88. Interview with Douglas Feith, August 9, 2006. Paul Pillar, who was National Intelligence Officer for the Near East and South Asia from 2000 to 2005, but not involved in the Khurmal decisionmaking, posited that the Bush administration decided against attacking Khurmal because "I think the White House didn't want to complicate the main event [regime change.]" Interview with Pillar, September 28, 2006.

89. Michael Gordon and Bernard Trainor, *Cobra II: The Inside Story of the Invasion and Occupation of Iraq* (New York: Pantheon Books, 2006), p. 52; and Bob Woodward, *State of Denial* (New York: Simon and Schuster, 2006), pp. 90–92.

90. Interview with senior administration official, March 2007.

91. Gordon and Trainor, *Cobra II,* p. 68; and Michael DeLong, with Noah Lukeman, *Inside CENTCOM: The Unvarnished Truth About the Wars in Afghanistan and Iraq* (Washington, DC: Regnery, 2004), p. 79.

92. Interview with Amb. Marc Grossman, December 8, 2006.

93. Interview with Amb. Richard Armitage, February 15, 2007.

94. Interview with Douglas Feith, April 5, 2007.

95. Interview with senior administration official, March 2007.

96. Interview with Gen. Jack Keane, September 27, 2006.

97. Gregory Fontenot, E. J. Degen, and David Tohn, *On Point: The United States Army in Operation Iraqi Freedom* (Annapolis, MD: Naval Institute Press, 2005), p. 250; Robinson, *Masters of Chaos*, pp. 296–323; and U.S. Army, interview by Operational Leadership Experiences Project with Major D. Jones, Combat Studies Institute, Ft. Leavenworth, Kansas, November 9, 2005.

98. Robinson, *Masters of Chaos*, pp. 296–323; Gordon and Trainor, *Cobra II*, p. 341; Greg Jaffe and David Cloud, "U.S. Sees Foreign Hand in Iraq," *Wall Street Journal*, October 29, 2003, p. A4; and U.S. Senate Select Committee on Intelligence, *Report of the Select Committee on Intelligence on Postwar Findings About Iraq's WMD Programs and Links to Terrorism and How They Compare with Prewar Assessments*, September 8, 2006, pp. 93–94.

99. Jeffrey Fleishman, "Militants' Crude Camp Casts Doubt on U.S. Claims," *Los Angeles Times*, April 27, 2003, p. A1.

100. Tenet, with Harlow, *At the Center of the Storm*, p. 278.

101. As one of al-Zarqawi's cohort later noted, "He had been planning for this for a long time." See Loretta Napoleoni, "Portrait of a Killer," *Foreign Policy* (November-December 2005), p. 41.

102. The report is dated March 12, 2003. See Report of a Committee of Privy Counsellors, chairman, The Lord Butler of Brockwell, *Review of Intelligence on Weapons of Mass Destruction* (London: The Stationery Office: July 14, 2004), p. 120.

103. Department of Defense, "DoD News Briefing-Secretary Rumsfeld, Mr. Di Rita and Lt. Gen. Schwartz," October 23, 2002.

104. Sean Naylor, "SpecOps Unit Nearly Nabs Zarqawi," *Army Times*, April 28, 2006.

105. U.S. Coalition Provisional Authority, "English translation of terrorist Musab al Zarqawi letter obtained by United States Government in Iraq," February 2004.

106. White House, "President Bush Delivers Commencement Address at United States Coast Guard Academy," May 23, 2007; and White House, "Fact Sheet: Keeping America Safe from Attack," May 23, 2007.

107. Karen DeYoung, "CIA Received Recent Detainee from Turkey, Al-Qaeda Says," *Washington Post*, May 25, 2007, p. A14; and Alexis Debat, "Osama Bin Laden's Heir," *National Interest* (Summer 2005), pp. 155–160.

108. David Cloud, "Elusive Enemy: Long in U.S. Sights, A Young Terrorist Builds Grim Resume," *Wall Street Journal*, February 10, 2004, p. A1.

109. As of 2004, at least 116 terrorist operatives had been arrested from Zarqawi's network outside of Iraq. See Matthew Levitt, "Untangling the Terror Web: Identifying and Counteracting the Phenomenon of Crossover Between Terrorist Groups," *SAIS Review* (Winter-Spring 2004), p. 38. See also Desmond Butler and Don Van Natta Jr., "Trail of Anti-U.S. Fighters Said to Cross Europe to Iraq," *New York Times*, December 6, 2003, p. A8; and Daniel Williams, "Italy Targeted by Recruiters for Terrorists," *Washington Post*, December 17, 2003, p. A35.

110. Mark Bowden, "The Ploy," *Atlantic Monthly* (May 2007), pp. 54–68; and "Litening [*sic*] Pod Used in Attack on Al Qaeda Brass," *Aviation Week and Space Technology*, June 12, 2006, p. 18.

111. Though the rumor of poison and toxin production at Khurmal was well-known before the UN Monitoring, Verification and Inspection Commission for Iraq teams entered the country in November 2002, the inspectors never visited Khurmal, because it was perceived as being outside of the control of Saddam Hussein's regime. Thus, had Hussein complied with the UN Resolutions and stayed in power, Ansar al-Islam could have continued operating outside of the watch of the international community. Interview with senior UNMOVIC official, October 2005; and Hans Blix, *Disarming Iraq* (New York: Pantheon Books, 2004). The CIA's *Comprehensive Report of the Special Advisor to the DCI on Iraq's WMD* also did not mention Khurmal because, as the report noted, "The goal of this report is to provide facts and meaning concerning the *Regime's* experience with WMD." Emphasis added. See *Comprehensive Report*, September 30, 2004, p. 1.

112. Interview with senior administration official, March 2007.

113. Robert Jervis, *Perception and Misperception in International Politics* (Princeton, NJ: Princeton University Press, 1976), pp. 217–282.

114. Tim Weiner and James Risen, "Decision to Strike Factory in Sudan Based on Surmise Inferred from Evidence," *New York Times*, September 21, 1998, p. A1; James Risen, "To Bomb Sudan Plant, or Not: A Year Later, Debates Rankle," *New York Times*, October 27, 1999, p. A1; Risen, *State of War*, p. 153; interview with Clinton administration intelligence official, July 2006; and interview with Paul Pillar, September 28, 2006.

Chapter 7

1. Frederick W. Kagan, *Finding the Target: The Transformation of American Military Policy* (New York: Encounter Books, 2006), p. 358.

2. Jon Meacham, "A Conversation with Barack Obama," *Newsweek*, May 25, 2009, p. 38.

3. George Stephanopoulos, *All Too Human: A Political Education* (Boston: Little, Brown, 1999), p. 312.

4. Covert DMOs are, by definition, not officially acknowledged or explained. Nevertheless, determining and evaluating their military and political objectives is fairly simple ex post facto on the basis of news reports, anonymous administration quotes, and acknowledgments of the attack by the targeted group, such as Al Qaeda's "martyr" announcements.

5. Although the Dual Key arrangement frustrated U.S. military officials who sought autonomy of action for their targeting procedures in Bosnia, it is unclear that the Serbs took advantage of the overlapping command and control relationship. Interview with Professor Kori Schake, U.S. Military Academy, July 22, 2006.

6. Using only in-theater assets did, however, have the positive effect of achieving

tactical surprise since the Iraqis did not have advanced warning to disperse its targeted assets. See Michael Knights, *Cradle of Conflict: Iraq and the Birth of Modern U.S. Military Power* (Annapolis, MD: Naval Institute Press, 2005), p. 201.

7. According to Zinni, President Clinton gave the commander the final decision to suspend the four-day campaign. See Knights, *Cradle of Conflict,* p. 205.

8. Interview with Clinton administration Pentagon official, June 2009.

9. See Chapter 1, note 6.

10. Office of the Director of National Intelligence, National Intelligence Estimate, *The Terrorist Threat to the U.S. Homeland,* July 2007; and Statement by the Director of National Intelligence, John D. Negroponte, to the Senate Armed Services Committee, *Annual Threat Assessment of the Director of National Intelligence,* February 27, 2008. As Admiral Michael Mullen, Chairman of the Joint Chiefs of Staff, warned in June 2008, "I believe fundamentally if the United States is going to get hit, it's going to come out of the planning that the leadership in the FATA is generating, their planning and direction." Peter Spiegel, "Michael Mullen Says Action Unlikely Against Militants in Pakistan," *Los Angeles Times,* June 11, 2008, p. A1.

11. Griff Witte and Joby Warrick, "Insurgents Forced Out of Pakistan's Tribal Havens Form Smaller Cells in Heart of Nation," *Washington Post,* December 19, 2009, p. A1; and Matthew Rosenberg and Siobhan Gorman, "U.S. Puzzles Over Top Militant's Fate," *Wall Street Journal,* February 5, 2010, p. A10.

12. Transcript of Daniel Benjamin, U.S. Department of State Coordinator for Counterterrorism, briefing with the Defense Writers Group, Washington, D.C., January 20, 2010.

13. Josh Meyer, "Militants' Rise in Pakistan Points to Opportunity Lost," *Los Angeles Times,* June 8, 2008, p. A1; Ann Mulrine, "Bad Guys in the Border Badlands," *U.S. News and World Report,* June 23, 2008, p. 39; and Craig Cohen and Derek Chollet, "When $10 Billion Is Not Enough: Rethinking U.S. Strategy Toward Pakistan," *The Washington Quarterly,* Vol. 30, no. 2 (Spring 2007), pp. 7–19.

14. Government Accountability Office, April 2008; Government Accountability Office, Statement of Gene Dodaro before the Subcommittee on Near Eastern and South and Central Asian Affairs, Committee on Foreign Relations, U.S. Senate, "U.S. Efforts to Address the Terrorist Threat in Pakistan's Federally Administered Tribal Areas Require a Comprehensive Plan and Continued Oversight," May 20, 2008; and Mark Mazzetti and David Rhode, "Amid U.S. Policy Disputes, Qaeda Grows in Pakistan," *New York Times,* June 30, 2008, pp. A1, A10–11.

15. Interview with Gen. David Petraeus, February 10, 2010; and Department of State, Office of the Special Representative for Afghanistan and Pakistan, *Afghanistan and Pakistan Regional Stabilization Strategy,* updated February 2010.

16. Kagan, *Finding the Target: The Transformation of American Military Policy;* David Mets, *The Long Search for Surgical Strike: Precision Munitions and the Revolution in*

Military Affairs (Maxwell, AL: Air University Press, 2001); Michael Rip and James Hasik, *Precision Revolution: GPS and the Future of Aerial Warfare* (Annapolis, MD: Naval Institute Press, 2002); and Bill Owens, with Ed Offley, *Lifting the Fog of War* (New York: Farrar, Straus & Giroux, 2000), pp. 97–149.

17. According to a senior Clinton NSC official closely involved in the planning and debates surrounding Desert Fox: "Civilians wanted a clear four-day 'that's it' operation." Interview with senior Clinton administration official, September 27, 2006.

18. Elliot Cohen and John Gooch, *Military Misfortunes: The Anatomy of Failure in War* (New York: Free Press, 1990), p. 25.

19. Seymour Hersh, "Preparing the Battlefield," *New Yorker*, July 7, 2008; Gareth Porter, "Commander's Veto Sank Threatening Gulf Buildup," *IPS News Service*, May 15, 2007; and Mark Thompson, "Iran Dissent Cost Fallon His Job," *Time*, March 12, 2008.

20. Karen DeYoung and Joby Warrick, "For Obama Administration, Fatal Blows Take Precedence," *Washington Post*, February 14, 2010, p. A1.

21. William Hawkins, "Imposing Peace: Total vs. Limited Wars, and the Need to Put Boots on the Ground," *Parameters* (Summer 2000), pp. 72–82; and Thom Shanker, "U.S. Pushes to Rely More On Remotely Piloted Craft," *New York Times*, June 5, 2008, p. A12.

22. Department of Defense, *Deterrence Operations: Joint Operating Concept, Version 2.0*, December 2006. See also Defense Science Board, *Report of the Defense Science Board on Future Strategic Strike Forces* (Washington, DC: Undersecretary of Defense for Acquisition, Technology, and Logistics, 2005); National Research Council, *Conventional Prompt Global Strike Capabilities: Letter Report* (Washington, DC: National Academy of Sciences, 2007); and Government Accountability Office, *DoD Needs to Strengthen Implementation of Its Global Strike Concept and Provide a Comprehensive Investment Approach for Acquiring Needed Capabilities*, April 2008.

23. Interview with James Steinberg, February 27, 2007; interview with Lt. Gen. Donald Kerrick, November 2, 2006; and interview with Lt. Gen. Gregory Newbold, August 29, 2006.

24. A.J.P. Taylor, *The Origins of the Second World War* (New York: Atheneum, 1962), p. 92.

25. Interview with Lt. Gen Gregory Newbold, August 29, 2006.

26. Interview with Col. Kevin Benson, April 4, 2008.

27. Eliot A. Cohen, *Supreme Command: Soldiers, Statesmen, and Leadership in Wartime* (New York: Anchor Books, 2002), pp. 257–258.

28. Interview with Gen. Barry McCaffrey, February 13, 2007; and interview with Gen. Jack Keane, September 27, 2006.

29. Department of Defense, *Fiscal Year 2010 Budget Request Summary Justification* (Washington, DC: Office of the Assistant Secretary of Defense, Public Affairs, May 2009); and International Institute for Strategic Studies, *The Military Balance: 2009* (London: Routledge, 2009).

30. Interview with Gen. Richard Myers, October 8, 2007.

31. Interview with Gen. Anthony Zinni, February 13, 2008.

32. Gary Goertz, *Social Science Concepts: A User's Guide* (Princeton, NJ: Princeton University Press, 2006), pp. 177–210.

33. DeYoung and Warrick, "For Obama Administration, Fatal Blows Take Precedence."

34. Risa Brooks provides an excellent overview of the necessity of open civil-military dialogue: "The quality of debate between political and military leaders is the best measure of the healthiness of civil-military relations. Political leaders may bring to the table their own biases and preexisting conceptions about military strategy and activity. Military leaders may also exhibit their own preconceived notions. Consequently, both must participate fully in comprehensive dialogue at the apex of decision making to expose flawed reasoning, hidden and contradictory assumptions, and alternative views in the analytical process. Both sides must share their private views and information and engage with open minds different arguments, even those that are marginal or unpopular, without prejudging their merits." Brooks, *Shaping Strategy: The Civil-Military Politics of Strategic Assessment* (Princeton, NJ: Princeton University Press, 2008), p. 269. For how secrecy can allow "deeply embedded flaws" in the civil-military decisionmaking process, see Ted Gup, *Nation of Secrets: The Threat to Democracy and the American Way of Life* (New York: Doubleday, 2007), pp. 76–79.

Appendix I

1. Michael Gordon, "Iraq Given Friday Deadline on Missiles," *New York Times*, January 7, 1993, p. A8.

2. Ann Devroy and Barton Gellman, "Military Action Against Iraq Signaled by Administration," *Washington Post*, January 13, 1993, p. A1; Michael Gordon, "Bush Said to Plan Airstrike on Iraq Over Its Defiance," *New York Times*, January 13, 1993, p. A1; and Paul Bedard, "Fog Gave Saddam One-Day Reprieve from Allied Planes," *Washington Times*, January 14 , 1993, p. A8.

3. Department of Defense news briefing, Gen. Joseph Hoar, January 13, 1993. All dates and times in this appendix are representative of the location where the DMO occurred.

4. Barton Gellman and Julia Preston, "Targets in Iraq Missed, Building Hit, U.S. Says," *Washington Post*, January 15, 1993, p. A1.

5. Ann Devroy and Julia Preston, "Allies, Iraq Again Near Brink Over U.N. Inspector Flights," *Washington Post*, January 16, 1993, p. A1; and David Fulghum, "Pentagon Criticizes Air Strike on Iraq," *Aviation Week and Space Technology*, January 25, 1993, p. 47.

6. Thomas Ricks, "Allied Planes Destroyed Single Iraqi Missile Site," *Wall Street Journal*, January 15, 1993, p. A7.

7. David Fulghum, "Pentagon Criticizes Air Strike on Iraq," *Aviation Week and*

Space Technology, January 25, 1993, p. 47; and White House, press briefing with Marlin Fitzwater, January 13, 1993.

8. UN Security Council Resolution 687, April 3, 1991.

9. The term was first used by White House Press Secretary Marlin Fitzwater on September 26, 1991.

10. White House, "Remarks and an Exchange with Reporters on the Situation in Iraq," January 15, 1993.

11. Eric Schmitt, "The Day's Weapon of Choice, the Cruise Missile, Is Valued for Its Accuracy," *New York Times,* January 18, 1993, p. A8; David Fulghum, "Clashes with Iraq Continue After Week of Heavy Air Strikes," *Aviation Week and Space Technology,* January 25, 1993, p. 38; and Michael Knights, *Cradle of Conflict: Iraq and the Birth of Modern U.S. Military Power* (Annapolis, MD: Naval Institute Press, 2005), p. 135.

12. Barton Gellman and Ann Devroy, "U.S., Allied Jets Batter Iraq's Air Defenses," *Washington Post,* January 19, 1993, p. A1.

13. Michael Gordon, "U.S. Leads Further Attacks on Iraqi Antiaircraft Sites," *New York Times,* January 19, 1993, p. A1; and Knights, *Cradle of Conflict,* p. 137.

14. Fulghum, "Clashes with Iraq Continue After Week of Heavy Air Strikes," p. 38; and Gordon, "U.S. Leads Further Attacks on Iraqi Antiaircraft Sites," p. A1.

15. White House, "Status Report on Iraq's Non-Compliance with UN Resolutions," letter from President Clinton to the Speaker of the House of Representatives and the President Pro Tempore of the Senate, March 22, 1993.

16. Charles Duelfer, *Hide and Seek: The Search for Truth in Iraq* (New York: Public Affairs, 2009), p. 147.

17. R. Jeffrey Smith, "Iraqi Officer Recruited Suspects in Plot Against Bush, U.S. Says," *Washington Post,* July 1, 1993, p. A18.

18. Warren Christopher, *Chances of a Lifetime* (New York: Scribner, 2001), pp. 233–234; and Bill Turque et al., "Striking Saddam," *Newsweek,* July 5, 1993, p. 15.

19. Thomas Friedman, "An Assessment: The Missile's Message," *New York Times,* June 28, 1993, p. A1; and Eleanor Clift et al., "Seven Days," *Newsweek,* July 12, 1993, p. 18.

20. Taylor Branch, *The Clinton Tapes: Wrestling History with the President* (New York: Simon and Schuster, 2009), p. 136.

21. George Stephanopoulos, *All Too Human: A Political Education* (Boston: Little, Brown, 1999), pp. 156–161.

22. William J. Clinton, *My Life* (New York: Knopf, 2004), p. 526; and Colin Powell, with Joseph Persico, *My American Journey* (New York: Random House, 1995), p. 584.

23. President Clinton initially ordered the strike on Friday, June 25, 1993, but it was delayed so that it would not occur on the Muslim Sabbath. See Tim Weiner, "Attack Is Aimed at the Heart of Iraq's Spy Network," *New York Times,* June 27, 1993, p. 1.

24. Department of Defense news briefing, June 26, 1993.

25. David Von Drehle and R. Jeffrey Smith, "U.S. Strikes Iraq for Plot to Kill Bush," *Washington Post*, June 27, 1993, p. A1.

26. Weiner, "Attack Is Aimed at the Heart of Iraq's Spy Network," p. 1.

27. Department of Defense news briefing, June 26, 1993; and David Fulghum, "Low Tomahawk Kill Rate Under Study," *Aviation Week and Space Technology*, July 5, 1993, p. 25.

28. Richard Clarke, *Against All Enemies: Inside America's War on Terrorism* (New York: Free Press, 2004), p. 84.

29. Department of Defense news briefing, June 27, 1993.

30. Ibid.; and John Lancaster and Barton Gellman, "U.S. Calls Baghdad Raid a Qualified Success," *Washington Post*, June 28, 1993, p. A1.

31. Government Accountability Office, *Cruise Missiles: Proven Capability Should Affect Aircraft and Force Structure Requirements* (Washington, DC: Government Printing Office, April 1995), p. 28.

32. UN Security Council, resolution 781, October 9, 1992.

33. UN Security Council, resolution 816, March 31, 1993.

34. NATO, "Operation Deny Flight," Allied Forces Southern fact sheet, updated July 18, 2003. The UN Security Council declared six safe areas: Sarajevo, Tuzla, Zepa, Gorazde, Bihac, and Srebrenica. See resolution 824, May 6, 1993.

35. NATO, "Operation Deny Flight," updated July 18, 2003.

36. Craig Covault, "AWACS, Command Chain Key to NATO Shootdown," *Aviation Week and Space Technology*, March 7, 1994, p. 25; and John Lancaster, "U.S. Jets Down 4 Serb Bombers Over Bosnia," *Washington Post*, March 1, 1994, p. A1.

37. Ivo Daalder, *Getting to Dayton: The Making of America's Bosnia Policy* (Washington, DC: Brookings Institution Press, 2000) p. 32; and John Pomfret, "U.N. Rejects NATO Request to Bomb Serb Airfield After 'No-Fly' Violations," *Washington Post*, June 22, 1995, p. A22.

38. Covault, "AWACS, Command Chain Key to NATO Shootdown," p. 25.

39. UN, "Seventh periodic report on the situation of human rights in the territory of the former Yugoslavia, submitted by Mr. Tadeusz Mazowiecki, Special Rapporteur of the Commission on Human Rights, Situation of Human Rights in the Territory of the Former Yugoslavia," June 10, 1994.

40. Paul Lewis, "U.N. Warns Serbs on Gorazde," *New York Times*, April 10, 1994, p. 1.

41. Jonathan Randal, "U.S. Jets Strike Serb Forces Near Bosnian Town," *Washington Post*, April 11, 1994, p. A1; and Laura Silber and Allan Little, *Yugoslavia: Death of a Nation* (New York: Penguin Books, 1997, revised and updated), pp. 327–328.

42. Chuck Sudetic, "U.S. Planes Bomb Serbian Position for a Second Day," *New York Times*, April 12, 1994, p. A1.

43. Steven Burg and Paul Shoup, *The War in Bosnia-Herzegovina: Ethnic Conflict and International Intervention* (Armonk, NY: M.E. Sharpe, 1999), pp. 146–153.

44. John Harris, "Bad Weather, Rugged Terrain Blunt Sophisticated Air Weaponry in

Bosnia," *Washington Post,* April 12, 1994; Michael Gordon, "Modest Air Operation in Bosnia Crosses a Major Political Frontier," *New York Times,* April 11, 1994, p. A1; and Jonathan Randal, "U.S. Planes Blast Serb Forces Again," *Washington Post,* April 12, 1994, p. A1.

45. NATO, "Operation Deny Flight," July 18, 2003; and John Pomfret, "U.S. Jets Hit Serbs After Raid on Arms," *Washington Post,* August 6, 1994, p. A1.

46. Tom Post et al., "Mission Accomplished—Barely," *Newsweek,* August 15, 1994, p. 55.

47. Ibid.

48. Chuck Sudetic, "U.S. Hits Bosnian Serb Target in Air Raid," *New York Times,* August 6, 1994, p. A4; and Post et al., "Mission Accomplished—Barely," p. 55.

49. Pomfret, "U.S. Jets Hit Serbs After Raid on Arms," p. A1.

50. Burg and Paul, *The War in Bosnia-Herzegovina,* pp. 154–157; and John Pomfret, "Serb Planes Launch New Strike," *Washington Post,* November 20, 1994, p. A1.

51. UN Security Council, Resolution 958, November 19, 1994.

52. Michael Gordon, "NATO Set to Bomb Serbs in Croatia," *New York Times,* November 21, 1994, p. A1.

53. Craig Covault, "NATO Hits Missile Sites," *Aviation Week and Space Technology,* November 28, 1994, p. 25; and John Pomfret, "NATO Jets Bomb Serb Airfield," *Washington Post,* November 22, 1994, p. A1.

54. William Drozdiak, "NATO Jets Attack Serb Air Defenses," *Washington Post,* November 24, 1994, p. A1.

55. William Drozdiak, "Bosnian Serbs Defy Threats, Move on Bihac," *Washington Post,* November 25, 1994, p. A1; and Daalder, *Getting to Dayton,* p. 32.

56. Ed Vulliamy, "How the CIA Intercepted SAS Signals," *The Guardian,* January 29, 1994, p. 9.

57. Pomfret, "NATO Jets Bomb Serb Airfield," p. A1.

58. Michael Gordon, "U.S. and Bosnia: How a Policy Changed," *New York Times,* December 4, 1994, p. 1.

59. John Pomfret, "Bombed Croatian Serb Airfield Repaired and Possibly in Use," *Washington Post,* December 5, 1994, p. A25.

60. UN, *Report of the Secretary-General Pursuant to General Assembly Resolution 53/35 (1998): Srebrenica Report,* November 15, 1999, p. 46; and Daalder, *Getting to Dayton,* p. 41.

61. Joel Brand, "NATO Strikes Threatened in Sarajevo," *Washington Post,* May 25, 1995, p. A33.

62. UN, *Srebrenica Report,* p. 46.

63. Joel Brand, "NATO Jets Hit Serb Site in Bosnia," *Washington Post,* May 26, 1995, p. A1; and "NATO Aircraft," *Aviation Week and Space Technology,* May 29, 1995, p. 17.

64. NATO press conference with Adm. Leighton Smith, Commander in Chief, Allied Forces Southern Region, May 26, 1995.

65. Roger Cohen, "U.S. Set to Offer Aid to Reinforce U.N. Bosnian Troops," *New York Times*, May 31, 1995, p. A1.

66. Rupert Smith, *The Utility of Force: The Art of War in the Modern World* (New York: Alfred A. Knopf, 2007), pp. 353–354; and UN, *Srebrenica Report*, November 15, 1999, p. 46.

67. NATO press conference with Adm. Leighton Smith, May 26, 1995.

68. Bob Woodward, *The Choice: How Clinton Won* (New York: Simon and Schuster, 1996), pp. 253–270; and Burg and Shoup, *The War in Bosnia-Herzegovina*, p. 325.

69. NBC, *Meet the Press*, with Brian Williams, August 27, 1995.

70. Steven Greenhouse, "U.S. Officials Say Bosnian Serbs Face NATO Attack If Talks Stall," *New York Times*, August 28, 1995, p. A1.

71. Robert Owen (ed.), *Deliberate Force: A Case Study in Effective Air Campaigning*, Final Report of the Air University Balkans Air Campaign Study, School of Advanced Airpower Studies (Maxwell, AL: SAAS, 1998). Pp. 349–350.

72. John Tirpak, "Deliberate Force," *Air Force*, October 1997.

73. Richard Sargent, "Aircraft Used in Deliberate Force," in Owen (ed.), *Deliberate Force*, p. 264; and Bradley Graham, "U.S. Fires Cruise Missiles at Bosnian Serb Sites," *Washington Post*, September 11, 1995, p. A1.

74. Burg and Shoup, *The War in Bosnia-Herzegovina*, pp. 351–352.

75. Richard Holbrooke, *To End a War* (New York: The Modern Library, 1998), pp. 101–158.

76. David Halberstam, *War in a Time of Peace: Bush, Clinton, and the Generals* (New York: Scribner, 2001), pp. 348–351.

77. Andrew Cockburn and Patrick Cockburn, *Out of the Ashes: The Resurrection of Saddam Hussein* (New York: HarperCollins, 1999), p. 232.

78. Kenneth Pollack, *The Threatening Storm: The Case for Invading Iraq* (New York: Random House, 2002), p. 81

79. Interview with Bruce Riedel, January 23, 2007; Tara Soneshine and John Barry, "Putting Iraq on Notice," *Newsweek*, September 9, 1996, p. 48; and testimony of Riedel before the House Committee on National Security, September 26, 1996.

80. John Harris and Bradley Graham, "After Quick Response to Iraq, a Lengthy Debate on Motive," *Washington Post*, September 8, 1996, p. A29; and Knights, *Cradle of Conflict*, pp. 156–159.

81. Interview with Bruce Riedel, January 23, 2007; and Pollack, *The Threatening Storm*, p. 83.

82. Harris and Graham, "After Quick Response to Iraq, Lengthy Debate on Motive," p. A29. The decision to expand the southern NFZ was proposed by Ambassador Mark Parris, the NSC's senior director for Near East and South Asia. Interview with former Clinton administration official, September 27, 2006.

83. Alison Mitchell, "U.S. Launches Further Strike Against Iraq After Clinton Vows

He Will Extract," *New York Times*, September 4, 1996, p. A1; and Knights, *Cradle of Conflict*, p. 166.

84. Department of Defense news briefing, with Kenneth Bacon, September 10, 1996.

85. Testimony of John Deutch before the Senate Select Committee on Intelligence, September 19, 1996.

86. Department of Defense news briefing, with Kenneth Bacon, September 6, 1996.

87. David Fulghum and Paul Mann, "No Clear Winners Emerge from U.S.-Iraq Clash," *Aviation Week and Space Technology*, September 9, 1996, p. 35.

88. Knights, *Cradle of Conflict*, pp. 162–164; and David Fulghum, "Hard Lessons in Iraq Lead to New Attack Plan," *Aviation Week and Space Technology*, September 16, 1996, p. 24.

89. Reprinted in UN, "Letter dated 15 December 1998 from the Executive Chairman December of the Special Commission established by the Secretary-General pursuant to paragraph 9 (b) (i) of Security Council resolution 687 (1991) addressed to the Secretary-General," December 15, 1998.

90. UN, "Letter dated 15 December 1998."

91. Madeline Albright, with Bill Woodward, *Madame Secretary* (New York: Miramax Books, 2003), p. 286.

92. Knights, *Cradle of Conflict*, p. 201–205.

93. Robert Wall, "U.S. to Replenish Missile Stocks, Steps Up Strikes Against SAMs," *Aviation Week and Space Technology*, January 18, 1999, p. 24.

94. Department of Defense, news briefing with Sec. William Cohen, Gen. Anthony Zinni, and Rear Adm. Thomas Wilson, October 19, 1998.

95. Albright, with Woodward, *Madam Secretary*, p. 286.

96. U.S. Senate Select Committee on Intelligence, *Report on the U.S. Intelligence Community's Prewar Intelligence Assessments on Iraq*, July 7, 2004, pp. 258–260.

97. Wall, "U.S. to Replenish Missile Stocks, Steps Up Strikes Against SAMs," p. 24.

98. U.S. Senate Armed Services Committee, "Hearing on Military Readiness," statement of Gen. Hugh Shelton, January 5, 1999; and Tom Clancy, with Tony Zinni and Tony Koltz, *Battle Ready* (New York: G.P. Putnam's Sons, 2004), pp. 16–19.

99. Steven Lee Myers, "Signs of Iraqi Arms Buildup Bedevil U.S. Administration," *New York Times*, February 1, 2000, p. 1.

100. Warren Strobel, "Bush Didn't Realize International Weight of Iraq Bomb Raid," *Knight Ridder Tribune*, April 26, 2001; and Knights, *Cradle of Conflict*, pp. 235–237.

101. David Fulghum and Robert Wall, "Strikes Hit Old Targets, Reveal New Problems," *Aviation Week and Space Technology*, February 26, 2001, p. 24; Thomas Ricks, "Bombs in Iraq Raid Fell Wide Of Targets," *Washington Post*, February 22, 2001, p. A1; and Knights, *Cradle of Conflict*, p. 237.

102. Thom Shanker, "Rumsfeld Says Iraq Has Improved Air Defenses Since February," *New York Times*, August 4, 2001, p. A6; Thomas Ricks, "U.S., British Jets Attack

Three Iraqi Air Defense Sites," *Washington Post*, August 11, 2001, p. A16; and Knights, *Cradle of Conflict*, pp. 238–243.

103. Thomas Ricks, "Iraq Bombing Errors Blamed on Poor Data," *Washington Post*, February 24, 2001, p. A20; Ricks, "Bombs in Iraq Raid Fell Wide of Targets," p. A1; and Department of Defense news briefing with Rear Adm. Craig Quigley, February 22, 2001.

104. Bob Woodward, *Plan of Attack* (New York: Simon and Schuster, 2004), pp. 380–399; and George Tenet, with Bill Harlow, *At the Center of the Storm: My Years at the CIA* (New York: HarperCollins, 2007), pp. 389–395.

105. Richard Myers, with Malcolm McConnell, *Eyes on the Horizon: Serving on the Front Lines of National Security* (New York: Threshold Editions, 2009), p. 238.

106. Tommy Franks, with Malcolm McConnell, *American Soldier* (New York: HarperCollins, 2004), p. 453; Rajiv Chandrasekaran and Thomas Ricks, "U.S. Opens War with Strikes On Baghdad Aimed at Hussein," *Washington Post*, March 20, 2003, p. A1; Michael Gordon and Bernard Trainor, *Cobra II: The Inside Story of the Invasion and Occupation of Iraq* (New York: Pantheon Books, 2006), p. 175; and Michael DeLong, with Noah Lukeman, *Inside CENTCOM: The Unvarnished Truth About the Wars in Afghanistan and Iraq* (Washington, DC: Regnery, 2004), pp. 97–98.

107. Gordon and Trainor, *Cobra II*, p. 175.

108. Mark Kinkade, "The First Shot," *Airman*, July 2003, Web edition (http://www.af.mil/news/airman/0703/air.html); and Gordon and Trainor, *Cobra II*, p. 174.

109. Kinkade, "The First Shot."

110. Gordon and Trainor, *Cobra II*, p. 177.

111. *CBS Evening News*, reported by David Martin, "Whether U.S. Attempt to Kill Saddam Was Successful," May 28, 2003.

112. Tenet, with Harlow, *At the Center of the Storm*, pp. 239–240; David Kaplan et al., "Playing Offense," *U.S. News and World Report*, June 2, 2003, p. 18; and Dana Priest and Ann Scott Tyson, "Bin Laden Trail 'Stone Cold,'" *Washington Post*, September 10, 2006, p. A1.

113. ABC News, reported by Brian Ross, "Al Qaeda Leader Killed in Secret Operation," May 13, 2005; Dana Priest, "Surveillance Operation in Pakistan Located and Killed Al Qaeda Official," *Washington Post*, May 15, 2005, p. A25; Douglas Jehl, "Remotely Controlled Craft Part of U.S.-Pakistan Drive Against Al Qaeda, Ex-Officials Say," *New York Times*, May 16, 2005, p. A12; and Mark Mazzetti, "U.S. Aborted Raid Against Al Qaeda in Pakistan in '05," *New York Times*, July 8, 2007, p. 6.

114. "Blast Kills Two in Pakistan's Waziristan," *The News* (Pakistan), Web edition from World News Connection, May 9, 2005; and Jehl, "Remotely Controlled Craft Part of U.S.-Pakistan Drive Against Al Qaeda, Ex-Officials Say," p. A12.

115. Testimony of John Negroponte, "Annual Threat Assessment," Senate Select Committee on Intelligence, January 11, 2007; and Carlotta Gall and Ismail Khan, "Taliban and Allies Tighten Grip in North of Pakistan," *New York Times*, December 11, 2006, p. A1.

116. Priest, "Surveillance Operation in Pakistan Located and Killed Al Qaeda Official," p. A25; and "Blast Kills Two in Pakistan's Waziristan," *The News* (Pakistan).

117. Craig Whitlock and Kamran Khan, "Blast in Pakistan Kills Al Qaeda Commander," *Washington Post*, December 4, 2005, p. A1.

118. Rahimullah Yusufzai, "Dead al-Qaeda No 3 Not on FBI's Most Wanted List," *The News* (Pakistan), December 4, 2005.

119. Amnesty International, "Pakistan: U.S. Involvement in Civilian Deaths," January 31, 2006; and Yusufzai, "Dead al-Qaeda No. 3 Not on FBI's Most Wanted List."

120. Testimony of Negroponte, "Annual Threat Assessment,"; and Gall and Khan, "Taliban and Allies Tighten Grip in North of Pakistan," p. A1.

121. Ismail Khan, "Senior Al Qaeda Commander Killed," *Dawn* (Pakistan), December 3, 2005, Web edition (http://www.dawn.com/2005/12/03/top4.htm); and *NBC Nightly News*, reported by Jim Miklaszewski, "U.S. officials Claim That Al-Qaeda's Third in Command, Abu Hamza Rabia, Killed by U.S. Missile," December 3, 2005.

122. Aparisim Ghosh, "Can Bin Laden Be Caught?," *Time*, January 30, 2006, p. 24; and Gretchen Peters, "Drone Said to Have killed Al Qaeda's No. 3," *Christian Science Monitor*, December 3, 2005, p. 4.

123. Josh Meyer, "CIA Expands Use of Drones in Terror War," *Los Angeles Times*, January 29, 2006, p. A1.

124. Amnesty International, "Pakistan: Human Rights Ignored in the 'War on Terror,'" September 29, 2006.

125. Zulfiqar Ali and Paul Watson, "Pakistani Journalist Abducted from Northern Tribal Area," *Los Angeles Times*, December 8, 2005, p. A5.

126. Evan Thomas, "Into Thin Air," *Newsweek*, September 3, 2007, p. 24.

127. Testimony of Negroponte, "Annual Threat Assessment,"; and Gall and Khan, "Taliban and Allies Tighten Grip in North of Pakistan," p. A1.

128. Peters, "Drone Said to Have Killed Al Qaeda's No. 3," p. 4.

129. "Musharraf Confirms Al-Qaeda Commander Killed in Pakistan," *Agence France Presse*, December 3, 2005.

130. Mohammed Khan, "Attack Kills 8 in Pakistan," *New York Times*, January 8, 2006, p. 13; and Pazir Gul and Zulfiqar Ali, "8 FC Men Among 16 Killed in Waziristan: 'Cleric's House Hit by U.S. Copters,'" *Dawn* (Pakistan), January 8, 2006, Web edition (http://www.dawn.com/2006/01/08/top3.htm).

131. Gul and Ali, "8 FC Men Among 16 Killed in Waziristan"; and Behroz Khan, "22 Killed in Tank, Miranshah Attacks," *The News* (Pakistan), January 8, 2006, Web edition (http://www.jang.com.pk/thenews/jan2006-daily/08-01-2006/main/main2.htm).

132. Pamela Constable and Dafna Linzer, "Confusion Shrouds Pakistan Attack," *Washington Post*, January 18, 2006, p. A10.

133. Priest and Scott Tyson, "Bin Laden Trail 'Stone Cold,'" p. A1; and Aparisim Ghosh, "The Blunt Instruments of War," *Time*, January 23, 2007, p. 17.

134. Carlotta Gall and Ismail Khan, "American Strike in January Missed Al Qaeda's No. 2 by a Few Hours," *New York Times*, November 10, 2006, p. A8.

135. Kamran Khan and Griff Witte, "Pakistanis Say Airstrike Killed Al Qaeda Figures," *Washington Post*, January 19, 2006, p. A19; Sami Yousafzai et al., "Al Qaeda: 'Got to Take That Shot'," *Newsweek*, January 23, 2006, p. 6; and *NBC Nightly News*, reported by Jim Miklaszewski, "Pakistan Claims Civilian Casualties in CIA Drone Attack," January 13, 2006.

136. Griff Witte and Kamran Khan, "Attacks Strain Efforts On Terror," *Washington Post*, January 23, 2006, p. A1.

137. Gall and Khan, "American Strike in January Missed Al Qaeda's No. 2 by a Few Hours," p. A8.

138. Craig Whitlock and Walter Pincus, "Zawahiri Taunts Bush After Attack Misses Him," *Washington Post*, January 31, 2006, p. A1.

139. Josh Meyer, "Al Qaeda Said to Focus on WMDs," *Los Angeles Times*, February 3, 2008, p. A1.

140. One of the three senior Al Qaeda leaders, Egyptian operative Abu Obaidah al-Masri, died from hepatitis C in early 2008. See Eric Schmitt, "Attack Planner for Al Qaeda Reported Dead," *New York Times*, April 20, 2008, p. A8; Craig Whitlock and Karen DeYoung, "Senior Al-Qaeda Commander Believed to Be Dead," *Washington Post*, April 10, 2008, p. A10; and Sebastian Rotella, "Alleged Al Qaeda Chief Dead, Officials Say," *Los Angeles Times*, April 10, 2008.

141. Josh Meyer, "U.S. Strike in Somalia Aims at Three Fugitives," *Los Angeles Times*, January 9, 2007, p. A1.

142. Testimony of Jendayi Frazer, Assistant Secretary for African Affairs before the House International Relations Committee, Subcommittees on Africa, Global Human Rights & International Operations, International Terrorism and Nonproliferation, June 29, 2006.

143. Michael Gordon and Mark Mazzetti, "U.S. Used Bases in Ethiopia to Hunt Al Qaeda in Africa," *New York Times*, February 23, 2007, p. 1; and Gordon and Mazzetti, "North Koreans Arm Ethiopians as U.S. Assents," *New York Times*, April 8, 2007, p. 1.

144. *NBC Nightly News*, reported by Jim Miklaszewski, "New U.S. Military Operation Against Suspected Al-Qaeda Terrorists in Somalia," January 9, 2007.

145. Gordon and Mazzetti, "U.S. Used Bases in Ethiopia to Hunt Al Qaeda in Africa," p. 1.

146. Alex Perry, "Somalia's Al Qaeda Link," *Time*, July 2, 2007, p. 17.

147. Edmund Sanders, "Somalia Targets Survived," *Los Angeles Times*, January 12, 2007, p. A3.

148. Stephanie McCrummen, "U.S. Troops Went into Somalia After Raid," *Washington Post*, January 12, 2007, p. A1; and "A Strike from the Skies That Missed," *U.S. News and World Report*, January 22, 2007.

149. "Somalia's Shahab Insurgents Split with Courts," *Jane's Terrorism and Security Monitor*, February 16, 2008; and Mohamed Olad Hassan, "Score Flee, 4 Dead in Somalia Fighting," *Associated Press*, March 22, 2007.

150. *CBS Evening News*, reported by Thalia Assuras, "U.S. Forces Attack Taliban and Al-Qaeda in Afghanistan," January 16, 2007; and Ishtiaq Mahsud, "Tribesmen: U.S. Launched This Week's Airstrike on Suspected al-Qaida Hideout in Pakistan," *Associated Press*, January 19, 2007.

151. Munir Ahmad, "Pakistan Army Hits Suspected al-Qaida Hideouts Near Afghan Border, Killing 10 People," *Associated Press*, January 16, 2007; and "Pakistan Strikes Militant Camps Near Afghan Border," *Agence France Presse*, January 16, 2007.

152. Karen DeYoung and Stephanie McCrummen, "U.S. Stages 2nd Airstrike in Somalia," *Washington Post*, January 24, 2007, p. A9; and Reuters, "U.S. Conducts a Second Airstrike Inside Somalia," *New York Times*, January 25, 2007, p. 11.

153. Alex Perry, "Somalia's Al Qaeda Link," *Time*, July 2, 2007, p. 17.

154. Gordon and Mazzetti, "U.S. Used Bases in Ethiopia to Hunt Al Qaeda in Africa," p. A1; and William Wallis, "Doubts Persist on al-Qaeda Casualties in Somalia Strike," *Financial Times*, February 5, 2007, p. 7.

155. Bashirullah Khan, "Missile Strike in Pakistan Kills 4," *Associated Press*, April 27, 2007; and Pazir Gul, "Missiles Fired from Across Border Kill Four in N. Waziristan," *Dawn* (Pakistan), April 27, 2007, Web edition.

156. Stephanie McCrummen, "U.S. Warship Fires Missiles at Fighters in Somalia," *Washington Post*, June 3, 2007, p. A18; and John Burgess, "Somali Leader Appeals for More American Aid," *Washington Post*, June 27, 2007, p. A16.

157. UN, "Letter dated 17 July 2007 from the Chairman of the Security Council Committee established pursuant to resolution 751 (1992) concerning Somalia addressed to the President of the Security Council," July 18, 2007, p. 17.

158. Perry, "Somalia's Al Qaeda Link," p. 17.

159. UN, "Letter dated 17 July 2007," p. 46.

160. Paul Salopek, "U.S. Helps Somalis Battle Insurgents," *Chicago Tribune*, June 3, 2007, p. 10; and Jeffrey Gettleman, "U.S. Strikes Inside Somalia, Bombing Suspected Militant Hide-Out," *New York Times*, June 3, 2007, p. 20.

161. Bashirullah Khan, "Uzbeks, Chechens, Arabs Among 30 Militants Killed in Pakistan-Afghan Border Attacks: Officials," *Associated Press*, June 20, 2007; and Griff Witte, "Blast Kills at Least 20 in Pakistan, *Washington Post*, June 20, 2007, p. A14.

162. Imtiaz Ali and Craig Whitlock, "Al-Qaeda Commander Moved Freely in Pakistan," *Washington Post*, February 4, 2008, p. A1.

163. Craig Whitlock, "The New Al-Qaeda Central," *Washington Post*, September 9, 2007, p. A1; Sara Carter, "Top-Tier al Qaeda Leader Killed," *Washington Times*, February 1, 2008, p. A1; and Alisa Tang, "Libyan Blamed for Bomb at Cheney Visit," *Associated Press*, May 3, 2007.

164. Josh Meyer, "Top Al Qaeda Commander Killed," *Los Angeles Times*, February 1, 2008.

165. *NBC Nightly News*, reported by Jim Miklaszewski, "Attack That Killed Kids Targeted al-Qaida Leader," June 17, 2007; Department of Defense news briefing with Col. Schweitzer and Maj. Gen. Khaliq via Video Conference from Afghanistan, June 20, 2007; and Craig Whitlock and Karen DeYoung, "Al Qaeda Figure Is Killed in Pakistan," *Washington Post*, February 1, 2008, p. A1.

166. Imtiaz Ali and Craig Whitlock, "Al-Qaeda Commander Moved Freely in Pakistan," *Washington Post*, February 4, 2008, p. A1.

167. Eric Schmitt and David Sanger, "Pakistan Shuns C.I.A. Buildup Sought by U.S.," *New York Times*, January 27, 2008, pp. 1, 10; Schmitt and Sanger, "Pakistan Shift Could Curtail Drone Strikes," *New York Times*, February 22, 2008, p. A1; and Robin Wright and Joby Warrick, "U.S. Steps Up Unilateral Strikes in Pakistan," *Washington Post*, March 27, 2008, p. A1.

168. Carter, "Top-Tier al Qaeda Leader Killed," p. A1; and Ali and Whitlock, "Al-Qaeda Commander Moved Freely in Pakistan," p. A1.

169. Joby Warrick and Robin Wright, "Unilateral Strike Called a Model for U.S. Operations in Pakistan," *Washington Post*, February 19, 2008, p. A1.

170. Jay Solomon and Siobhan Gorman, "Al Qaeda Chieftain Is Believed Killed By U.S. in Pakistan," *Wall Street Journal*, February 1, 2008, p. A16; Whitlock and DeYoung, "Al Qaeda Figure Is Killed in Pakistan," p. A1; and Warrick and Wright, "Unilateral Strike Called a Model for U.S. Operations in Pakistan," p. A1.

171. Warrick and Wright, "Unilateral Strike Called a Model for U.S. Operations in Pakistan," p. A1.

172. CNN, "U.S. Officials: CIA Kills Top al Qaeda Terrorist in Pakistan," January 31, 2008, Web edition (http://edition.cnn.com/2008/US/01/31/alqaeda.death).

173. Omar Sinan and Paul Schemm, "Al-Qaida Releases Video Showing Corpse of Its Slain Afghan strategist," *Reuters*, March 2, 2008.

174. Ismail Khan, "Missile Attack, Possibly by NATO, Kills 8 in Pakistan," *New York Times*, February 29, 2008, p. A6; Hafiz Wazir, Missile Hits Pakistan's Waziristan," *Reuters*, February 27, 2008; and Imtiaz Ali and Candace Rondeaux, "Missile Strike in Pakistan Kills 10 at Suspected Taliban Safe House," *Washington Post*, February 29, 2008, p. A14.

175. Khan, "Missile Attack, Possibly by NATO, Kills 8 in Pakistan," p. A6; and Mushtaq Yusufzai and Irfan Burki, "12 killed as Missile Hits House in S. Waziristan," *The News* (Pakistan) (online), February 29, 2008.

176. Jeffrey Gettleman and Eric Schmitt, "U.S. Forces Fire Missiles into Somalia at a Kenyan," *New York Times*, March 4, 2008, p. A9; and Jennifer Daskal and Leslie Lefkow, "Off-Target," *Los Angeles Times*, March 28, 2008.

177. Fred Baker, "U.S. Attacks Al Qaeda Terrorist in Somalia," *Armed Forces Press Service*, March 3, 2008.

178. FBI, "Saleh Ali Saleh Nabhan," (http://www.fbi.gov/terrorinfo/nabhan.htm, as of March 7, 2008); and Jeffrey Gettleman, "In Somalia, Government Once Hailed as Best Hope Is Teetering on Collapse," *New York Times*, March 29, 2008, p. A6.

179. Gettleman and Schmitt, "U.S. Forces Fire Missiles Into Somalia at a Kenyan," p. A9; Stephanie McCrummen, "U.S. Strike in Somalia Targets Terror Suspects," *Washington Post*, March 4, 2008, p. A13; Edmund Sanders, "U.S. Missile Strike in Somalia Kills 6," *Los Angeles Times*, March 4, 2008; and Daskal and Lefkow, "Off-Target," March 28, 2008.

180. Jeffrey Gettleman and Eric Schmitt, "American Raid In Somalia Kills Qaeda Militant," *New York Times*, September 15, 2009, p. A1.

181. Jane Perlez and Ismail Khan, "Airstrikes Kill 9 in Pakistan Region That Harbors Militants," *New York Times*, March 17, 2008, p. A3; Candace Rondeaux, "Airstrike Kills 18 in Pakistan," *Washington Post*, March 17, 2008, p. A13; and Irfan Barki and Akhtar Shehzad, "20 Killed in S. Waziristan Missile Strike; Foreigners Among Dead," *The News* (Pakistan) (online), March 17, 2008.

182. Perlez and Khan, "Airstrikes Kill 9 in Pakistan Region That Harbors Militants," p. A3.

183. Jane Perlez, "Pakistanis Signal Shift in Relationship with U.S.," *New York Times*, March 26, 2008, p. A7; and Robin Wright and Joby Warrick, "U.S. Steps Up Unilateral Strikes in Pakistan," *Washington Post*, March 27, 2008, p. A1.

184. Perlez and Khan, "Airstrikes Kill 9 in Pakistan Region That Harbors Militants," p. A3.

185. Rondeaux, "Airstrike Kills 18 in Pakistan," p. A13; Bashirullah Khan and Lauren Frayer, "Missiles Kill 20 in strike on Pakistani Tribal Area," *Associated Press*, March 16, 2008; and Jamal Khurshid, "Dr. Arshad Waheed killed in Wana," *The News* (Pakistan) (online), March 23, 2008.

186. Zulfiqar Ali and Laura King, "18 Killed in Pakistan Missile Strike," *Los Angeles Times*, March 17, 2008.

187. Eric Schmitt and Jeffrey Gettleman, "U.S. Says Strike Kills Leader of a Somali Militia Suspected of Ties to Al Qaeda," *New York Times*, May 2, 2008, p. A10.

188. Josh Meyer, "Slain Somali Was in U.S. Sights for Years," *Los Angeles Times*, May 2, 2008, p. A1.

189. Schmitt and Gettleman, "U.S. Says Strike Kills Leader of a Somali Militia Suspected of Ties to Al Qaeda," p. A10.

190. Stephanie McCrummen and Karen DeYoung, "U.S. Airstrike Kills Somali Accused of Links to Al-Qaeda," *Washington Post*, May 2, 2008, p. A12; and Meyer, "Slain Somali was in U.S. Sights for Years," p. A1.

191. Schmitt and Gettleman, "U.S. Says Strike Kills Leader of a Somali Militia Suspected of Ties to Al Qaeda," p. A10.

192. Sami Yousafzai and Ron Moreau, "Where 'The Land Is on Fire,'" *Newsweek*,

June 16, 2008, p. 42; Zahid Hussain and Yochi Dreazen, "Strike Kills Militant Tied to Europe Attacks," *Wall Street Journal*, May 20, 2008, p. A14; and Jason Burke, "Al-Qaeda Chief Dies in Missile Air Strike," *The Observer*, June 1, 2008, p. 33.

193. "Pakistan Army Takes Issue Over U.S. Missile Attack," *Reuters*, May 17, 2008.

194. Zulfiqar Ali and Laura King, "Pakistan Says It Has No Knowledge of Missile Strike," *Los Angeles Times*, May 16, 2008.

195. Yousafzai and Moreau, "Where 'The Land Is on Fire'," p. 42; Hussain and Dreazen, "Strike Kills Militant Tied to Europe Attacks," p. A14; and Burke, "Al-Qaeda Chief Dies in Missile Air Strike," p. 33.

196. Yousafzai and Moreau, "Where 'The Land Is on Fire'," p. 42.

197. David Sanger, *The Inheritance: The World Obama Confronts and the Challenges to American Power* (New York: Harmony Books, 2009), pp. 248–257; and Mark Mazzetti and Eric Schmitt, "U.S. Military Seeks to Widen Pakistan Raids," *New York Times*, April 20, 2008, p. 1.

198. Sanger, *The Inheritance*, pp. 248–257.

199. Julian Barnes and Greg Miller, "Pentagon May Step Up Raids in Pakistan," *Los Angeles Times*, September 5, 2008, p. A4; and Sanger, *The Inheritance*, p. 257.

200. Eric Schmitt and Thom Shanker, "Officials Say U.S. Killed an Iraqi in Raid in Syria," *New York Times*, October 28, 2008, p. A1; and Mark Hosenball, "Targeting a 'Facilitator'," *Newsweek* (online), October 27, 2008.

201. Ann Scott Tyson and Ellen Knickmeyer, "U.S. Calls Raid a Warning to Syria," *Washington Post*, October 28, 2008, p. A1.

202. Karen DeYoung, "Terrorist Traffic via Syria Again Inching Up," *Washington Post*, May 11, 2009, p. A1.

203. U.S. Department of the Treasury, Office of Foreign Assets Control, "Terrorism: What You Need to Know About U.S. Sanctions," May 27, 2009.

204. U.S. Department of the Treasury, "Treasury Designates Members of Abu Ghadiyah's Network Facilitates Flow of Terrorists, Weapons, and Money from Syria to al Qaida in Iraq," February 28, 2008.

205. Michael Shear, "An Early Military Victory for Obama," *Washington Post*, April 13, 2009, p. A9; Bill Gertz, "Obama OK'd 2 SEAL Teams for Pirates," *Washington Times*, April 22, 2009, p. 1; Kate Wiltrout, "Commander Shares His Pride in Bainbridge's Rescue Effort," *Norfolk Virginian-Pilot*, April 16, 2009; and Department of Defense, "DoD News Briefing with Vice Adm. Gortney From Bahrain," April 12, 2009.

206. Chip Cummins, "Pirate Threat Grows in Gulf," *Wall Street Journal*, June 15, 2009, p. A9.

207. Scott Wilson, Ann Scott Tyson, and Stephanie McCrummen, "'3 Rounds, 3 Dead Bodies'," *Washington Post*, April 14, 2009, p. A1.

Appendix II

1. James A. Baker III, with Thomas M. DeFrank, *The Politics of Diplomacy: Revolution, War and Peace, 1989–1992* (New York: G.P. Putnam's Sons, 1995); and Ivo Daalder, *Getting to Dayton: The Making of America's Bosnia Policy* (Washington, DC: Brookings Institution Press, 2000), pp. 6–7.

2. Hearing before the Senate Armed Services Committee, "Situation in Bosnia and Appropriate U.S. and Western Responses," August 11, 1992; and interview with Lt. Gen. Barry McCaffrey, February 13, 2007.

3. David Halberstam, *War in a Time of Peace: Bush, Clinton, and the Generals* (New York: Scribner, 2001), pp. 36–42.

4. Richard Haass, *War of Necessity, War of Choice: A Memoir of Two Iraq Wars* (New York: Simon and Schuster, 2009), pp. 150–151; and Patrick Tyler, "U.S. Said to Plan Raids on Baghdad If Access Is Denied," *New York Times*, August 16, 1992, p. 1.

5. Ashton Carter and William Perry, *Preventive Defense: A New Security Strategy for America* (Washington, DC: Brookings Institution Press, 1999), pp. 123–142; and "South Korea Stopped U.S. Strike on North Korea: Former President," *Agence France Presse*, May 24, 2000.

6. Kenneth Pollack, *The Persian Puzzle: The Conflict Between Iran and America* (New York: Random House, 2004), pp. 284–285, 291; Richard Clarke, *Against All Enemies: Inside America's War on Terrorism* (New York: Free Press, 2004), pp. 118–121; and interview with Col. Kevin Benson, April 4, 2008.

7. Anonymous (later revealed as Michael Scheur), note to the Members of the Senate Select Committee on Intelligence," date September or October 2004, as printed in "How *Not* to Catch a Terrorist," *Atlantic Monthly*, (December 2004), pp. 50–52; and Philip Shenon, *The Commission: The Uncensored History of the 9/11 Investigation* (New York: Twelve, 2008), pp. 191–194.

8. National Commission on Terrorist Attacks Upon the United States, *9/11 Commission Report* (New York: W.W. Norton, 2004), p. 351.

9. William J. Clinton, *My Life* (New York: Knopf, 2004), p. 925.

10. Ivo Daalder and Michael O'Hanlon, *Winning Ugly: NATO's War to Save Kosovo* (Washington, DC: Brookings Institution Press, 2000), p. 34.

11. Clinton, *My Life*, p. 803; and National Commission on Terrorist Attacks Upon the United States, *9/11 Commission Report*, p. 117.

12. Bradley Graham, "Senior Officials Split on Aborting Airstrikes," *Washington Post*, November 16, 1998, p. A1; John Harris and Dana Priest, "Off-Again Airstrikes May Be On Again Soon, Officials Suspect," *Washington Post*, November 17, 1998, p. A35; and Taylor Branch, *The Clinton Tapes: Wrestling History with the President* (New York: Simon and Schuster, 2009), p. 522.

13. Mark Mazzetti, "U.S. Aborted Raid Against Al Qaeda in Pakistan in '05," *New York Times*, July 8, 2007, p. 1; Evan Thomas, "Into Thin Air," *Newsweek*, September 3,

2007, p. 24; and Mark Mazzetti and David Rhode, "Amid U.S. Policy Disputes, Qaeda Grows in Pakistan," *New York Times*, June 30, 2008, p. A11.

14. National Commission on Terrorist Attacks Upon the United States, *9/11 Commission Report*, p. 436.

15. Mazzetti and Rhode, "Amid U.S. Policy Disputes, Qaeda Grows in Pakistan," p. A11.

16. David Sanger, *The Inheritance: The World Obama Confronts and the Challenges to American Power* (New York: Harmony Books, 2009), pp. 270–279; and David Fulghum and Robert Wall, "Cyber Combat's First Shot," *Aviation Week and Space Technology*, November 26, 2007, p. 28.

17. Sanger, *The Inheritance*, p. 69; White House, "Statement by National Security Advisor Stephen Hadley," Office of the Press Secretary, January 5, 2009; Nicholas Kristof, "A New Chance for Darfur," *New York Times*, December 28, 2008, p. WK10; and interview with Bush administration official.

INDEX

Note: Page numbers in *italic* type indicate illustrations.

Abbas, Athar, 150, 151
ABC News, 104
Abdulmutallab, Umar Farouk, 89
Abdul-Rahman, Omar, 54
Abramowitz, Morton, 32
Abu Sayyaf Group, 54
Acheson, Dean, 27
Afghanistan, 8, 46, 56–58. *See also* Khost,
    Afghanistan DMO
African Union, 158
Albania, 71
Albright, Madeline, 1, 69, 71, 156, 182*n*51
Algeria, 54
"All or nothing" use of force, 1, 12, 164*n*47
Ansar al-Islam, 14, 91–113, 199*n*59
Archidamus II, King of Sparta, 17
Armitage, Richard, 86, 88, 95, 108, 198*n*43
Art, Robert, 21
Assassination attempts: on Bush Sr., 132; on
    Musharraf, 148. *See also* Targeted killings
Atef, Mohammed, 82
Atta, Mohammed, 65
Atwah, Mushin Musa Matwalli, 59
Aum Shinrikyo, 62
Ayro, Aden Hashi, 20, 146, 151

Baker, James, 32, 34, 48
Bashir, Omar al-, 53
Benjamin, Daniel, 54, 89, 117

Berger, Samuel (Sandy), 59, 62–63, 66, 69,
    182*n*51
Betts, Richard, 10, 23
Biden, Joseph, 200*n*75
Bin Laden, Osama, 4, 9, 12, 13, 27, 52, 54, 55,
    57–63, 65–67, 70–72, 76–79, 83, 93, 101–2,
    109–10, 119, 142, 148
Blair, Tony, 107
Blechman, Barry, *Force Without War*, 21
Bosnia-Herzegovnia, 26–27, 51, 127–28,
    133–38, 155, 170*n*1
Boutros-Ghali, Boutros, 134
Branch Davidians, 6
Britain: and Bosnia-Herzegovina, 137; and
    Iraq, 13, 40, 42, 130, 140, 141. *See also*
    United Kingdom
British Joint Intelligence Committee, 109
Brooks, Risa, 206*n*34
Burke, Jason, 197*n*25
Bush, George H.W.: and Afghanistan, 56;
    assassination attempt on, 132; and Bosnia,
    26, 155; and coercive diplomacy, 20; and
    deterrence, 19; and DMOs, 27; DMOs not
    used by, 15, 155; and Iraq, 30–31, 33–34, 48,
    130, 131; and war on drugs, 5
Bush, George W.: and coercive diplomacy,
    20–21; critical of DMOs, 8–9, 72; and
    deterrence, 19; and DMOs, 27; DMOs not
    used by, 14, 91–113, 157; DMOs used by,
    9, 11; drone attacks authorized by, 159*n*6;
    foreign military assistance given by, 7; and
    Iraq, 94, 106, 200*n*82; and Iraqi no-fly zones,

Weapons of mass destruction (WMD):
bombing strategies for, 98; Bush on, 91; Iraq
and, 33, 37, 41–42, 131, 139–40; Khurmal
and, 91, 101–5, 108–9; Al Qaeda and,
61–63, 145; Syria and, 157. *See also* Nuclear
weapons, in DMOs
Whitman, Bryan, 150
Williams, Pete, 130, 131
Wolfowitz, Paul, 79, 87, 95, 97, 106
Woodhouse, John, 172*n*21
World Trade Center bombing (1993), 54
Worst-case planning, 8, 10

Yemen, 75; Americans threatened in, 77–78;
Bush administration demands on, 79–82;
DMOs against, 9; evacuation operations in, 6;
geostrategic location of, 74–76; logistics and

intelligence supplied to, 7; political objectives
in, 116–18, 117; and terrorism, 76–82, 89
Yemen DMO: account of, 84–86; aftermath
and assessment of, 86–90, 120–21; Khurmal
DMO compared to, 106; strategic setting of,
74–78; as turning point, 73–74
Yemeni, Haitham al-, 142
Yugoslavia, former, 26

Zarqawi, Abu Musab Al, 9, 94, 101–4, 109–10,
113, 199*n*59
Zawahiri, Ayman al-, 12, 15, 65, 77, 119, 142,
144–45, 157
Zelikow, Philip, 21
Zhawar Kili complex, 52, 60, 64, 64–65, 68
Zinni, Anthony, 41, 43, 49, 61, 63–64, 68, 70,
124, 185*n*107